Andrew O'Day is co-author, with
(2004). He received his PhD in
Holloway, University of London ar   ̄y ai
'classic' and 'new Who' to a range   ...cu chapters on
                                                 ...cu collections.

DOCTOR WHO

THE ELEVENTH HOUR

A CRITICAL CELEBRATION OF THE MATT SMITH AND STEVEN MOFFAT ERA

Edited by
Andrew O'Day

I.B. TAURIS

LONDON · NEW YORK

Published in 2014 by I.B.Tauris & Co Ltd
6 Salem Road, London W2 4BU
175 Fifth Avenue, New York NY 10010
www.ibtauris.com

Distributed in the United States and Canada Exclusively by Palgrave Macmillan
175 Fifth Avenue, New York NY 10010

ISBN: 978 1 78076 018 6 (HB)
       978 1 78076 019 3 (PB)

A full CIP record for this book is available from the British Library
A full CIP record is available from the Library of Congress

Library of Congress Catalog Card Number: available

Printed and bound by CPI Group (UK) Ltd, Croydon, CR0 4YY

MIX
Paper from
responsible sources
FSC
www.fsc.org   FSC® C013604

CONTENTS

FIGURES

CONTRIBUTORS

Dee Amy-Chinn is Lecturer in Film and Media at the University of Stirling. Her research focuses on representations of gender and sexuality in popular culture. Previous published works on *Doctor Who* include a chapter in *Ruminations, Peregrinations and Regenerations: A Critical Approach to Doctor Who* (ed. Christopher J. Hansen, Newcastle, 2010) and an article on Rose Tyler in *Science Fiction Film and Television*. Her work on *Torchwood* has appeared in the *Journal of Bisexuality*.

Jonathan Bignell is Professor of Television and Film at the University of Reading. He specialises in the history of television, especially British television drama. His publications relating to *Doctor Who* include *Terry Nation*, a study of the screenwriter co-written with Andrew O'Day, and the chapters 'The Child as Addressee, Viewer and Consumer in Mid-1960s *Doctor Who*', in the edited collection *Time And Relative Dissertations In Space* (ed. David Butler, Manchester, 2007), and 'Space for "Quality": Negotiating with the Daleks', in the collection that he co-edited with Stephen Lacey, *Popular Television Drama: Critical Perspectives*. He has also published on other telefantasy programmes and science-fiction cinema.

Piers Britton is Associate Professor and Director of Visual & Media Studies at the University of Redlands, Southern California. He has written extensively on design for the screen, with his work in this area ranging from an entry in the *Routledge Companion to Science Fiction* on design for SF film and television to *Reading* *between Designs* (co-authored with Simon J. Barker), the first book devoted to costume and production design in television series (including *Doctor Who*). He is currently working on *Immaterial Culture*, a wide-ranging volume addressing the ways that design becomes meaningful in the texts of television and film.

David Budgen received his PhD in 2010 for the thesis 'British Children's Books and the First World War, 1914–2007'. He is currently Associate Lecturer in History at the University of Kent, where his teaching is focused largely on areas of twentieth-century cultural and social history, with particular concentration on Britain during the two World Wars.

Brigid Cherry is Research Fellow in Communication, Culture and Creative Arts at St Mary's University College. Her research is focused on cult film and television, particularly fan cultures and practices. She has recently published work on horror fan canons, feminine handicrafting as fan production, projected interactivity in fan fiction for *Twilight* and *Supernatural,* and *Doctor Who* fans' responses to the return of the series. Her *Film Guidebook on Horror* was published by Routledge in 2009. She is co-editor of *Twenty-First-Century Gothic* published in 2011, and editor of a collection for I.B.Tauris on *True Blood* published in 2012.

Frank Collins edits and writes www.cathoderaytube.co.uk and has contributed to the Doctor Who Appreciation Society's magazine *Celestial Toyroom*, and the 'Behind the Sofa', 'Television Heaven', 'Tachyon TV' and 'British Television Drama' websites. He is the author of Classic TV Press' acclaimed *Doctor Who: The Pandorica Opens – Exploring the Worlds of the Eleventh Doctor* (2010). Educated at Newport School of Art and the University of Reading, he has worked for the British Market Research Bureau and the NHS, managed independent cinemas in Surrey and Brixton and, through Design Initiative, supported and promoted designers in the North West of England.

Ross P. Garner lectures at both the University of Glamorgan and the University of Worcester across a range of Media and Cultural Studies subjects but counts Television Studies as his area of specialist interest. He is completing a PhD in 'Nostalgia and Twenty-First Century Time Travel TV Dramas' at Cardiff University and is a co-editor of *Impossible Worlds, Impossible Things: Cultural Perspectives on Doctor Who, Torchwood and The Sarah Jane Adventures* (Newcastle, 2010).

Richard Hewett is a television historian and academic specialising in performance analysis, production technologies, genre and actor training. He completed his PhD thesis 'Acting for Auntie: From Studio Realism to Location Realism in BBC Television Drama, 1953–2008' at the University of Nottingham, where he has also taught undergraduate courses on film and television. His publications include the article 'Acting in the New World: Studio and Location Realism in *Survivors*' for the *Journal of British Cinema and Television*.

Vasco Hexel is the Area Leader of Taught Postgraduate Composition for Screen at the Royal College of Music, London, and the Music Consultant for the London Film School. His research interests include the role of contextual agents in recent Hollywood film music, a practice-led understanding of evolving music technology in the field of film and television music, as well as musical creativity and originality in competitive and collaborative environments. Vasco has composed scores for award-winning animations, short films, documentaries, commercials, production music and feature films. His clients include Music Sales, Gucci, RSA, Channel 4, Boden, Universal Music, ZDF and KanalD Romania. He can be found on the web at www.vascohexel.com.

Matt Hills is Professor in Film and TV Studies at Aberystwyth University. He is the author of five books, including *Fan Cultures* (2002) and *Triumph of a Time Lord: Regenerating Doctor Who in the Twenty-first Century* (2010). He has written widely on cult media, fandom and *Doctor Who*, most recently contributing a foreword to the *Doctor Who: Fan Phenomena* volume (Intellect, 2013) as well as writing regular book and TV reviews for Doctor Who News (www.doctorwhonews.net).

Matthew Kilburn has a doctorate in eighteenth-century British history from the University of Oxford. He is now an independent historian, writer and editor while remaining an associate member of the History faculty, University of Oxford. He is a former research editor at the *Oxford Dictionary of National Biography*, to which he continues to contribute articles, mainly on eighteenth-century history. In addition to having written for *The History of Oxford University Press, Volume 1: Beginnings to 1780* (2013), he has contributed a chapter to the edited *Doctor Who* collection *Time And Relative Dissertations in Space* (ed. David Butler, Manchester, 2007) and information text subtitles for BBC Worldwide's *Doctor Who* DVD releases.

Simone Knox is Lecturer in Film and Television at the University of Reading. Her research interests include the transnationalisation of film and television (including audio-visual translation), aesthetics and medium specificity (including convergence culture), representations of the body and postmodernism. She has published in the *Journal of Popular Film and Television*, *Critical Studies in Television* and *Film Criticism*. Forthcoming publications include the book *Transatlantic Television* (co-authored with Jonathan Bignell).

Andrew O'Day received his PhD in Television Studies from Royal Holloway, University of London. His thesis concentrated on metafiction in telefantasy with an emphasis on the 'classic' *Doctor Who* series. He is co-author (with Jonathan Bignell) of the book *Terry Nation* (Manchester, 2004), primarily investigating Nation's science-fiction work, and has contributed to edited collections on *Doctor Who*, both old and new, including Christopher J. Hansen's *Ruminations, Peregrinations and Regenerations* (Newcastle, 2010), and Matt Hills' *New Dimensions of Doctor Who* (London, 2013). Andrew's other research interests include Jack the Ripper in media and popular culture, and further afield Lesbian, Gay, Bisexual and Transgender (LGBT) Studies and the Law. He can be found on the web at www.hrvt.net/andrewoday.

Neil Perryman is an independent scholar who is currently studying for a PhD in Media Convergence at the University of Sunderland. He contributed the article 'Doctor Who and the Convergence of Media: A Case Study in Transmedia Storytelling' to the journal *Convergence* (2008) and can be found on the web at www.tachyon-tv.co.uk, www.behindthesofa.org.uk and www.wifeinspace.com.

NOTE ON TERMINOLOGY

There are two contentious issues regarding labelling the Steven Moffat/Matt Smith era. First, the revival of *Doctor Who* is sometimes referred to as 'NuWho'. Matt Hills has, in the past, though, drawn a distinction between the Russell T. Davies era as 'new *Who*' and the Steven Moffat era as 'new new *Who*'. However, throughout this book, the Moffat era, like the Russell T. Davies one, will be referred to as 'new *Who*'. Second, there is the issue of how to number the seasons, an issue which Matt Hills considers in his chapter for this volume. Some fans take into account the fact that there have been 30 previous seasons of the programme (including those of the 'classic' series) and begin the numbering for Moffat's seasons at 31. Others begin the numbering at 1. But this collection will follow the DVD numbering and refer to the seasons of the Moffat era thus far as 'series 5, 6 and 7'. (There were previously four series of the Russell T Davies era.)

ACKNOWLEDGEMENTS

Ever the enthusiastic scholar, I first proposed the idea for this volume to I.B.Tauris at the end of 2009, shortly before the first appearance of Matt Smith's Doctor on our television sets. I was encouraged every step of the way by commissioning editor Philippa Brewster's eagerness and I wish to extend my gratitude to her, to all at I.B.Tauris, and to all the contributors for making the editing process such a smooth one. I especially thank Professor Jonathan Bignell and Professor Matt Hills for their assistance. I'd also like to thank Professor James Chapman, Professor Leonée Ormond (the former Head of my MA from King's College, London), Professor Roberta Pearson and Dr Catherine Johnson for suggesting contributors. Outside of academia, Tim Harris, Adam Emmanuel and Simon Heritage have been a constant source of support. It is with great sadness that I write that another good friend of mine, Nicholas Courtney, who played Brigadier Lethbridge-Stewart in 'classic' *Doctor Who*, passed away while I was in the midst of working on the book.

During the later stages of producing this collection, I have been enrolled as a student in the LL.B for Graduates degree at the University of Birmingham. I offer my gratitude to both the staff and to my fellow students for providing such a comfortable environment, both in which to pursue my studies and in which to finish off this book. I also offer my thanks to Frogg Moody, Sue Parry and everyone at The Whitechapel Society for being patient in awaiting further articles on 'Jack the Ripper' while I completed this collection. Additional thanks must go to the Terrence Higgins

Trust Gay Men's Outreach team in Oxford with whom I worked on many a worthwhile and enjoyable Friday night and to members of the LGBT community.

Finally, this book would not have been possible without the love and support of my family, especially that of my parents and my two younger brothers Daniel and Matthew Englander. They have endured many hours of watching *Doctor Who* over the years and this collection is therefore dedicated to them.

INTRODUCTION

Andrew O'Day

Part of the charm of the 'classic' series of *Doctor Who* (1963–89) was the way in which it was constantly renewed every few years. This renewal was demonstrated not only by the phoenix-like ability of the Doctor to regenerate his appearance whenever it was necessary to cast a new actor in the role, but also occurred stylistically whenever a new producer, or sometimes script-editor, came to the programme. This stylistic renewal sometimes, but certainly not always, coincided with the change of lead actor.

This same pattern can be detected within new *Who*. In 2005, Russell T Davies was responsible for bringing back *Doctor Who*, which had been off-the-air as a continuous television series for 16 years, to the BBC's Saturday evening line-up to great critical acclaim. Davies had cast two actors in the title role – Christopher Eccleston (who remained for only one year) and David Tennant – and had breathed new life into the franchise. A regular pattern was established, up to Tennant's final season of four specials; each season comprised 13 (usually) 45-minute episodes, with 3 two-parters, roughly in the same position each year, including a finale which would resolve an ongoing season story arc. When Davies decided to leave, it was never in dispute that *Doctor Who* would continue and he asked Steven Moffat to take his place as executive producer. Moffat not only had experience in creating and writing for other television programmes (the children's series *Press Gang* for ITV (1989–93), and BBC situation comedies *Joking Apart* (1993–5), *Chalk* (1997) and *Coupling* (2000–4), as well as the horror serial

Jekyll (2007)). He also had an established and successful writing record for *Doctor Who*. Tennant had also decided to step down as the latest Doctor and it fell to Moffat to cast the younger Matt Smith in Tennant's place, first seen at the close of 'The End of Time' Part Two in a transition scene written by Moffat.

As new *Who*, Moffat's first 2010 season bears more structural – and even narrative – similarities with Davies's seasons than Davies's had with the 'classic' series, reminding the viewer that this is the same series:[1] it remained composed of 13 (mostly) 45-minute episodes, with 3 two-parters in roughly the same position of the season, and an ongoing story arc. The first episode, 'The Eleventh Hour', begins, just as Davies's first episode 'Rose' (amongst others) had done, with a shot of the Earth as seen from space and a zoom-in. Furthermore, episodes two and three involved the new companion – Amy Pond – being taken on a journey in the space and time machine, the TARDIS (short for Time And Relative Dimension In Space), to the future and the past respectively, much as had happened in the Davies era with companions Rose Tyler (series one) and Martha Jones (series three). The opening episode of the 2010 season, 'The Eleventh Hour', written by Moffat, also has a plot not dissimilar to the premiere of the 2007 season, 'Smith and Jones', penned by Davies, in which the 'space police' pursue a war criminal and threaten the eradication of innocent humans.

But beneath that surface, there are many changes. As this collection will show, these go beyond the fact that Moffat's second and third seasons are split in two, that Moffat plays with the number of, and placing of, the two-parters and that the story arcs run over multiple seasons. The 2011 season unusually opened with a two-parter, had 2 two-parters in the middle, with one stretched over the two halves of the season, and closed with a single episode, while the companions remained with the series longer, making for more complex arcs. The Autumn 2012 season, meanwhile, was untypically all composed of single-episode narratives.

As the programme reached its 50th anniversary, the Moffat/ Smith era continued the mainstream success of the Davies era and had its own fanbase. Along with fan conventions primarily featuring guests from the 'classic' series, 2012 saw an official BBC convention being held in Cardiff, with guests such as Moffat and

Smith, along with Karen Gillan (Amy Pond) and Arthur Darvill (Rory), while the weekend of 15–17 June saw the staging of *Doctor Who: The Eleventh Hour* at the Birmingham Hilton Metropole, featuring Matt Smith and a range of guest stars from series six. Fans – spanning the generations – attended talks and autograph sessions, had photographs taken with the celebrities and attended the parties, dressed as the Eleventh Doctor with fez and mop and sometimes eye-patch, or as River Song, or as the monstrous Weeping Angels and Silents. 2013 has followed suit.

About this Collection

Back in 1983, when *Doctor Who* was celebrating 20 years of continuous on-air broadcasting, John Tulloch and Manuel Alvarado published the first academic book about the series, *Doctor Who: The Unfolding Text*, a study of the programme since its 1963 origins.[2] But, despite the fact that Television Studies has valued the study of popular television as it is the television that people watch the most, academics were slow to recognise the importance of the programme, partly as the discipline of Television Studies was in its infancy, yet not helped by the fact that, bar a 1996 TV movie, starring Paul McGann, the programme proper was out of production at the BBC between the period of 1989–2004. The 1980s, 1990s and early 2000s saw but a scattering of articles on the series by scholars like John Fiske,[3] Nicholas Cull[4] and Alan McKee,[5] as well as John Tulloch and Henry Jenkins' monograph *Science Fiction Audiences: Watching Doctor Who and Star Trek*.[6] It may seem hard to believe now but *Doctor Who* scholarship was to all extents and purposes finished before it had even got off the ground until David Butler boldly announced in his call for papers for a 2004 conference to be held at Manchester University that much had happened in the intervening years since Tulloch and Alvarado's book, including the production of audio dramas by professionalized fans. This conference coincided roughly with the publication of Jonathan Bignell and Andrew O'Day's study of the screenwriter Terry Nation which crossed programme boundaries.[7] Since then, along with the revival of the series in 2005, has come an explosion of *Doctor Who* scholarship; some books by the likes of James Chapman,[8] Matt Hills[9] and Piers Britton,[10] too many journal articles and conference papers to list, and more and more edited collections.[11] This book materialises for the 50th anniversary year of *Doctor Who* but, unlike Tulloch and Alvarado's for the 20th anniversary, it is an edited collection of essays and part of I.B.Tauris' wider series of *Who Watching* books. Thirteen chapters are contained within by 13 different scholars; there are many more new *Doctor Who* scholars than this now which just goes to show how the field has grown. This time the academics have been ready for a programme celebrating its 50th anniversary and can join the chorus of fans who are raising a glass and saying 'Happy 50th *Doctor Who!*'

To date, however, there have not been many analytical studies of the Steven Moffat/Matt Smith era and those that there are tend to be fan-orientated. Books by Frank Collins,[12] by Steven Cooper and Kevin Mahoney,[13] and by Telos Publishing provide an episode-by-episode analysis of series five (and in the latter cases the first Matt Smith Christmas special). Cooper and Mahoney have also released a follow-up study of series six and the second Matt Smith Christmas special.[14] By contrast, this collection is divided up according to issues. This book is also far more wide-reaching in that it is not limited to textual analysis of the episodes themselves.

The first part of the book, however, 'Performance, Genre and Gender', focuses on the episodes. Spearheading the volume is a chapter by Richard Hewett which concentrates on how Matt Smith brings the role of the Doctor to life and also on Steven Moffat's own input into the role. In order to do this, Hewett draws a comparison with casting in Moffat's other series *Sherlock*. Performance has, until recently, been much neglected in Television Studies,[15] and so this chapter fills a gap in scholarship. The following chapters in the section identify 'signatures' running across Moffat's era as well as focusing on other issues in Television Studies. Frank Collins and Matthew Kilburn turn to examine the particular characteristics of Gothic and fairy-tale storytelling and the use of history in the Moffat era, and Collins draws comparisons with Moffat's *Jekyll*. Collins positions his examination of the Gothic in relation to television as an uncanny medium at the heart of the home and considers possible audiences, while Kilburn reflects on the institution of the BBC as well as authorship in his discussion of history. Dee Amy-Chinn then looks at representations of gender and sexuality in the Moffat Whoniverse.

The second section of the collection focuses on 'Wider Broadcasting Contexts'. In a most intriguing chapter, David Budgen ventures into a largely unchartered area of space and considers Moffat's *Doctor Who* Christmas specials. Budgen places these in the context of Christmas storytelling and Christmas television as being for the family. Budgen's approach differs to Collins', then, since while Collins sees television as an uncanny medium located in the home, Budgen views television as a more comforting one. Following this, Simone Knox considers the transnational dimensions of television and of Moffat's *Who*.

The third section of the book, 'Sights and Sounds', moves to probe elements of production such as the technologies used to make new *Doctor Who*. Jonathan Bignell engages with debates concerning whether visual style overrides character and story and concludes that in Moffat's *Who* it does not. Bignell also develops on Knox's chapter, pointing out that spectacle in the Moffat era, associated with US science fiction, is greatly reduced because of budgetary constraints. Meanwhile, Piers Britton focuses on design. Britton focuses on a number of key designs for the Moffat era and, arguing that design eludes single authorship and bleeds meanings beyond the frame, examines varying conflicting statements made about these by authorising figures and some of the consequences of not putting legitimating weight behind a particular design. Britton does, however, note that, while the showrunner does not exercise complete control, there is a 'Moffat era aesthetic'. Vasco Hexel then proceeds to examine the work of another authorial figure in the context of television generally: composer Murray Gold.

The final section of the volume, 'Beyond the Episodes', concerns the much neglected area of publicity for the programme (by Matt Hills), fan reaction and particularly the way in which fans are resistant to the changes that a new era ushers in (by Brigid Cherry) and the *Doctor Who Adventure Games* and *Sarah Jane Adventures* episode 'Death of the Doctor' (by Neil Perryman and Ross P. Garner, respectively). Returning to the theme of authorship, Perryman argues that *The Adventure Games* are given official status in a number of ways including by Moffat's seal of approval, while Garner looks at how publicity for *The Sarah Jane*

Adventures episode shifts between emphasising episode writer Russell T Davies's authorship and Moffat's.

Not only has *Doctor Who* changed over time but television is a constantly evolving form and the discipline of Television Studies must therefore evolve with it. This collection is very much a product of its time and looks very different than such a book would have done 30 years ago. I am often asked whether I prefer the 'classic' or new series of *Doctor Who*. The answer I truthfully offer is that there is no comparison since while maintaining the same basic format, new *Who* is so different, both in form and content. Not only are Christmas specials, for example, a hallmark of new *Who*, but the use of music, considered by Vasco Hexel, has changed markedly. Similarly, the *Doctor Who* spin-off is primarily a twenty-first-century phenomenon (the episode leading from the 'classic' series, *K9 and Company*, never generated a spin-off series). In terms of the evolution of television, when discussing whether visual style has been allowed to override character and story in Moffat's *Who*, Jonathan Bignell must take into account the newer production technologies used to make the programme for a variety of viewing platforms other than the typical model of a television set being watched in the home. Likewise, Neil Perryman must continue to look at the way in which *Doctor Who* is available in new media forms. Furthermore, the culture around the programme has changed, including fan practices, in the Internet age.

The collection is designed to be read in two ways. One is that readers can dip into the volume at any point to engage with their interests. The other rewards reading from start to finish where chapters build on one another. So, for example, all the chapters read together provide a picture of Moffat's authorship and sometimes his lack of authority. Another of the connections between chapters in the first part of this collection is that some of them explore the notion of family in Moffat's *Who* from a series of perspectives. Frank Collins, for instance, scrutinises the inclusion of the theme of family from a Gothic perspective, while Dee Amy-Chinn disentangles the way in which *Who*, under Moffat, both liberalises gender roles and provides a conservative model of the family. Conversely, David Budgen considers the nature of Christmas television generally and the *Doctor Who* Christmas special more specifically as being for the family.

Furthermore, while there is not a chapter devoted solely to Moffat's use of the story arc *per se*, the story arc perhaps fittingly becomes a running theme across many of the contributions. For example, Richard Hewett explores the effect of the story arc on the characterisation of the Doctor as performed by Matt Smith; Frank Collins and Matthew Kilburn look at the connections between the story arc, with its timey-wimey secretive nature, and the Gothic and history respectively; Dee Amy-Chinn observes that gender relations are at the centre of Moffat's story arc; Simone Knox notes the way the story arc reflects transnational influences; and Vasco Hexel probes the use of music to support the arc, as well as to provide tonal variations between scenes. David Budgen and Neil Perryman, however, take a different approach. Budgen argues that Moffat's Christmas specials are largely detached from the main seasons so as not to alienate the more family-orientated Christmas audience, while Perryman asserts that the *Doctor Who Adventure Games* are not so connected with the series that both cannot be appreciated independently.

Writing this Introduction has led me to ponder just why academics so frequently turn to the genre of the edited collection when bringing out a book about *Doctor Who*. Along with the fact, noted above, that *Doctor Who* scholarship has grown to the point of making such volumes practical, one of the reasons (tied in with this) is that edited collections pool on a wide range of expertise of people working in different areas of Television and Cultural Studies and indeed in other disciplines. And writing about *Doctor Who* seems to demand this variety. So, for instance, tying into the list of chapters above, Dee Amy-Chinn's tromping ground is primarily in the area of gender and sexuality; Simone Knox's in transnational television; Brigid Cherry's in qualitative studies of fandom; Neil Perryman's in New Media; while Ross P. Garner has a long-standing academic interest in the antics of those from Bannerman Road in the spin-off *Sarah Jane Adventures*. Matthew Kilburn, meanwhile, undertook his PhD in History, while Piers Britton teaches in a Department of Art History, and Vasco Hexel at the Royal College of Music. Indeed, *Doctor Who* scholarship had to all extent ignored the vital role of music in the programme until David Butler's edited collection *Time And Relative Dissertations In Space* in 2007, which included contributions from musicologists Kevin Donnelly and Louis Niebur.

Finally, this book has gone to press before the end of the Steven Moffat/Matt Smith era and the viewer will since have enjoyed more adventures of the Time Lord and his new companion, played by Jenna-Louise Coleman ('The Snowmen'). On the one hand, this leaves a space for further scholarship. On the other hand, I wrote a review (and may I say a very positive one) of Matt Hills' 2010 volume *Triumph of a Time Lord*.[16] Hills' book, also published by I.B.Tauris, concentrated on the Russell T Davies era of the programme and the manuscript was obviously delivered before the final run of four David Tennant specials had been screened (2009–10). But such was the strength of Davies's authorial signature that the final four specials could easily be tied in to Hills' analysis. It remains to be seen to what degree the arguments made here are applicable to the remainder of Steven Moffat's era and what occurs in the discourses surrounding the programme. But while there are similarities with the Davies era, Steven Moffat and his team have consciously announced that a different Eleventh Doctor set of stories has arrived.

Notes

1. Matt Hills, 'New New *Doctor Who*: Brand Regeneration', 19 April 2010. Available at www.blog.commarts.wisc.edu/2010/04/19/new-new-doctor-who-brand-regeneration (accessed 26 June 2012).
2. John Tulloch and Manuel Alvarado, *Doctor Who: The Unfolding Text* (Basingstoke, 1983).
3. John Fiske, 'Dr Who: Ideology and the Reading of a Popular Narrative Text', *Australian Journal of Screen Theory* 13/14, pp. 69–100.
4. Nicholas Cull, 'Bigger on the Inside: *Doctor Who* as British Cultural History', in Graham Roberts and Philip M. Taylor (eds), *The Historian, Television and Television History* (Luton, 2001), pp. 95–111. Also Nicholas Cull, 'Tardis at the OK Coral,' in John R. Cook and Peter Wright (eds), *British Science Fiction Television: A Hitchhiker's Guide* (London, 2006), pp. 52–70 (originally published in Swedish-language version as 'Värreän Dalekerna? Doctor Who och USA' ('Worse than Daleks: Doctor Who and the USA') *Filmhäftet* 112/ 4 (2000), pp. 26–39.
5. Alan McKee, 'Is *Doctor Who* Political?', *European Journal of Cultural Studies* 7/2, pp. 201–17.
6. John Tulloch and Henry Jenkins, *Science Fiction Audiences: Watching Doctor Who and Star Trek* (London, 1995).

7. Jonathan Bignell and Andrew O'Day, *Terry Nation* (Manchester, 2004).
8. James Chapman, *Inside the TARDIS: The Worlds of Doctor Who* (London, 2006).
9. Matt Hills, *Triumph of a Time Lord: Regenerating Doctor Who in the Twenty-first Century* (London, 2010).
10. Piers D. Britton, *TARDISbound: Navigating the Universes of Doctor Who* (London, 2011).
11. Examples following David Butler's edited collection *Time And Relative Dissertations In Space: Critical perspectives on Doctor Who* (Manchester, 2007) include Ross P. Garner, Melissa Beattie and Una McCormack (eds), *Impossible Worlds, Impossible Things: Cultural Perspectives on Doctor Who, Torchwood and The Sarah Jane Adventures* (Newcastle, 2010); Christopher J. Hansen (ed.), *Ruminations, Peregrinations and Regenerations: A Critical Approach to Doctor Who* (Newcastle, 2010); Simon Bradshaw, Antony Keen and Graham Sleight (eds), *The Unsilent Library: Essays on the Russell T Davies Era of the New Doctor Who* (2011); *Doctor Who in Time and Space* (Gillian I. Leitch, ed., Jefferson, 2013); and *Fan Phenomena* (Paul Booth, ed., Wilmington, 2013). A volume *New Dimensions of Doctor Who* (ed. Matt Hills) has just been published (London, 2013). There are also collections on *Doctor Who* and myth (*Mythological Dimensions of Doctor Who*, Anthony Burdge, Jessica Burke and Kristine Larsen, eds, Crawfordville, 2010) and *Doctor Who* and philosophy (*Doctor Who and Philosophy*, Courtland Lewis and Paula Smithka, eds, Chicago, 2011), with one expected on *Doctor Who* and religion (*Time And Relative Dimensions In Faith*, Andrew Crome and James McGrath, eds, London, 2013), highlighting the way in which scholarship on the programme crosses over subject boundaries.
12. Frank Collins, *Doctor Who: The Pandorica Opens: Exploring the Worlds of the Eleventh Doctor* (Cambridge, 2010).
13. Steven Cooper and Kevin Mahoney, *Steven Moffat's Doctor Who 2010* (London, 2011).
14. Steven Cooper and Kevin Mahoney, *Steven Moffat's Doctor Who 2011* (London, 2012).
15. See, for example, Christine Cornea (ed.), *Genre and Performance: Film and Television* (Manchester, 2010).
16. Andrew O'Day, 'Matt Hills, Triumph of a Time Lord', *Journal of British Cinema and Television* 7/2 (2010), pp. 352–4.

PART ONE

PERFORMANCE, GENRE AND GENDER

1

WHO IS MATT SMITH?
Performing the Doctor

Richard Hewett

In terms of lead characters, the Doctor is unique in television drama. Possessed of the ability to physically 'regenerate' his body, the nine-centuries-old Time Lord can be portrayed by actors who are both physically dissimilar to and – perhaps more significantly – personologically distinct from each other, each actor cast in the role having provided a marked contrast with his predecessor. However, while each Doctor is a 'new man',[1] he simultaneously inherits the life experiences and memories of his predecessors, as made clear by executive producer and lead writer Steven Moffat's vigorous assertion that 'there's no such thing as eleven Doctors; there's one Doctor with eleven faces. He is the same man.'[2]

This combination of re-casting and continuity presents a dichotomy in terms of characterisation. For an incoming Doctor such as Matt Smith, the question of which traits remain essential to the character must be of primary consideration, while at the same time seeking to establish those facets which will distinguish his version from what has gone before. Several elements of the Doctor remain unaltered throughout his television incarnations: essentially altruistic, he is a wanderer in time and space who, despite often paying lip service to the fact that he is forbidden to interfere, in practice cannot resist becoming involved in the affairs of other life forms. He is possessed of a huge intellect, vast scientific knowledge and an insatiable curiosity, and frequently finds himself drawn to the planet Earth and its inhabitants. The Doctor's status as a humanoid alien – another of the constants throughout the series[3] – acts as an additional complicating factor. David Lavery has argued that in portraying fantasy characters – or characters involved in fantasy scenarios – any human actor is limited in terms of the personal experiences upon which he or she can draw, positing the question: 'How do you prepare, as an actor, for something like that? What instructions could a director give? What method would suffice?'[4] However, Lavery overlooks an important point; given that the Doctor's behaviour may seem alien to human viewers, his emotional reactions deriving from entirely different impetuses, they are no less real to him for that. There is no reason that an actor versed, for example, in Stanislavski's system of emotion memory and adaptation[5] cannot apply these methods, summoning an appropriate response from personal history and applying it to the Doctor's situation to create a character who, in the words of Sixth Doctor Colin Baker, '[is] not always going to behave in the way human beings would expect him to behave … like not crying when a person dies, but becoming extremely angry about other things'.[6]

Matt Smith's succession to the role of the Doctor was first announced in a January 2009 edition of *Doctor Who Confidential* (BBC, 2005–11), Steven Moffat accurately predicting that the 'brilliant, but not famous' actor would swiftly be seized upon as an 'unknown' by the press.[7] The success of Moffat's reign as executive producer hinged to a great extent on his new lead actor, and whether Smith's performance chimed with the public in the same way as those of David Tennant and Christopher Eccleston under previous show runner Russell T Davies. Drawing on primary source material in the form of interviews conducted by magazines and television documentaries, this chapter will first attempt to situate Smith's interpretation alongside those of his predecessors, before using textual analysis to identify the approaches he uses in his performance as the Doctor. Finally, I will offer an examination of the executive producer's role in the formation of characterisation, partly via comparison with

Sherlock (2010-), the drama production which Steven Moffat co-helmed for BBC1 alongside *Doctor Who*. In this way the chapter will attempt to negotiate the complex question of authority and authorship in relation to characterisation in television drama, although there is insufficient space to fully examine such complicating factors as the input of other writers, and the role played by individual directors. As to the vexed question of actual intent – either on the part of the actor Matt Smith or executive producer Steven Moffat – this is difficult to state with total certainty; interview material offers a potential indication, but is always open to question. However, the use of performance analysis provides a useful methodological balance, for if we cannot definitively establish authorial aims in the creation of the Eleventh Doctor, we are able at least to analyse the on-screen realisation of the character.

'Being' the Doctor?

Doctor Who's production turnaround has always been rapid. In the days of the original series, one 25-minute episode would be rehearsed and recorded every week (in the 1960s up to 11 months of the year), while the modern production – in which each 50-minute episode is allocated a fortnight, usually as one half of monthly production 'blocks' – has dispensed altogether with the rehearsal process which typified the old multi-camera studio drama process. Such pressures leave little time for actors and directors to work together on characterisation, and it could be argued that it is in fact the role of the script editor and producer (in the original series) and the lead writer (in the re-launch) to maintain continuity of character and plot developments. However, I contend that this is only half the case; rather, in *Doctor Who* the input of the lead actor has always been the central contributing factor in the depiction of the main character. This could take various forms; several of the actors to have played the Doctor have either subsequently been identified as, or have freely admitted to, drawing upon aspects of their own personality when creating their characterisation. Original series actor William Russell has claimed that William Hartnell, when playing the First Doctor, was 'in his own character: a bit scratchy, and a bit unpredictable; and these things came over, and he used them',[8] while comedian Jon Pertwee confounded viewer expectations by providing a 'straight' characterisation of the Third Doctor which he later confessed was 'more or less me',[9] even wearing items from his own wardrobe. In the case of Fourth Doctor Tom Baker, this process seems to have worked in reverse, the actor admitting to having carried the persona of the Doctor into his personal life, never allowing himself to be seen with a cigarette or pint of beer while in the presence of children for fear of destroying their perception of the character.[10]

Doctor Who's lead actors drawing on aspects of themselves in performance could be seen as a direct result of the programme's tight production schedule, but it was not an approach employed by all. Second Doctor Patrick Troughton avoided any discussion of his own personality in relation to his acting, stating simply: 'I'm a character actor and I play a lot of characters … in the end it's still just a job.'[11] Troughton claimed to have created a character separate from himself, while still injecting aspects of his own choosing when planning with the production team what form this character would take: 'I have a wicked glint in my eye for comedy and so we decided on that.'[12]

The extent to which viewers identify actors with a particular role or type can also be a factor in characterisation. Prior to becoming the Doctor, Troughton had largely avoided playing any one character for longer than the duration of a finite serial, but later leads Peter Davison and Colin Baker were already well known to television viewers when they embarked upon their respective tenures: Davison as vet Tristan Farnon in *All Creatures Great and Small* (BBC, 1978–91), and Baker as ruthless accountant Paul Merroney in *The Brothers* (BBC, 1972–76). Rather than battle such strong audience associations, their interpretations could be read as having subtly incorporated aspects of their existing television personae alongside the established characteristics of previous Doctors. Davison later admitted that an early influence on his portrayal was the suggestion by a young fan that he play his Doctor 'like Tristan, but brave',[13] while Colin Baker's creation of an initially darker, less accessible Doctor, if not a deliberate extension of Merroney – the man viewers 'loved to hate' – might well have struck audiences of the time as similarly unsympathetic. Significantly, Davison and Colin Baker were the first leads to have watched the programme regularly prior to becoming actors and upon being cast, both actively conducted research by watching recordings of their predecessors.[14] Each could be seen as having incorporated Pertwee's physicality into their characterisations, though while Davison tended towards the seeming fallibility of Troughton, Baker's performance recalled much of Hartnell's irascibility. By the time Sylvester McCoy took over the role in 1987, there was less of a preparation period, and though the actor watched some old episodes, he admitted that 'the only time there's been is to learn the lines and try not to bump into the...furniture'.[15] In the event, the production team's initial decision to base McCoy's Doctor on aspects of Troughton's template gave way to a deliberately darker, more mysterious characterisation when the actor returned for his second year.

Like Tom Baker, whose few high-profile roles had been in film rather than television, Matt Smith was not well known to viewers when his appointment was announced. Despite appearances on the BBC in *The Ruby in the Smoke* (2006), *Party Animals* (2007) and *The Shadow in the North* (2007), Smith's lack of an established small-screen persona with which audiences could identify or draw comparisons provided him with a blank canvas upon which to create. Interviewed by *Doctor Who Magazine* in the months leading up to Smith's first series, Steven Moffat was keen to align his star with actors such as Tom Baker who had used their own personalities, while positioning predecessor David Tennant alongside those who kept characterisation and personal identity separate: 'David Tennant is a brilliant, vibrant, *huge*, quite theatrical Doctor, but in reality he's a kindly, modest man. He's not at all like that, he's quite gentle. He's not 'Doctor-y' at all.'[16] According to Moffat, Matt Smith represented the opposing part of the binary; contrasting the actor's performance as career detective Dan Twentyman in *Moses Jones* (2009) – broadcast on the BBC shortly after the announcement of Smith's appointment – with his acting as the Doctor, Moffat observed: 'He's brilliant in *Moses Jones*, but he's trying to play a geezer. Matt's so *not* a geezer. When you see him play the Doctor, you'll just see him let that part of himself out to play.'[17] In support, Moffat cites aspects of Smith the man which are also

DOCTOR WHO, *THE ELEVENTH HOUR*

instantly recognisable in Smith the Doctor, such as the actor's now infamous clumsiness:

> Sometimes you can't take your eyes off him cos you think there's a sense of incipient disaster about him. ... You think he's about to fall over or bump into something. And generally speaking ... you're right! He's the clumsiest man I've ever seen! I mean, despite the fact that he's a superb athlete, he knocks over coffees, falls over and breaks props![18]

However, while Smith concurs that he is somewhat accident-prone as an individual, he sees a clear distinction between his own clumsiness and that of the Doctor: 'There's an elegance to his clumsiness! He just has an absent-mindedness about his body. He's still getting used to it! ... His hands are very interesting – there's a weird fluidity about the way he moves them.'[19] Smith's identification of a physical characteristic, endemic to him personally, which he chooses to use in his performance and to justify for narrative or dramatic reasons, makes Moffat's assertions regarding the actor's characterisation difficult to sustain, and it is probable that they were intended as a form of interest-generating promotion rather than serious analysis. It is difficult, if not impossible, to ascertain to what extent actors may or may not be 'playing themselves' in a role. Even the glimpses of Smith 'the man' that viewers are given in *Doctor Who Confidential* comprise another form of performance, the actor shown indulging in time-filling games and conducting impromptu 'interviews' with cast and crew members between takes.

Certainly Smith's at times mesmerising use of his hands – arcing, fluttering and swooping to emphasise or illustrate what he is saying – is a trait present both in his performance as the Doctor and when the actor is being interviewed on screen. His reflection on the Doctor's 'weird fluidity' shows that he is clearly aware of this element to his characterisation, suggesting either that it is a deliberate choice or that he has noted it while watching himself in playback. His comment while making his opening episode, 'The Eleventh Hour', that 'hopefully, physically, it's all quite kind of sporadic and weird'[20] to describe the Doctor's acclimatisation to his new body indicates a calculated performance choice; how such choices inform Smith's performance will now be investigated further.

Creating the Doctor

One factor which definitively sets Smith apart from his predecessors is that, born in October 1982 – just seven years before the original series' cancellation – he had little prior knowledge of the programme when he accepted the role: 'You always remember the Doctor you grew up with – which makes it terrible that *Doctor Who* wasn't on TV when I was a kid. But I'm experiencing it now, as an adult – and I get to be a kid every day!'[21] Like Davison and Colin Baker, however, Smith embarked on a period of research, and in his first *Doctor Who Confidential*, he clearly relishes the process of investigation that is to come:

> I love that part of being an actor; I love the discovery of it, the being a detective bit….This next six months for me is about preparation and learning…about the history of the show, the world of the show, and soaking it all up.[22]

Smith subsequently spoke enthusiastically of original series serials including Patrick Troughton's 'The Tomb of the Cybermen' (1967) and Tom Baker's 'City of Death' (1979),[23] and it is possible to detect elements of each – Troughton's impishness, Baker's other-worldliness – in his characterisation. The research the actor conducted represents a clear desire to retain a core consistency of character, and the elements outlined earlier are all present in the Eleventh Doctor. However, Smith also emphasised that 'you can only ever be true to your identity as an actor',[24] and this is ultimately key to distinguishing his characterisation from what has gone before – as the actor confirmed when discussing his initial audition: 'I just think it's important…to be brave enough to make my own choices…choices that are based on me and my personality, and my life.'[25]

One of the most important of these choices was the Eleventh Doctor's first costume, the finished version of which Smith described as 'a bit of Indiana Jones, a bit of a professor, and a bit of the explorer….I think it has to feel like an extension of your personality, and this does, for me'.[26] As Moffat has said, with the addition of a bow tie 'you could tell that [Matt Smith]...for the first time since the costume fitting started, was leaping around the room pretending his pen was a sonic screwdriver, and absolutely believing it!'[27] Again, Smith's description – while centring round his own personality – neatly includes several of the key, unchanging elements to the Doctor's character: the adventurer, the scientist and the curiosity of the explorer. The actor's suggestion of braces and a bow tie could be seen as a direct result of his research into past episodes and a particular liking for Troughton, but Smith did not limit himself to the series' history when formulating his character:

> I had six months to kill, so I felt I needed to connect with the Doctor in some way. ... So I thought, 'Who's been the most intelligent human being on the planet?'... Then I saw that photograph of Albert Einstein poking his tongue out and it just clicked. I found this book of quotes by Einstein...and I started writing stories about Einstein and the Doctor.[28]

It is intriguing that the image Smith latched onto when considering his characterisation – the elderly Einstein famously indulging in a playful, childish gesture – is the inverse of a quality particular to the Eleventh Doctor: that of an aged individual, most often described in the new series as being around nine hundred years old, personified in the body of a man in his late twenties. Much was made in the media of the fact that, at 26, Smith was the youngest actor to have been cast in the role,[29] but his Doctor is portrayed as anything but a youth. Matthew Sweet was one of the first to note this performance potential aspect to Smith: '[He] has got a fascinating face. It's long and bony, with a commanding jaw. ... He has a quality of the old man trapped in the young man's body.'[30]

This element provides the cornerstone of Smith's performance, but when questioned as to how he manages to convey the weight of nine-hundred-plus years' experience on his twenty-something shoulders, he frustratingly relies on the actor's common standby: 'You just play the truth – the Doctor's a...907-year-old guy. ... So I just play the truth via me. And then whatever gravitas a 907-year-old man has will reveal itself.'[31] Such a deceptively simple response would seem to contradict Lavery's assertions regarding the impossibility of realising the fantastic through the Stanislavskian technique of employing personal experience, without providing evidence of a concrete process or approach on the part of Smith, who as the youngest actor in the role arguably had the least experience upon which to draw. The idea that his performance is a purely instinctive response to the text, however, is challenged by the amount of consideration which the actor evidently gives to his portrayal; when pondering the Time Lord's motivation for his travels, the implications of his longevity and the amount of suffering that he has seen in his life, Smith reflects:

> I think the Doctor ignores death and keeps going and moving and never really dwells on it, to be honest. He recognises it, but I think he moves on quite quickly, because if he didn't, think of all the death that is on his hands.[32]

Performing the Doctor

As noted by Matthew Sweet, Matt Smith's physiognomy is a definite advantage in his portrayal of an old man 'trapped' in a young body. However, Smith's own comments suggest an actor very aware of his own physicality and presence, and the ways in which he employs his face in performance are notable in several respects. The 'long, bony jaw' is made use of in moments of confusion or pondering, mouth often hanging slackly open as the Doctor processes a new piece of information or considers his next move. This expression, which lengthens and seemingly ages Smith's face, is in marked opposition to the Cheshire cat grin that more often splits and widens it when he is seen 'off duty'[33] in *Doctor Who Confidential*, giving him a more youthful aspect. Smith also makes use of his prominent brow, often keeping his eyebrows slightly raised and so creating furrows and wrinkles which belie his late twenty-something years.

However, such factors are grace notes to the overall use Smith makes of his body when playing the Doctor. One trope consistently used in his portrayal from 'The Eleventh Hour' onward is a habit of craning his body forward when engaged in one-to-one conversation, head slightly lowered so that his eyes are raised upwards to peer into the face of his fellow actor. This 'peer' is used variously in moments of concentration, interrogation and – occasionally – anger, but is always suggestive of other-worldly intensity, and it is noticeable that directors have increasingly favoured shots from slightly above Smith's eye-level to maximise the effect.

Such moments usually arrive as the calm between the various storms of Smith's more physical performance, his diffuse energy often dominating the screen. This is seen most obviously in the spasmodic scenes in 'The Eleventh Hour' as the post-regenerative Doctor struggles to adapt to his new body, and the paroxysms he undergoes in 'Let's Kill Hitler' as he succumbs to River Song's poison. These are examples of the Doctor in extremis, but Smith's frequently unconventional use of his body – Steven Moffat observing that he walks 'like a drunk giraffe'[34] – is suggestive both of the Doctor's alien-ness and the fact that, although his mind may be centuries-old, it is currently housed in a body that possesses all the vigour of youth.[35] Moffat's comment that 'the lovely thing you get with Matt is a hot young bloke – a very, very handsome young man – who is nonetheless just genetically a little bit like Magnus Pike [sic]. ... There's an immediate tension',[36] that, while again redolent of promotional hyperbole, ties in with my earlier description of the actor's conscious use of his hands in performance. Moffat's comparison of Smith with British scientist Magnus Pyke, whose enthusiastic waving of his arms when explaining science for a lay audience made him a popular television figure in the 1970s, supports his assertion that, 'of the three new Doctors, he's the most convincing boffin'.[37]

There is insufficient space here to unpack Smith's performance style in full, but I hope that this brief description shows how its various components comprise different facets of the Eleventh Doctor's character, from his alien-ness to his boundless energy. However, the actor's input, while crucial to the realisation of the on-screen character, also depends on the text itself, as Smith made clear when first embarking on his period of preparation: 'I'm just going to concentrate on the words in the page, and let the rest unfold.'[38] As lead writer and executive producer of the series, Steven Moffat can legitimately be considered the co-creator, with Smith, of the Eleventh Doctor.

His role will now be examined partly via comparison with the other series on which he was working simultaneously with the first year of *Doctor Who*: his twenty-first-century re-imagining of Arthur Conan Doyle's *Sherlock*.

The Role of the Executive Producer

Co-conceived with Mark Gatiss, *Sherlock* reached British television screens in the summer of 2010, shortly after the conclusion of Matt Smith's opening series as the Doctor. First to be cast was Benedict Cumberbatch, previously BAFTA-nominated for his lead performance in *Hawking* (BBC, 2004), who took up the mantle of the Baker Street sleuth. However, the search for a suitable foil proved more problematic:

> We'd already cast Benedict Cumberbatch and the very first person we saw for Dr Watson was Matt [Smith], who came in and gave a very good audition. But he didn't have a chance in hell of getting it cos he was clearly more of a Sherlock Holmes than a Dr Watson. There was also something a bit barmy about him – and you don't want that for Dr Watson, you want somebody a bit straighter. But he gave a very good account of himself and you could feel the effort in him clamping down on his barminess, you know, in order to do the audition! ... Then I saw him about a week later, for *Doctor Who*, on our first day, the third person through the door. And, you know, as much as he was a struggling, but brilliantly accomplishing, Dr Watson, he just utterly *got* the Doctor. ... It was like he could just act in the way he always *wanted* to, as opposed to the way he always *tried* to.[39]

The idea of Smith as Watson to Cumberbatch's Holmes is as intriguing as the possibility, subsequently hinted at by the latter,[40] of Cumberbatch playing the Doctor; however, the role of Watson ultimately went to Martin Freeman, whose on-screen chemistry with Cumberbatch became an integral part of *Sherlock*'s success.

Steven Moffat was involved in pre-production and production on *Doctor Who* and *Sherlock* over the same period. An un-broadcast pilot for the latter was made in January 2009, with filming for the initial series of three episodes eventually taking place in early 2010; work on Matt Smith's first series had begun in July 2009, not concluding until March the following year. Moffat's authorial hand can therefore be detected in both series; as executive producer, he was chiefly responsible for casting the lead actors for each, and as lead writer on *Doctor Who* and author of the opening episode of *Sherlock,* he also created the initial character templates. There are certainly elements common to both Time Lord and detective, not least their enormous intellect; in their respective introductory adventures, both the Doctor and Sherlock encounter a companion who is impressed by their abilities and, although less cerebral, helps compensate for their 'lack' in terms of humanity. Mentally, both men exist in a world inaccessible to those around them, and behave in a manner that, while seeming eccentric to others, is normality itself to them. Each is an animated talker in moments of excitement – words tumbling over themselves faster than their thoughts can form – and both frequently converse with themselves; they are usually the only people capable of understanding their train of thought. Indeed, some sections of script from the two series are almost interchangeable; Sherlock's gabbled line 'Oh that was clever. Was it clever? Why was it clever?' might just as easily have emerged from the mouth of the Eleventh Doctor, and both respond to newly discovered challenges and perils alike with the delighted exclamation 'This is Christmas!'

However, there are also several points of departure. While the Doctor is other-worldly yet amiable, often literally embracing those around him, Sherlock is by turns unworldly – unaware, for example, that the Earth revolves around the sun – and isolated, disdainful of a world to which he feels superior. However, he is also capable of at least playing at normality, as for instance when bluffing his way into a flat, or feigning sympathy with the wife of a presumed murder victim; a feat of which the Doctor would be quite incapable. Perhaps surprisingly given the amount of time that his former selves have spent on Earth,[41] the Eleventh Doctor at times displays a notable naivety regarding its inhabitants and their foibles; in 'The Lodger' it is the Doctor's inability to blend in as a 'normal' human being which provides the impetus for much of the narrative, and in that episode and 'Night Terrors', the Doctor's adoption of 'air kissing' as a mode of greeting is used to comedic effect.[42] Equally, while the Eleventh Doctor is increasingly depicted as a man prepared to condone and even resort to physical violence to defend his friends, and exhibits a certain ruthlessness more generally in episodes like 'Dinosaurs on a Spaceship', it is difficult to imagine him torturing a dying man for information, as Sherlock does in 'A Study in Pink'. There are clearly similarities and divergences in Moffat's conception of each which extend into and influence the actors' characterisations; Moffat's were, after all, the scripts from which Smith and Cumberbatch read for their auditions.

Matt Smith at least admits that much of his creative impetus derives from Moffat. Speaking of the moment in one of his first recorded episodes, 'Flesh and Stone', when the Doctor threatens the Weeping Angels should they kill his imperilled companion Amy Pond, he observed: 'All of that vulnerability, and the rage of this Doctor as well which is in there somewhere, is all Steven.'[43] The fact that, under Moffat, a new dimension to the Time Lord's characterisation has fed into Smith's performance has been recognised by those who worked on the programme in its previous incarnation, Alex Kingston observing of Matt Smith's performance in the same episode:

> There were moments where I could see that he had tears in his eyes, and he was so angry; it was quite shocking because I've never seen any former Doctors be quite that angry and passionate and vulnerable all at the same time, and slightly lost.[44]

The character's use of the word 'cool' in 'The Eleventh Hour' to describe and defend his choice of bow tie – subsequently extended to include a variety of head-gear, including a fez and a Stetson – also raises the problematic notion of whether the Eleventh Doctor's defining and often comedic traits derive from Moffat or Smith. The fact that it is difficult to imagine the adjective being used by any of the previous incarnations[45] makes it particular to Smith's version, but while it could be argued that the word sprang from Moffat's pen, it is also possible that, given Matt Smith's frequent use of it 'in person' as seen on *Doctor Who Confidential*, the writer included it after observing his lead in conversation. Its continuing incorporation as a key element of the character – in much the same vein as the Second Doctor's 'When I say run, run!', the

Ninth's use of 'Fantastic!', or indeed the Eleventh's 'Geronimo!' – indicates a scripting choice, as with the repetition in 'Closing Time' of the Doctor's earlier claim to be fluent in 'baby', which becomes a claim to be fluent in 'horse' in 'A Town Called Mercy'. However, it is also possible that it was a more organic development, similar to the Third Doctor's references to 'reversed polarity'; an easily remembered phrase which Jon Pertwee chose to substitute for any more complex scripted technological terminology.

Under Steven Moffat, there have been a greater number of overt references in *Doctor Who* to the programme's past. Visual material has been incorporated from both the original series and the programme's more recent history (holograms of Rose, Martha and Donna appearing in 'Let's Kill Hitler'). This trope has also been extended to performance, as when Matt Smith mimes to Tom Baker's voice issuing from the Flesh Doctor's mouth in 'The Almost People'. However, there are also less explicit moments, some of which once again raise the question of authorial intention. The Eleventh Doctor's habit of referring to Amy Pond by her last name is reminiscent of the First Doctor's (frequently incorrect) mode of address to companion Ian Chesterton, while his use of a jammy dodger to threaten the Daleks in 'Victory of the Daleks' recalls the Fourth's similarly menacing employment of a jelly baby in 'The Face of Evil' (1977). Whether the latter was a deliberate intra-textual reference is difficult to ascertain, and it is as likely to have originated with episode writer Mark Gatiss (like Moffat, a long-time fan of the original series) as with the executive producer.

However, the increased prominence of the lead writer, based on the American showrunner model, is one of the most notable distinguishing features between 'new' *Doctor Who* and the original series. Since the programme's return in 2005, there has been a more structured development of character, as evidenced in the process of healing that took place in Russell T Davies's first year as executive producer between Rose Tyler and the 'damaged' Ninth Doctor, still raw from the Time War, and maintained through the Tenth's subsequent relationships with his various companions. In the Steven Moffat era, such development has been taken a stage further; the Doctor is evidently still learning about himself as much as others in episodes such as 'The Almost People', and is by turns delighted and intrigued to discover that he can experience new feelings and emotions in 'The Doctor's Wife', 'A

Good Man Goes to War' and 'The Doctor, the Widow and the Wardrobe'. One feature particular to the Eleventh Doctor is an element of self-loathing, as revealed by his alter ego the Dream Lord in 'Amy's Choice', while in 'Let's Kill Hitler' it becomes clear that he in fact regards himself as a somewhat negative force in the lives of his companions: 'There must be someone left in the universe I haven't screwed up yet.' Rather like in the Russell T Davies era, he also finds it hard to let his companions go. Perhaps the most obvious example of the Doctor's continuing character development as conceived by Moffat is the process of discovery that is his relationship with River Song, which commenced even before Matt Smith took over the role of the Time Lord.

The Eleventh Doctor's character arc, as conceived and planned by Moffat and realised by Smith, sets this particular era of the programme apart both from the original series, when such character development was seldom attempted,[46] and even the Russell T Davies era, in which the Doctor's mourning for his lost home world, once established as a basis for the Ninth's rehabilitation, was seldom developed under the Tenth other than being used as a default dramatic counterpoint to his more manic moments. Smith's Doctor is superficially offhand when referencing the destruction of Gallifrey in 'The Beast Below', but his controlled anger at Silurian Alaya's pretence that she is the last of her species in 'The Hungry Earth' gives the lie to this seeming indifference. Such character beats are developed further in 'The Doctor's Wife', the Doctor's barely contained excitement at the possibility that fellow Time Lord the Corsair may be alive turning to cold anger when he discovers the truth. The frequent Davies-era positioning of the Doctor as the much-feared 'Oncoming Storm' is deflated in 'A Good Man Goes to War', River Song poignantly pointing out that his doctoral title has now become synonymous on some worlds with 'mighty warrior': 'When you began all those years ago, sailing off to see the universe, did you ever think you'd become this?' In 'The Wedding of River Song', Moffat's script has the Doctor admitting that he has become 'too big', the faking of his death allowing him to return to the comparative anonymity of becoming once again a simple wanderer in time and space, while reinstating the air of mystery that first surrounded William Hartnell's incarnation in 1963: 'Doctor *who*?'

Conclusion

Each actor to have played the Doctor has brought a new dimension to the character while maintaining the essential continuities, outlined at the outset of this chapter, and from the evidence presented here Matt Smith could certainly be seen as continuing in that tradition. The development of the Doctor in the era of Moffat and Smith has in one sense seen the character brought full circle, while simultaneously adding layers and complexities not possible in the classic series due to the limitations imposed by its relentless production cycle. As a result of changes in the climate of television drama which have taken place over the last two decades, such character considerations are now virtually *de rigueur* for a continuing drama such as *Doctor Who*, and form a primary consideration for production team and lead actor alike. As Smith states:

> I've come to think that this role is a bit like Hamlet: your own personality has to go into it, in a way. And it takes a whole process for it to come out clearly. There's an evolution to the way I'm playing the Doctor. A gradient. I hope the Doctor's identity will become clearer and clearer throughout the series.[47]

As has been shown, the formation of the Doctor's on-screen persona, although complicated by various contributing factors, represents a combination of inputs, drawing upon previously established traits while simultaneously exploring new aspects and areas of the character. In light of the evidence provided here it seems probable that as the Eleventh Doctor era draws to a close further significant developments will take place under the combined aegis of actor and executive producer.

Notes

1. However, the ability of a Time Lord to switch gender was established by the Doctor's reference to the Corsair having changed sex in 'The Doctor's Wife'.
2. Steven Moffat, *Doctor Who Confidential: Call Me the Doctor*, (BBC), 3 April 2010.

3. In the 2006 television movie (BBC/Fox), it was established that the Doctor is in fact half-human, though this has never been referenced subsequently.

4. David Lavery, 'What's My Motivation? The Method Goes Fantastic in Television Acting'. Available at http://cstonline.tv/telegenic-method (accessed 1 July 2012).

5. Constantin Stanislavski, *An Actor Prepares*, trans. Elizabeth Reynolds Hapgood (London, 2008).

6. Colin Baker, 'Colin Baker Interview', *Doctor Who Magazine* 118 (1986), p. 18.

7. Steven Moffat, *Doctor Who Confidential: The Eleventh Doctor*, (BBC), 3 January 2009.

8. William Russell, 'Commentary on An Unearthly Child', *Doctor Who: The Beginning* (BBCDVD1882, 2009).

9. Jon Pertwee. Available at http://drwhointerviews.wordpress.com/2009/09/18/jon-pertwee-1990/ (accessed 1 July 2012).

10. Tom Baker, 'Interview: Tom Baker', *Doctor Who Magazine* 92 (1984), p.20.

11. Patrick Troughton, 'Patrick Troughton Interview', *Doctor Who Magazine* 102 (1985), p. 10.

12. Patrick Troughton, 'Doctor Who Interview: Patrick Troughton', *Doctor Who Monthly* 78 (1983), p. 18.

13. Peter Davison, 'New TV Comedy: It's *Sink or Swim* for Dr. Who', *The Listener* (1983), p. 13.

14. Davison commented in *Doctor Who Magazine* 106 (1986) that 'I decided that I'd like to take elements of all the previous Doctors and mould them into one (p. 9), while in *Doctor Who* Magazine 97 (1985), Colin Baker admitted to having watched 'between twenty and thirty old stories' (p. 21).

15. Sylvester McCoy, 'Sylvester McCoy Interview', *Doctor Who Magazine* 130 (1987), p. 8.

16. Steven Moffat, 'The Time is Now! The DWM Interview: Steven Moffat', *Doctor Who Magazine* 418 (2010), p. 18.

17. Ibid.

18. Ibid., p. 20.

19. Matt Smith, 'Eleven Plus! The DWM Interview: Matt Smith', *Doctor Who Magazine* 420 (2010), p. 25.

20. Matt Smith, *Doctor Who Confidential: Call Me the Doctor* (BBC), 3 April 2010.

21. Smith, 'Eleven Plus!', p. 24.

22. Smith, *Doctor Who Confidential: The Eleventh Doctor* (BBC), 3 January 2009.

23. Matt Smith, 'Just Like Starting Over', *Doctor Who Magazine Special Edition: The Doctor Who Companion – The Eleventh Doctor: Volume 1*, p. 12.

24. Smith, *Doctor Who Confidential: Call Me the Doctor.*

25. Smith, *Doctor Who Confidential: The Eleventh Doctor.*

26. Smith, *Doctor Who Confidential: Call Me the Doctor.*

27. Moffat, 'The Time is Now!', p. 21.

28. Matt Smith, *The One Show* (BBC), 1 April 2010.

29. In fact Peter Davison was only two years older when his appointment was announced in late 1980.

30. Caroline Davies and David Smith, 'Dr Who? Big Names Lose Out to Matt Smith', *Guardian*, 3 January 2009. Available at www.guardian.co.uk/media/2009/jan/03/doctor-who-matt-smith (accessed 1 July 2012).

31. Smith, 'Eleven Plus!', p. 25.
32. Matt Smith, *Doctor Who Confidential: Take Two* (BBC), 28 May 2011.
33. However, as noted earlier, the actor at these moments is still very much 'giving a performance' for the cameras.
34. Moffat, 'The Time is Now!', p. 20.
35. The fact that the Doctor's body can grow both younger and older is established in 'The Power of the Daleks' (1966), where Patrick Troughton's Doctor discovers that he no longer requires the more elderly William Hartnell's spectacles.
36. Moffat, 'The Time is Now!', p. 18.
37. Ibid.
38. Smith, *Doctor Who Confidential: The Eleventh Doctor.*
39. Moffat, 'The Time is Now!', p. 18.
40. Catriona Wightman, 'Cumberbatch Hints at *Dr Who* Role', *Digital Spy*, 22 July 2010. Available at www.digitalspy.co.uk/tv/s7/doctor-who/news/a248556/cumberbatch-hints-at-doctor-who-role.html (acccessed 1 July 2012).
41. The Third Doctor was exiled to the planet for the majority of Jon Pertwee's first three years with the programme.
42. By the later episode he has at least learned to apply it only to females.
43. Matt Smith, *Doctor Who Confidential: Blinded by the Light* (BBC), 1 May 2010.
44. Alex Kingston, *Doctor Who Confidential: Blinded by the Light* (BBC), 1 May 2010.
45. David Tennant's Doctor is a possible exception.
46. Colin Baker's 'seven year plan' to mellow his initially unsympathetic Sixth Doctor was ultimately frustrated by his sacking from the programme after just two seasons.
47. Smith, 'Eleven Plus!', p. 24.

2

MONSTERS UNDER THE BED

Gothic and Fairy-Tale Storytelling in Steven Moffat's *Doctor Who*

Frank Collins

Since its beginnings, *Doctor Who* has juxtaposed the ordinary with the extraordinary, finding horror in familiar and domestic settings, what Alec Charles refers to in the series as 'the convergence of the domestic and familiar with the alien and repressed'.[1] Freud introduced the concept of the 'uncanny', of the *unheimlich* and *heimlich* – the unfamiliar within the familiar – and Charles argues that television is the perfect medium for conveying this state:

> The projection or broadcast of desires and fears might be considered central to the processes of television; and television, that familiar stranger at the heart of one's home, that box of infinite revelations, may therefore seem a particularly suitable medium for such uncanny explorations. Jeffrey Sconce, who describes television as 'an uncanny electronic space in and of itself'...argues that 'electronic media in the age of television became a crucible for an uncanny electronic space capable of collapsing, compromising and even displacing the real world'.[2]

Freud's concept is identified by Gina Wisker as a strategy within Gothic texts that destabilises and dislocates 'places, people, our sense of reality' and which preys on our need for security.[3] Helen Wheatley defines Gothic television as one concerned with 'the structures and images of the uncanny; homes and families which are haunted by events/figures from the past; complex narrative organisation (flashbacks, dreams, memory montages); dark *mise en scène*; and subjective or impressionistic camerawork and sound recording'.[4] As Wheatley emphasises, 'Gothic television, with its emphasis on the uncanny, joins together the homely or familiar elements of the medium and its domestic spaces with the unfamiliar, unsettling, and often supernatural elements of Gothic storytelling'.[5]

The Gothic genre and *Doctor Who* have long been comfortable bedfellows, the relationship achieving its peak in the original series during the three seasons produced by Philip Hinchcliffe and script-edited by Robert Holmes between 1975 and 1977. While this era moved away from the everyday, it, like other periods in the programme's history, saw *Doctor Who* undergo intense scrutiny over its acceptable use of horror and the effect it had on the child viewer. Along with its emphasis on a series of Gothic conventions such as a common insistence on archaic settings, a prominent use of the supernatural and the presence of highly stereotyped characters, the era was defined and vilified for its 'portraying the terrifying',[6] and its appreciation of Edmund Burke's marriage of the sublime, of phenomena that powerfully affect emotions, with responses such as fear, dread and horror.

Judging by a number of recent newspaper reports and online debates, the reception of *Doctor Who* since its revival in 2005 is still being scrutinised over its suitability for children. As if in response to such concerns, current head writer and executive producer Steven Moffat offered, in March 2010, that '*Doctor Who* is how we warn our children that there are people in the world who want to eat them'.[7] It is a remark consistent with his personal vision for the series, a sensibility developed while writing under the remit of former executive producer Russell T Davies. A 2008 *Radio Times* interview characterised Moffat as the 'Dark Man', already acknowledging his reputation as a writer whose award-winning scripts for the series were regarded as 'the Scary Ones'. Again, Moffat defined the series' power to influence the imaginations of children and the major tenets of his manifesto: 'Doctor Who doesn't really take place in outer space, it takes place under children's beds....'[8] Recognisable horror motifs continue to appear, alongside references to classic fairy tales and children's fantasy literature, where the use of the Gothic deposits the uncanny and the monstrous into a familiar domestic viewing environment.

Writing about the Davies era, Matt Hills sees this as part of the series' appeal to a trans-generational audience where the child watches for traditional scares, and can indeed play games around the narratives, and the adult is able to return to such a mode of viewing, to a symbolically child-like state.[9] Hills, however, points out that this argument is 'based on imagined audiences' since 'very little focus-grouping was done for the series'.[10] There are also wider themes contained in the Moffat era, which Hills would see as making the narratives 'double coded', appealing to older viewers. Some (but certainly not all) of these are connected to the notion of childhood fears, to the family and to growing up and forming sexual relationships, which Jonathan Bignell has argued were themes associated with Susan Foreman in 1960s Doctor Who, enabling a dual address to children and adults.[11] Catherine Spooner sees contemporary use of Gothic as able to 'deal with a variety of themes just as pertinent to contemporary culture as to the eighteenth and nineteenth centuries'[12] and as having a fluidity that allows for a Gothic presence to appear in other, non-related texts. In addition to examining the Gothic and fairy tale in Moffat's writing, both for the Russell T Davies era and his own, this chapter will probe how his signature extends to Doctor Who episodes he has commissioned from other writers and to his series Jekyll made entirely for an adult audience. The chapter will then conclude by examining Moffat's use of a Gothic structure for his story arc.

Gothic Chills

The structural components of Moffat's narratives are heir to many familiar Gothic tropes including the use of space, which often substitutes for the Gothic castle or house: hospitals, libraries, bedrooms, caverns and asylums are places of unease in his writing both for the Davies era and his own. Furthermore, the Weeping Angels are stone figures associated with the many external manifestations of the Gothic – haunted houses, castles, ruins, graveyards, catacombs, tombs and vaults. The depiction of various caverns, libraries and archives also foreshadows the museum in 'The Big Bang' and the damp warehouses and tunnels of 'The Impossible Astronaut' that house the bat-like Silents who hang from the ceilings. The threatening Gothic space of Graystark Hall Orphanage in 'Day of the Moon', with its allusions to the Dickens of *Oliver Twist* and the Gotham of *Batman*, is presented as a storm-lashed architecture drenched in psychological unease that Amy and Canton access via a huge staircase, another iconographic element of screen horror.

Moffat's *Who* also plays with the notion of uncanny sights and sounds. In 'The Eleventh Hour', not only is there a crack in the wall in Amy Pond's bedroom but also the adult Amy and the audience are made aware of a mysterious door in her house leading to a room that can only be perceived in the corner of one's eye. The uncanny gaze is also central to 'The Impossible Astronaut'/'Day of the Moon'. The Silents manipulate mankind's history through their ghostlike ability to appear before their victims who, the instant they avert their gaze in fear, forget their encounter with these monsters incongruously wearing suits and ties. The notion of detecting the uncanny in familiar surroundings is prominent in Amy's first sight of a Silent at Lake Silencio and later in the Oval Office and White House bathroom. This detection culminates in 'Day of the Moon' with the use of the tattoos as markers, an aide memoir of the uncanny, of uncovering the sightings of the Silents.

Meanwhile, in 'The Eleventh Hour' the sound of voices originates from behind the crack in Amy Pond's bedroom; and in 'The Impossible Astronaut' the telephone is an object of unease as President Nixon receives calls from an abandoned child and records them on tape. These instances tie in with Moffat's earlier fascination with sound. Jamie's plaintive question 'Are you my mummy?' during 'The Empty Child' is transmitted through a number of ordinary objects (the TARDIS's defunct emergency telephone, a tape machine, a period radio set, even a typewriter), transforming their function and rendering them uncanny. In 'The Girl in the Fireplace' Moffat codifies personal space through familiar objects such as a doll's house and a rocking horse, but a loud ticking sound is used to pre-empt the unseen danger lurking in the darkness of the bedroom. Telephones also take on a threatening and uncanny significance in Cal's bright, cheerful domestic reality in 'Silence in the Library'/'Forest of the Dead', alerting her to the Doctor's presence in the library.

Watching Telly, Playing Games and Haunting Themes

A key element in Moffat's *Who* is the use of games, songs and nursery rhymes, subverting their innocent qualities to underline the threat posed by apparently normal objects and people. Furthermore, the audience, and children particularly, would associate them with the viewing of a narrative and the child could emulate them in the home or playground. These work in unison with a series of memes and catchphrases that Moffat often employs. Moffat has stated that 'you're always looking for ... games [children] can play. You want to know what the next playground game is – how they're going to play at it the next day.'[13] This is also a development of the way in which children played at being Daleks in the school playground after watching the 'classic' series[14] and what Hills refers to as the contextualising of the monstrous in children's imaginative play.[15]

In Moffat's writing for the Davies era, a series of refrains occur, from the 'Are you my mummy?' of 'The Empty Child'/'The Doctor Dances', to Sally Sparrow in 'Blink' seeing the Doctor on television issuing a warning about the Weeping Angels ('Don't turn your back, don't look away and don't blink'); to 'Silence in the Library'/'Forest of the Dead' where the signature mantra is 'Hey, who turned out the lights?' Similarly, echoes of games appear along with songs and rhymes which highlight the sudden appearance of the pursuing monster or offer humorous relief to terror. For example, in 'The Doctor Dances' a game of hide-and-seek begins when Jamie suddenly announces through the speaker grille that Jack later uses to talk to the Doctor, 'I can hear you. Coming to find you. Coming to find you.' After Nancy is handcuffed to a table next to the infected Private Jenkins, who undergoes a traumatic transformation into a gas-masked zombie, the only way Nancy can redact the monstrous is to reinforce a sense of childhood security by singing to him the lullaby 'Rock-a-bye Baby'. In 'Silence in the Library'/'Forest of the Dead', fears of the Vashta Nerada are identified by recourse to a game as the Doctor and Donna are exhorted to 'Count the shadows. For god's sake, remember. If you want to live, count the shadows.' A variation of the playground game of shadow tag, where players try to step on the shadow of another player to tag them, is how expedition members Proper Dave and Other Dave are codified as victims. After one of them sprouts two shadows, others in the room are directed, as if in a game children would follow, 'Don't cross his shadow'. Earlier, 'Blink' was also inspired by a traditional children's game to which Moffat refers in an episode of *Doctor Who Confidential*: ' "Blink" is basically that statues game isn't it? That Grandma's Footsteps game which I always found frightening. I know kids find it exciting and interesting.'[16]

These motifs run throughout Moffat's own era where the catchphrase is 'Silence will fall'. In 'The Beast Below', the cryptic 'Vator Verse' with its fable of the Star Whale, the Smilers and the topsy-turvy world in which they exist develops the idea that the series is a dream fantasy, part of a story told to or sung to children using sing-song nonsensical rhymes. It implies a universe where initially everything is transposed but then stabilised by Amy reciting a new verse to bookend the episode. There is also the deadly game of Blind Man's Buff in the episode 'Flesh and Stone', as Amy, blind, wanders through a forest filled with deadly Angels. The fear of looking and glimpsing something extraordinary in the corner of your eye becomes the primal, childhood fear of monsters springing to life and creeping up on you, the uncanny suddenly generated in our ordinary, everyday surroundings.

Furthermore, Moffat suggests that a child's imagination is shaped, and fear is sublimated, by watching television, particularly *Doctor Who*. In his episode for the Davies era, 'Forest of the Dead', the little girl Cal, in a state of excitement and anxiety, watches the horrific events in the library on a television set. When Miss Evangelista reveals her monstrous transformation to Donna, Cal cringes behind a cushion, alluding to the iconic position of 'behind the sofa' viewing assumed by the young audience at home. The trope of watching television appears again in 'The Time of Angels' where Moffat imbues the Weeping Angels with ferocious new attributes and abilities, complicating the nature of our curiosity and desire to gaze at them. The sequence of Amy watching the Angel emerge from the television monitor in the Byzantium's vault involves a further doubling of the gaze and the act of blinking as the viewing audience and Amy watch together. This suggests that the Angels can pop out of the television screen after their victims or their viewers and also alludes to Nakata Hideo's *Ringu* (1998) and its story of an urban legend surrounding a cursed videotape from which a vengeful spirit emerges, out of the television screen and into the real world.

These sequences use the act of looking and the art of capturing images to provide what Barbara Creed refers to as 'the uncanny gaze' that she believes is central to experiencing horror films. Creed suggests that 'As the horrified spectator focuses on the scenario unfolding on the screen, the uncanny gaze is constructed at that point at which the familiar becomes unfamiliar'.[17] This replicates our own intense fascination with viewing the fearful and the horrific in *Doctor Who*.

In addition to having a Gothic atmosphere, Moffat's *Who* deals with key themes. These include the horror of our own materiality and mortality. In 'The Beast Below' the Smilers come complete with the double aesthetic of whirring, clicking mechanical gears and as in the earlier episodes, 'The Empty Child' and 'The Girl in the Fireplace', of machines meshing flesh and technology together. The fear of death is also transferred onto the fanged faces of the Gorgon-like Weeping Angels, and the feral face of Prisoner Zero, just as they were onto the victims of the Vashta Nerada. Characters achieve an undead status as a result of this sublimation. When Miss Evangelista disappears into darkness in 'Silence in the Library' and becomes a victim of the Vashta Nerada, she becomes undead, a 'data ghost' as the technology of her suit's intercom is overlapped on the dying human body and her fading consciousness. This prefigures Amy's own loss of control at Graystark Hall in 'Day of the Moon', where she is reduced to the state of ghost, a lone voice left crying from the nano recorder she had embedded in her hand, left behind on the bedroom floor. And in 'Asylum of the Daleks', while she dreams of a normal domestic life, it is revealed that Oswin Oswald has been converted into a Dalek.

Indeed, with its emphasis on homes and families, Moffat's *Who* explores the dysfunction between parents and their children and their eventual reconciliation. The ability to maintain, or restore, a normal family life forms the trajectory of the narrative arc, focusing on Amy and Rory, throughout the fifth and sixth series. In 'A Good Man Goes to War', Amy is (re)united with her daughter Melody in the form of River Song. In this sense, Moffat revisits the themes of his earlier writing. In 'The Empty Child'/'The Doctor Dances', confused parent Nancy attempts to assuage her own guilt, and a secret which the Doctor uncovers, over the death of her abandoned son Jamie and the shame of social nonconformity as 'a teenage single mother in 1941'. Ultimately Nancy and Jamie are united, not as sister and brother but as mother and son. The imperative of a normal family life is explored in Donna's domestic fantasy during 'Forest of the Dead', while Cal, an almost dead child hooked into the mainframe of a library's vast computer system, is living the dream of a normal life with a loving father.

Scares and Enchantment: A Dark Fairy Tale

At the end of 'Flesh and Stone', River Song acknowledges *Doctor Who* itself as a tale reiterating an idea from 'Forest of the Dead', where River, in Cal's data world, looks directly at the camera and at the audience, after she has told children the story of the Doctor, saying 'sweet dreams everyone'. In 'Flesh and Stone', the Doctor refers to the Pandorica, too, as a fairy tale. 'Oh, Doctor. Aren't we all?' River replies with a twinkle in her eye.

In 'The Girl in the Fireplace', Reinette views the Doctor as her imaginary friend, a childhood fantasy that later gains greater relevancy in the friendship between Amy and the Doctor. Through the Doctor's intervention, Reinette matures into a woman capable of confronting and defying the clockwork monsters invading the court as 'merely the nightmare of' her 'childhood, the monster from under' her 'bed'. The Doctor tells her that 'everyone has nightmares' and reassures her, and by extension the viewer, that he will defeat this nightmare, because nightmares are there to test us and enable us to overcome our fears.

The abandoned Amelia in 'The Eleventh Hour' shows how children can interpret and dissolve their anxieties through dream, fantasy and adventure. Amelia's stories, drawings and dolls become sublimated into her adult life where the yearning for such adventure still exists but has not been fulfilled. The adult Amy in her nightie, joining the Doctor in the TARDIS, sees Amelia's personal, long-held fantasies, and those of many viewers, acted out.

Moffat's vision of *Doctor Who* as a dark fairy tale often references classic tales and children's fantasy literature and involves the pivotal theme of children growing into adults. In 'The Eleventh Hour', the garden and Amy's house, which echo Frances Hodgson Burnett's *The Secret Garden* (1910) or Philippa Pearce's *Tom's Midnight Garden* (1958), is a powerful primal arena from which Amy and the Doctor launch their journey through the series. It is the place in which they are both shaped and changed uniquely, and to which they both return in 'The Big Bang', completing the cycle of the journey. The triad of Amy, River and the Doctor also reflects Barrie's *Peter Pan* (1904) with the interrelationships between the characters of Peter, Wendy and Tinker Bell. Peter is one of the Lost Boys of Neverland as much as the Doctor is the Last of the Time Lords of Gallifrey. Like Peter Pan, the eternal, childlike Doctor prefers freedom to stuffy, adult conformity. In *Doctor Who*, Amy makes the journey from immaturity to maturity, running away with the Doctor the night before her wedding but eventually, at the end of series five, marrying Rory. In this sense, Moffat retraces ideas from 'The Girl in the Fireplace', which features the familiar portal or gateway of classic children's fantasy literature that separates realities as apparent in Burnett's *The Secret Garden*, C.S. Lewis's *The Lion, the Witch and the Wardrobe* (1950) and Pearce's *Tom's Midnight Garden*, and sees Reinette grow into a sexually active adult.

Joining in the Game: Moffat's Commissioned Writers

The themes and motifs employed by Moffat clearly inform many of the scripts that he has commissioned from other writers. Simon Nye's 'Amy's Choice' will be focused on later in this collection by Dee Amy-Chinn but for now suffice it to say that its depiction of gender and sexuality is presented through a fantasy, injected with humour: the Doctor's doppelganger, the Dream Lord, forces Amy to grow up and decide whether life on board the TARDIS with the Doctor or life married to Rory in Leadworth is a reality. The comic Gothic forms much of the structure of two scripts by Gareth Roberts, 'The Lodger' and its sequel 'Closing Time'. 'The Lodger' focuses on the homosocial bond between the Doctor and Craig and his role in bringing the lovelorn Craig and Sophie together (themes that will also be drawn upon later in this collection by Amy-Chinn). Craig's flat is occupied by a time engine that devours people. Gothic space is represented in Craig's flat. The disturbances from the time engine are realised in the ever-growing damp patch on the ceiling. It is a sign that the rest of the house, quite different in atmosphere and tone, is invading Craig's light and airy bachelor pad and that something odd and threatening is encroaching on the normal space that he occupies. The Doctor, however, has detected the abnormalities at the heart of the domestic scene, literally and symbolically, and must put them right.

The queer architecture of the house, and the title of the episode 'The Lodger', alludes in specific ways to the cinema of director Alfred Hitchcock. Steven Jacobs proposes that 'specific architectural motifs such as stairs and windows are closely connected to Hitchcockian narrative structures, such as suspense, or typical Hitchcock themes, such as voyeurism'.[18] The repetition of Gothic visuals, such as the figure behind the closed door, are also connected to Hitchcock where 'the motif of the closed door ... relates to the theme of a secret hidden within the house ... activating a dialectic of concealing and revealing' that can be found in many of Hitchcock's classic films.

Time is also behaving oddly, queerly folding back on itself, disturbing the modes of natural behaviour. Linear, normal time and space are bent completely out of shape in 'The Lodger' and symbolically match the way that characters are misshaped too, where everyone, from the Doctor, Craig and Sophie to Amy in the TARDIS, are at the mercy of the architecture of the house and the freefalling fluctuations in linear time that occur whenever 'the man upstairs' attempts to find a pilot for the time engine. The emergency program's burning up of potential pilots also fills the house with crashing and exploding noises that signify something odd and abnormal occurring within a space full of Gothic atmosphere.

Tapping into Moffat's concerns about parents and children, Roberts' sequel 'Closing Time' is an exploration of Craig's strengths and weaknesses as a father during a crisis brought about by a temporarily absent mother and an invasion by Cybermen and shares many of its attitudes about the father and son bond with Mark Gatiss's 'Night Terrors' (see below). Craig's home life is again the centre of what could best be described as Gothic farce where humour is mixed with horror and combines the uncanny and melodrama to comic effect.

Similarly, the environs of the Sanderson and Grainger store and the house Craig and Sophie now live in are rendered uncanny by the presence of the Cybermen and their rat-like Cybermats. The Cybermat at loose in the toy department and in Craig's house offer a locus for abjection as a 'metal rat... [with a] real mouth' and, as an extension of the Cybermen, a symbol of the merging of flesh and technology. The Cybermen interrupt the ordinary world from behind hidden doors, walls and mirrors to kidnap their victims and as they investigate, the Doctor and Craig make the transition from the colour and light of the store into the dark, forbidding space of the Cybermen's ship. The uncanny, however, is replaced by Craig's secure bonding with his son.

Neil Gaiman is well versed in the subversion of traditional myths and fairy tales and with 'The Doctor's Wife' he develops many of the primary symbols of the series, specifically the TARDIS located in a junkyard, echoing the opening episode from 1963. His predilections for dysfunctional families, displaced children and supernatural creatures in his fiction mirror Moffat's own subject matter, and Gaiman's take on the mythology of *Doctor Who* looks at the dichotomy between the materialist and spiritual worlds, between flesh and soul while using familiar tropes such as haunted houses and possession. The episode's themes deal with the philosophical questions about the reanimation of a family of bodies that evolves from the structure of Mary Shelley's *Frankenstein* (1818).

The bizarre family of Idris, Auntie, Uncle and Nephew is in effect one created out of reanimated corpses. Dickensian characters, they exist in a land Steven Marcus aptly sums up with Dickens's depiction of England as 'a vast necropolis. Those who are not yet in their graves soon will be – they are the living dead',[19] and one that could be appropriated for the asteroid's locus as a graveyard full of dead Time Lords and their TARDISes. They are merely living dead Prometheans, commanded by an external,

41

malevolent force called House and are material from which the life essence can be removed and replaced. The attempted preservation from decay is filtered through the effigies of Auntie and Uncle and into the slow decay of Idris as the TARDIS matrix burns up her body.

Auntie and Uncle have been repaired countless times from the remains of Time Lord castaways who have crashed onto the graveyard asteroid constructed by House, and Idris is an empty vessel, with little in the way of personal identity beyond a visual allusion to the Elsa Lanchester figure of the Bride in *Bride of Frankenstein* (1932), into which the 'soul' of the TARDIS is deposited. Not only does this acknowledge the transposition and possession of flesh or bodies by an unseen entity and the interface between living machine and human soul as seen in 'The Empty Child' but it also discusses the infinite nature of the soul in comparison to the eventual limits of matter, as Idris, now housing the TARDIS matrix, points out to the Doctor that people are also so much bigger on the inside.

The episode also uses the idea of the possessed TARDIS as a site to 'unhouse' the main characters, particularly Rory and Amy, and House subjects them to terrifying psychological ordeals that reveal their innermost fears and anxieties. The TARDIS literally becomes a 'madhouse', the antithesis of the welcoming home, inhospitable and haunted. Under House's incumbency, it is shaded in sickly green. Sharon Packer sees the symptoms of 'madness' as akin to the strangeness of 'mad houses' where madness is close enough to ordinary human behaviour to resemble daily actions but it is also different enough from average activity to make it uncanny.[20] In 'The Doctor's Wife' it could be said that Rory and Amy become *unheimlich*, trapped in TARDIS corridors that change configuration and shift in time. Rory is transformed into an embittered, rapidly ageing inmate as House turns the TARDIS into a part asylum, part maze, part fun house where Rory claims 'they come for me at night, every single night they come for me and they hurt me'. He has been driven mad by the experience of abandonment and his psychosis has developed to the extent that he seeks the death of Amy.

Compare this psychosis with that other madness, of the TARDIS matrix 'unhoused' and in control of the flesh and blood Idris. Idris is constantly regarded as 'off 'er head', 'doolally' or the 'bitey, mad lady' and represents the TARDIS as an unfettered female self, albeit temporarily. Her madness is defined by the release, after hundreds of years of silence, of a once confined intelligence and an exhilarating assertion of self-hood. She literally is the female Gothic heroine trapped in the castle, suddenly released and able to find her sense of self, limited by the painful decay of Idris's body before 'She's back in the box again' and 'rehoused' in the TARDIS. This allusion is visually symbolised by the prison in which Idris is locked, a prison that resembles a human-sized bird cage and again is a metaphor for the barely contained female Other that the TARDIS has become, the curious wife of the episode's title.

House is 'unhoused' evil to the TARDIS's 'housed' good and representative of everything the Doctor and his TARDIS are not. House floats in an uncanny pocket universe that borders the one more familiar and home to the Doctor, Amy and Rory. House is unable to escape his state of *unheimlich* and remains trapped as the proximate 'Other' to the Doctor and the TARDIS, which in contrast are always in continual flux and undergo repeated change. When House attempts to change, he seals his own fate and is re-possessed by the TARDIS matrix. As the Doctor indicates, the TARDIS is 'Bigger on the inside! See, House. That's your problem. Size of a planet but inside you are just so small.'

Matthew Graham's 'The Rebel Flesh'/'The Almost People', meanwhile, is one of the series' most explicit explorations of 'Other' as self. It returns to the theme of bioengineering the body and the self and the consequences of technologically reproducing the human form. This reinterpretation of the self occurs within Gothic spaces – the disused chapels of an island monastery – uses grotesque, abject body horror to question the ethical and sentient status of the doppelgangers in the story and shows the 'gangers' confronting their human counterparts to demand their rights to be in the world.

Mark Gatiss's 'Night Terrors' also fits in with the 'signatures' associated with Moffat identified in this chapter. The episode expands upon the notion of the home as *unheimlich* centring around the dysfunctional little boy George. The flat where George lives is a domestic space where two parents have been chosen to foster an alien child. A perception field created by George shapes his parents' memories and, although outwardly normal, there is something not quite right in this domestic setting. The story explores the Gothic within a run-down housing estate where tenants live in fear of a threatening landlord and Social Services, and the ordinary becomes uncanny – an old woman wheeling her trolley down the corridor, a noisy lift, a pile of refuse (which swallows the old woman) and 'the scariest place in the universe – a child's bedroom'.

George is an analogue to many child viewers, fearful of everything and requiring rituals carried out by parents to reassure him that he will be safe in the dark. The light switch must be switched on and off five times before he goes to sleep, while the noises in the night and the toys threatening to come to life must be locked up in an old cupboard. George articulates the particular desire of many children watching *Doctor Who* and entreats the Doctor: 'please save me from the monsters'. This correlation reflects the many ways that fairy tales, fables and stories tell children that although monsters, both supernatural and human, may exist they can also be conquered, that fears will be controlled and anxieties resolved.

'Night Terrors' articulates *Doctor Who*'s own possible effects on the child viewer when George's 'father' attempts to blame television for his woes. The lines 'May be it was things on telly. Scary stuff. Getting under his skin. Frightening him. So we stopped letting him watch', are a metatextual nod to the scariness of *Doctor Who* and recent concerns from parents about the show. 'Oh, you don't want to let him do that,' counters the Doctor. He winks at George, but it is also a wink of self-awareness at the watching audience. Reading is also blamed, but the Doctor suggests, 'Reading's great. You like stories George? Yeah?' The idea of moral storytelling at the heart of the series, to disarm and deal with the fears of the modern world, is acknowledged by the Doctor and his bedtime stories from a thousand years ago: 'I loved a good bedtime story. The Three Little Sontarans, The Emperor Dalek's New Clothes, Snow White and the Seven Keys to Doomsday, eh? All the classics.' *Doctor Who* is again emphasised as fairy tale and Gatiss merges classic fairy-tale stories with elements of the series' mythology.

In 'Night Terrors', characters are ultimately plunged into a nightmarish world. This is supplemented by a score often based upon the nursery-rhyme-styled song 'Tick Tock Goes the Clock' which also ties in with the series' story arc. George's fears are internalised within the bedroom cupboard and specifically within a doll's house kept inside it. Here is an unreal world of life-sized dolls, glass eyes, fake clocks and wooden frying pans. The wooden inhabitants of the doll's house also reflect the uncanny quality of marionettes, dolls and automatons that Packer sees as 'close enough to real human forms to remind us of humans'.[21] There is a long tradition of children's fiction in which the protagonists become part of the world of the doll's house, from the work of Beatrix Potter and Frances Hodgson Burnett to the books and stories of Rumer Godden, Helen Clare and William Sleator 'where the domestic can change into the Gothic, or as Freud would call it, the *unheimlich*'.[22] The child positioned within the transitional spaces of the doll's house narrative has 'deep desires beyond loneliness' and the house's 'structures seem to be designed or altered by the child to meet their [sic] inner needs'.[23] George puts everything that frightens him in the doll's house and uses it as a psychic repository for all his fears because he feels rejected and abandoned by his foster father. As with many of our unconscious anxieties, he is unaware that he is the cause of this and has started a cycle of fear that can only be resolved by opening the cupboard door. Similarly, Alex and Claire's need to have a child was sensed by this alien cuckoo and the solution to this crisis is for Alex to embrace George and declare his love for his son. The episode, like many doll and toy narratives, is concerned with the socialisation of the child and the acceptance of the real world in which the child's parents exist, despite the child's disillusionment and fears.

Toby Whithouse's 'The God Complex' depicts a hotel as a shifting maze full of rooms that expose specific fears of objects, people and situations: of parents, clowns, of being eaten, the Weeping Angels and male inadequacy with the opposite sex. A sinister Gothic space, monitored by CCTV and filled with muzak, nursery rhymes, manic laughter and screams, it alternatively functions as a prison. Significantly, the episode disinters the Doctor's unresolved fear of error or failure, even in the face of intractable problems or impossible tasks. He accepts his fear of change, resolving to let Amy take responsibility for a life devoid of travelling in time and space.

Questioning the Monstrous

The monstrous, the potential of horror and the ambiguous roles of heroes and villains have become points of enquiry within the current series, questioning the 'classic' series' reductive codification of monsters or villains as simply evil or bad, where now, as Hills suggests, ' "monsters ... can be understood rather than narratively repressed or destroyed" '.[24] In Moffat's universe, the monstrous is often deceptive, an accidental effect of something going awry – where 'gangers' gain sentience through a freak thunderstorm (in 'The Rebel Flesh'); a siren (in 'The Curse of the Black Spot') is really a virtual doctor and an alien child only seeks the unconditional love of a parent (in 'Night Terrors') – or monsters can subvert their traditional definitions and roles – a Silurian is transformed into a Victorian investigator tracking Jack the Ripper and a Sontaran becomes a frontline nurse (in 'A Good Man Goes to War').

The abstractions of Gothic narrative allow Moffat to also examine the divided nature of the hero/villain. The Doctor, for example, uses his own death to create subjective distance from his troubling transformation into the 'mighty warrior', the villain that Madame Kovarian and the Silents fear and then wage war against. His very accessibility and ubiquity, his *heimlich* you could say, becomes destabilised, or *unheimlich*, in 'A Good Man Goes to War' and as a result, the subtext in series six is concerned with restoring this balance.

Television for Adults: *Jekyll*

Unlike *Doctor Who*, Moffat's *Jekyll* (2007), screened after the watershed on BBC1, was aimed entirely at adults, with its strong language, its scenes of an explicit sexual nature and its graphic violence. Yet Moffat's psychological 'sequel' to Robert Louis Stevenson's *The Strange Case of Dr Jekyll and Mr Hyde* displays many of the signatures identified in this chapter. Hyde's emergence is signalled when Jackman's eyes turn black and his predilection for violence and sexual dominance are manifested through games and rhymes, and he acquires a repeated signature tune, in the form of the nursery rhyme 'Boys and Girls Come Out to Play'. Here Moffat's characteristic use of singsong dialogue and nursery rhymes define Hyde's status as an immature, monstrous child. As in 'Blink', partially uncovered messages alert Jackman to the imminent arrival of Hyde, who projects himself into dictaphones, telephones and computers to send messages and warnings. Jackman, recovering from his first controlled transformation, wakes up and plays back a recording of these messages on a television monitor. His own face stares back at him and asks, just as Jamie earlier asked of his estranged parent Nancy in 'The Empty Child', 'Daddy? Is that you, Daddy? Are you my daddy?'[25] The confrontation is so intense for Jackman that he visualises Hyde reaching out through the television set and strangling him.

Marriage, parents and children are markers of normalcy and abnormalcy in *Jekyll*. It is not only a battle of wills between Jackman and his doppelganger, but also one fought between 'daddy' Jackman and 'son' Hyde to preserve the domestic status quo and prevent the 'unhousing' of Jackman from his family life. Hyde is eventually exposed as an incomplete superman, needful of the emotional maturity found within Jackman's family, and who must accept that, as half of one complete man, Jackman is essential to this maturity. To this end, the drama takes place in stereotypically Gothic spaces, such as cells, laboratories, old houses, cellars and basements. When Claire explores the Klein and Utterson mansion, *Jekyll* recognises the function of such space as a repository of 'family secrets and the immediate past of its transgressive protagonists'.[26] She finds a makeshift ward where several Jackman/Hyde doppelgangers are kept confined, monsters created by failed attempts to clone the original Jekyll. This manipulation of Jekyll through technological means also references Moffat's fascination with the impact of science and technology on the body. *Jekyll* further ties in with what Fred Botting sees as the Gothic tendency to render monsters more sympathetically,[27] that we have seen at work in *Doctor Who*. The serial ends with a typical Moffat twist where here Jackman's mother is revealed to be a 'Hyde' creature.

Hidden Meanings: The Gothic and Moffat's Story Arc

There remains one more important element of the Gothic to consider in *Doctor Who* and this is in relation to Moffat's use of the story arc. Non-linear narrative structures increasingly become important to Moffat in *Doctor Who*. He has acknowledged and experimented with them in previous dramas and comedies, such as *Joking Apart* and *Coupling*,[28] and in earlier work within the *Doctor Who* canon (like 'The Girl in the Fireplace' which begins *in medias res*) but it is with 'Blink', like *Jekyll*, that Moffat consolidated the combination of horror and non-linear storytelling. Steven Peacock argues that Moffat's pre-2010 narratives for the programme have 'puzzle-box' story structures[29] and Charles suggests that 'the meanings behind his mysteries are all already there, hidden immediately beneath the surface'.[30] This includes twist endings as in 'The Girl in the Fireplace'.[31] 'Blink's structure is determined by clues Sally Sparrow finds in messages hidden behind peeling wallpaper, in old letters and phone calls from the past and the Easter eggs in her DVD collection. At the climax of the episode, Sally and Lawrence return to Wester Drumlins and play back the messages in their entirety, arranging and presenting them in linear order. Non-linear clues, obfuscating messages, incomplete and hidden narratives and audience expectation now emerge as a visible linear story and redolent of what Jay Clayton sees as the experimentation in which late-eighteenth-century Gothic writers indulged.[32] It reflects the sensations of the Gothic horror narrative where rooms, objects and people convey secrets, hidden messages and clues used to solve or make sense of a particular mystery. Examples include Ann Radcliffe's female protagonist attempting to solve *The Mysteries of Udolpho* (1794). Philippa Gates notes that this early example of female Gothic 'offers a heroine who must assert self-control and rely on her intelligence and moral strength to overcome the tests, confrontations, or entrapment she faces'.[33]

It is in Moffat's 'Silence in the Library'/'Forest of the Dead', and Moffat's own era, however, that non-linear puzzles are associated with a story arc. As Peacock has observed, River Song's diary contains mysteries – spoilers – which can only be revealed in time.[34] The journey through the Aplan Mortarium in 'The Time of Angels' is an opportunity to use the trappings of the Gothic to allow characters to reveal secrets, wrongdoings and, in reflecting Freud's 'return of the repressed', exorcise their own long dormant psychological phantoms. As the Doctor, Amy, River and the Clerics led by Octavian penetrate the maze, all manner of confessions are overheard where the truth is as hard to find as 'a stone angel on the loose amongst stone statues'. This episode again, in typically Gothic fashion, litters the plot with clues, secrets, lies and truths about the Doctor's relationship with River. We are left to ponder River's identity and are told that she went to prison for killing a 'good man'.

In 'The Impossible Astronaut', too, she and Rory explore the tunnels beneath a warehouse, discussing the bifurcated nature of her relationship with the Doctor, his first and her last experiences. At the same time, Amy reveals her own secret, a pregnancy that exists across similarly bifurcated time and space and the nature of which is left unresolved until later in the sixth series. In 'Day of the Moon', Amy's status as mother is traumatically explored at the Graystark Hall orphanage, the walls of which are scattered with messages resembling those in 'Blink'. This is accompanied by the first of many appearances from Madame Kovarian, a woman who constantly appears through a series of concealed openings to utter cryptic clues.

Finally, in 'The Angels Take Manhattan', the Doctor reads the delayed narrative of Melody Malone's detective novel back to Amy, a book to which she has already added an afterword that is only revealed at the end of the episode. The afterword is a summation of her own adventures and she asks the Doctor to tell her stories to the Amelia waiting in the garden at Leadworth. Moffat self-reflexively uses the novel's form to conclude Amy's story and construct Amelia's childhood recreations of her future adventures with the Raggedy Doctor.

Conclusion

As in much of 'classic' *Doctor Who*, fear of the ordinary and the everyday is pushed forward in Moffat's narratives. Fear is, to a degree, a very child-centric component, either expressed through Moffat's recall of his own childhood fears and what also scares his own children, whom he consults on a regular basis, or by dint of specific child characters placed in central roles. The cathartic thrills of Holmes and Hinchcliffe's serials are certainly a potent memory for Moffat but, unlike his own work, there were very few child characters in serials produced during that era and much of the horror and threat was targeted at adult characters and involved genre pastiche rather than the everyday. Although the companion was the proxy child identification figure, narratives did not focus very much on the maturing of such figures or the emotional impact upon them of fear until the programme's closing seasons.

Moffat was an adolescent during the Hinchcliffe era but it could be argued that his focus on childhood fears and the development of child characters into maturity is also a reflection of other children's television of the period. During the decades spanning the Letts and Hinchcliffe productions, a number of contemporary and period Gothic dramas featuring child protagonists were also transmitted. In the 1970s and 1980s, serials such as *Escape into Night* (ATV, 1972), *Children of the Stones* (HTV, 1977), *King of the Castle* (HTV, 1977) and *The Clifton House Mystery* (HTV, 1978) rubbed shoulders with adaptations of *The Secret Garden* (BBC, 1975), *Tom's Midnight Garden* (BBC, 1974, 1989) and *The Box of Delights* (BBC, 1984). Even Russell T Davies's highly regarded dramas for children *Dark Season* (BBC, 1991) and *Century Falls* (BBC, 1993) hark back to this period by putting pre-teen and teenage characters and their anxieties at the centre of the drama. Wheatley sees these television dramas as reflections of children's Gothic that 'challenges the view that childhood is a time of innocence, safety, and protection, and instead sees the world as full of threat and menace'.[35] At the same time, Moffat's *Who*, while not designed solely for adults like *Jekyll*, appeals to older viewers, the idea of what is monstrous can be questioned, and his approach to the story arc can be tied into the Gothic.

Notes

1. Alec Charles, 'The Crack of Doom: The Uncanny Echoes of Steven Moffat's *Doctor Who*', *Science Fiction Film and Television* 4/1 (2011), p. 4.
2. Charles, 'The Crack of Doom', p. 3.
3. Gina Wisker, *Horror Fiction: An Introduction* (New York, 2005), pp. 146–7.
4. Helen Wheatley, 'Uncanny Children, Haunted Houses, Hidden Rooms: Children's Gothic Television in the 1970s and 80s', *Visual Culture in Britain* 13/3 (2012), p. 5.
5. Wheatley, 'Uncanny Children', p. 6.
6. David Punter, *The Literature of Terror: A History of Gothic Fictions* 1 (London, 1980), p. 1; also see Mary Whitehouse's complaints about horror in *Doctor Who*.

7. 'Interview: Steven Moffat, Screenwriter', *The Scotsman Magazine*, 20 March 2010. Available at www.scotsman.com/news/interview_steven_moffat_doctor_who_screenwriter_1_474813 (accessed 12 February 2012).
8. Nick Griffiths, 'Dark Man', *Radio Times*, 7–13 June 2008, p. 11.
9. Matt Hills, *Triumph of a Time Lord: Regenerating Doctor Who in the Twenty-First Century* (London, 2010), pp. 119–21.
10. Hills, *Triumph of a Time Lord*, p. 121.
11. Jonathan Bignell, 'The Child as Addressee: Viewer and Consumer in Mid 1960s *Doctor Who*', in David Butler (ed.), *Time And Relative Dissertations In Space* (Manchester, 2007), pp. 43–55.
12. Catherine Spooner, *Contemporary Gothic* (London, 2008), p. 8.
13. Griffiths, 'Dark Man', p. 11.
14. Gary Gillatt, *Doctor Who: From A to Z* (London, 1998).
15. Hills, *Triumph of a Time Lord*, pp. 122–3.
16. 'Do You Remember the First Time?', *Doctor Who Confidential*, BBC Three, 9 June 2007.
17. Barbara Creed, *Phallic Panic: Film, Horror and the Primal Uncanny* (Melbourne, 2005), p. 29.
18. Steven Jacobs, *The Wrong House: The Architecture of Alfred Hitchcock* (Rotterdam, 2007), p. 12.
19. Steven Marcus, *Dickens: from Pickwick to Dombey* (London, 1965), p. 145.
20. Sharon Packer, *Movies and the Modern Psyche* (Connecticut, 2007), p. 69.
21. Ibid.
22. Lois R. Kuznets, *When Toys Come Alive: Narratives of Animation, Metamorphosis, and Development* (Connecticut, 1994), pp. 123–5.
23. Ibid.
24. Hills, *Triumph of a Time Lord*, p. 135.
25. Charles, 'The Crack of Doom', p. 5.
26. David Punter and Glennis Byron, *The Gothic* (Oxford, 2004), pp. 261–2.
27. Fred Botting, *Gothic Romanced: Consumption, Gender and Technology in Contemporary Fictions* (Oxford, 2008), p. 15.
28. Charles, 'The Crack of Doom', p. 4.
29. Steven Peacock, 'Steven Moffat: Time Lord', *Critical Studies in Television*, December 2008. Available at www.criticalstudiesintelevision.com/index.php?siid=8605 (accessed 2 July 2012).
30. Charles, 'The Crack of Doom', p. 7.
31. Ibid., p. 10.
32. Jay Clayton, *Romantic Vision and the Novel* (Cambridge, 2009), p. 48.
33. Philippa Gates, *Detecting Women: Gender and the Hollywood Detective Film* (New York, 2011), p. 19.
34. Peacock, 'Steven Moffat'.
35. Wheatley, 'Uncanny Children', p. 7.

3

GENEALOGIES ACROSS TIME

History and Storytelling in Steven Moffat's *Doctor Who*

Matthew Kilburn

S ince its revival in 2005, *Doctor Who* has been engaged with human history to a level not sustained throughout the original series. As noted in the Introduction to this collection, a visit to Earth's past has been established as an early rite of passage for each of the Doctor's twenty-first-century human companions and these have been followed by at least one other historical adventure per season. All the historical adventures in the post-2005 period of *Doctor Who* would be termed 'pseudo-historicals' in the conventions of *Doctor Who* criticism as they include science-fiction and fantasy elements. During Russell T Davies's period as executive producer and head writer, these took forms including what Matt Hills calls 'the celebrity historical', focusing on celebrated figures like Charles Dickens, Agatha Christie and even Shakespeare,[1] genre parody and depictions of past societies constructed in part from existing representations in popular culture. These trends have continued in the series written under the aegis of Steven Moffat, although his era deals differently with 'the celebrity historical'. The Moffat era draws on a number of different genealogies. The programme's treatment of history has often suggested that Moffat has been conscious of the programme's status as a television institution often identified as somehow distinctively British. Furthermore, Moffat's *Doctor Who*, with its emphasis on character, allows a space for historically sensitive, mildly polemical drama, drawing on a different lineage. However, under Moffat, the programme's storytelling nature has shaped its perception of history with use from different source material.

History ... and a Very British One at That!

The first episode of the Steven Moffat era to make substantive use of historical signifiers is, appropriately perhaps for a time-travel series, not one of the historical episodes at all. 'The Beast Below' depicts a future Britain (minus Scotland) escaping an Earth ravaged by solar flares. Britain is eventually revealed to be travelling on the back of a whale-like spacefaring creature, the eponymous beast. This future imagined community has retreated into a selectively reconstructed mid-twentieth century of red telephone boxes and school uniforms. English counties are housed in tower blocks, clockwork plaster heads from amusement arcades are arbiters of moral conformity and a beloved monarch speaks in comedic Cockney. The queen, Liz Ten (Elizabeth the Tenth), is a stylised representation of the New Elizabethanism of the 1950s, the remote and mystical depersonalisation dreamed of by romantic conservatives in the early years of the reign of Elizabeth II combined with a faith in national renewal through technology. Liz Ten seeks to avenge the oppression of her people by their administrators, but a political and cultural critique is revealed by her failure to do so, as Liz Ten herself is responsible for building the system with which all the people of Starship UK are collaborators, based on the enslavement and torture of the Beast.

In Mark Gatiss's 'Victory of the Daleks', *Doctor Who* pits a symbol of its own cultural endurance – the Dalek – against another mythologised element of British history. 'Victory of the Daleks' authenticates its wartime setting substantially through the inclusion of Winston Churchill as a character. The war of 'Victory of the Daleks' is introduced as centrally directed by the Prime Minister and the staff of the Cabinet War Rooms, continuing the struggle for the collective good despite the suffering and death of loved ones. Loyalty to Britain is equated with loyalty to the Prime Minister, a charismatic and selectively charming figure who talks in catchphrases, but whose judgment is clouded by his single-minded desire to win the war. The Churchill of 'Victory' is ruthless but his willingness to think the unthinkable (the setting is the London Blitz, so several years before the bombing of Dresden) is presented in fantastical terms, through his demand for the TARDIS key and his belief in Professor Bracewell and the 'Ironsides', the patriotically refashioned Daleks.

In casting Churchill, 'Victory of the Daleks' co-opts an earlier portrayal, that by Ian McNeice, in Howard Brenton's play *Never So Good*.[2] This was variously described as 'pugnacious',[3] 'wicked'[4] and 'nice comic relief'.[5] Over its run at the National Theatre in London in 2008, *Never So Good* was seen by a much smaller number of people than watched 'Victory of the Daleks' on television, but McNeice's experience in playing Churchill was mentioned in *Doctor Who Magazine* as relevant to his casting.[6] *Doctor Who*'s status as 'quality' television, established under the Russell T Davies production regime, was reinforced by association with a stage play which proposed arguments about twentieth-century British history.[7] While it has been alleged that the repeated resort to catchphrases renders the Churchill of 'Victory' 'a pretty superficial portrait',[8] these habits are used as markers of documentary authenticity.[9] However sketchily, McNeice's characterisation of Churchill is contextualised both in the history of World War II and the history of television portrayals of Churchill. It is this context which lends Churchill the authority to challenge Bracewell, broken in mind and robotic body, to prove his humanity and thus reject the materialist determinism of identity comparable to the eugenics practiced by both Dalek and Nazi opponents.

Moffat's *Doctor Who* relies on the saturation of the audience by media representations of the past to make its points through familiarity. In 'Victory of the Daleks', Bracewell enables the rescue of the Doctor by Royal Air Force aeroplanes, rapidly and unfeasibly made spaceworthy. The sequence acts as a commentary upon World War II's impact on British science fiction in mass entertainment media. The squadron leader's call sign is 'Danny Boy', perhaps not only a reference to Frederic Weatherly's elegiac ballad (1907) and the call signs used in the film *Where Eagles Dare* (1968),[10] but also a nod to the RAF officer in space, Dan Dare of the original *Eagle* (1950–69). The depiction of British soldiers raising the Union flag above Whitehall in the manner of the United States soldiers in Joe Rosenthal's photograph 'Raising the Flag on Iwo Jima' co-opts and rebuffs the early twenty-first-century sub-genre of films where British initiatives have been attributed to the United States. The historical outlook of 'Victory of the Daleks' is grounded in *Doctor Who*'s role as a specifically British cultural product and in its awareness of the portrayal of World War II in a postwar British popular culture from which *Doctor Who* and the Daleks themselves emerged. The effect is to associate Britishness with an emotionally literate humanism, and project it into an imagined 1940, though the emphasis on central organisation over the individual (the Cabinet War Rooms staff receive little characterisation) leaves the episode's historical perspective confused. In 'Let's Kill Hitler', the Doctor's brief confrontation with Hitler is presented as a statement of Britishness, although River's transformation from assassin in a Nazi jacket to heroine-archaeologist owes something to the American precedent of the Nazi-fighting Indiana Jones.[11]

'Vincent and the Doctor': *Doctor Who* as Campaigning Biographical Drama

As *Doctor Who*'s depiction of Churchill was placed in a tradition of fictional depictions of Churchill, 'Vincent and the Doctor' is placed in a genealogy of biographical dramas about Vincent van Gogh, fitting in with Steven Moffat's interest in exploring a small ensemble of characters in his episodes. Its title alludes to an earlier television series and film, Robert Altman's *Vincent and Theo* (1990). It acknowledges established conventions about van Gogh's life; though early evening restrictions based on *Doctor Who*'s responsibilities to its child audience presumably prevented a realisation of the amputation of van Gogh's ear by the artist himself, van Gogh is represented as unappreciated by contemporaries and troubled by profound mental illness. So far, the episode panders to general knowledge about van Gogh, perhaps building upon it by introducing the viewer to some of the context of the artist's methods of production – multiple paintings of lilies, the canvases hung out to dry – or paintings of which they were previously unaware. However, it goes further than the other historical settings in the series by relating the plight of the character based on the historical van Gogh to issues contemporaneous with the viewer.

While the episode evidences a 'Moffat signature', it also bears that of its writer, Richard Curtis. Richard Curtis's dramatic interpretations of history make passionate arguments which take clearly delineated sides. *Blackadder Goes Forth* (BBC, 1989) aroused the ire of revisionist historians of World War I in depicting senior British military officers as sending ill-prepared subordinates to their deaths in the obstinate pursuit of a badly conceived strategy. *The Boat that Rocked* (2009) presented an idealised view of offshore pirate radio in the 1960s, ignoring the gangsterish nature of some operators and replacing the cultural, intellectual and economic concerns of the ministerial opponents of the 'pirates' with a farcical representation of reactionary prejudice. *Doctor Who* forces Curtis to be more even-handed. Van Gogh's enemies among the townspeople elicit some sympathy: the daughter of one of van Gogh's critics is killed during the episode by the Krafayis, and even the Doctor, in the privacy of the TARDIS, regrets that van Gogh doesn't paint in the (implicitly more photo-realist) style of Thomas Gainsborough. This allows the viewers to build some sense of historical development – though they are not told that Gainsborough painted in an earlier period than van Gogh – and it identifies van Gogh as an 'Impressionist' (though 'Post-Impressionist' is the classification preferred by art historians).[12]

Curtis omits Vincent's friends and family, beyond brief mentions, to allow the Doctor and Amy prominence. They circulate around Vincent as intimates and as interrogators of the historical problem (Vincent's depression and lack of acclaim or material prosperity) and the science-fictional one (the mysterious shape in the painting of the church at Autun, a somewhat Gothic location, and the revelation of the Krafayis). The slaying of the Krafayis by Vincent is also an answer to the problem of Vincent's identity and his alienation from his contemporaries: he is not mad, but gifted in a fashion coded both as science fictional – his synaesthesia allows him to see the Krafayis – and more readily perceived by different cultures to his own, as illuminated and expounded by the Starry Night sequence which is placed after the 'monster' component of the plot.

This last detail emphasises the importance to the episode of historical dissonance. This is achieved not only through the distinction between van Gogh as an artist unappreciated in his own day and the laudatory reception he has received after his death, but also the failure of his society to provide a method for the alleviation of his depression or to interpret it and his synaes-thesia as anything other than a variety of alcoholism. 'Vincent and the Doctor' uses the Doctor and Amy to contrast modern com-prehension of depressive illness with the disdain and dismissal of the nineteenth century. The shock of bringing Vincent van Gogh briefly into the twenty-first century is for viewers as well as van Gogh. The innovation encourages complacency about the bene-ficial effects of praise and an appreciative environment upon the depressive in both Amy and the viewer. The failure of the Doctor and Amy to change van Gogh's fate hints at the complexities of depressive illness. While 'Vincent and the Doctor' is open to the charge that it condescends to the past as unenlightened, Amy's naive faith in her ability to restore Vincent's self-esteem bears some comparison to Barbara Wright's belief that she can eradicate human sacrifice in pre-Hispanic Mexico in 'The Aztecs' (1964). In both cases, human nature is obstinate and unpredict-able in the face of an individual whom the programme positions as the agent of human moral values.

While superficially conforming to the 'celebrity historical' form and thus repudiating the insistence of early Doctor Who that its historical stories should concentrate on people at the margins of great events, 'Vincent and the Doctor' turns the assumptions behind this maxim on its head by recognising that reputation itself evolves and changes through time. This plays into the con-ventional charge that biographical drama sinks easily into hagiog-raphy by presenting Vincent as an impoverished and persecuted martyr ultimately elevated into a communion of creative saints. The episode adds a cautionary note which restrains its drive to canonise Vincent. If Vincent is a prophet of unrestrained artistic expression, then on leaving his own country he is a prophet rec-ognised by the van Gogh scholar and museum curator Dr Black. Black, ignorant of the Doctor's time-travelling ways, immediately dismisses his identification as impossible. The gag illustrates the gap between the mythologised van Gogh and the often alcohol-sodden, lustful persona represented as the reality in Doctor Who. The art historian's truth is only one facet of the human experi-ence which the Doctor and Amy can share, and through them the viewer; the gesture is almost a rebuke to a school of revisionist historian who wishes to present van Gogh as a controlled professional frustrated at his lack of recognition rather than a marginalised figure suffering from undiagnosed mental illness.

The continuity announcement which followed the original BBC 1 transmission referred viewers who had been 'affected' by the issues raised in the programme to a Helpline. This service might have been more familiar to viewers from single dramas or episodes of more overtly socially conscious drama series such as *EastEnders*, focusing on 'difficult or distressing issues' in the terminology of the BBC Editorial Guidelines. The Guidelines state:

> We must seek to ensure that information provided is impartial, objective and accurate. We should give details of and/or links to a wide range of agencies, charities and statutory organisations. No single body should be unduly promoted at the expense of others.
>
> We must ensure that any helpline, whether provided by the BBC or an outside agency, is capable of offering a robust service.[13]

While van Gogh's death was only alluded to as part of events, rather than portrayed, the episode still shows signs of having been governed by BBC editorial policy on 'Suicide, Attempted Suicide, Self-Harm and Eating Disorders'. This policy is described as follows:

> Suicide, attempted suicide and self-harm should be portrayed with great sensitivity, whether in drama or in factual programmes. Factual reporting and fictional portrayal of suicide, attempted suicide and self-harm have the potential to make such actions appear possible, and even appropriate, to the vulnerable.[14]

There is no tradition in British television of the 'very special episode' of a popular fictional series, widely trailed as addressing social concern. Nevertheless the positioning of this announcement after 'Vincent and the Doctor' suggests that as far as this episode's presentation was concerned, the most popular television drama was one which demonstrated social utility, and perhaps that the best history is the kind which is most socially useful;

an aspiration perhaps in keeping with *Doctor Who*'s origins at Sydney Newman's BBC Television Drama Group, remembered for its patronage of 'social issue' drama[15] and with the BBC's public service remit.[16] In the case of 'Vincent and the Doctor', science fiction is periphery, used to comment on the idea of those with mental illnesses as somehow 'alien' and 'other'.

History and Telefantasy

However, in most cases, Moffat's *Doctor Who* subordinates history to his fantasy narratives and story arcs, drawing on a different lineage of source material. 'Victory of the Daleks' can be seen as a means of introducing newly designed Daleks to the programme. Toby Whithouse's 'The Vampires of Venice', meanwhile, seeks recognition in a different set of genres: historical drama, travelogue history and the postwar British horror film. The narrative plays obliquely on the factual history of its period. In the episode, Venice's isolation is the result of plague. Historically, plague struck the city in 1576 and 1577, though Doge Alvise Mocenigo I did not abandon Venice in the way the story suggests its rulers did. The population fell from approximately 175,000 in 1575 to 124,000 in 1581.[17] However, the development is given no context in political history. There is no mention of the triumphant Battle of Lepanto in 1571, or the humiliating peace treaty with the Ottoman Empire of 1573 which bound Venice to pay 100,000 ducats in tribute to the Turkish sultan for three years and surrender her claims to Cyprus, a blow to the very maritime pride which 'Vampires of Venice' celebrates.

Yet, 'The Vampires of Venice' does express some of the preoccupations of the historical Venice of 1580. The historical Venetian convents, which took in boarding-girls from the Venetian nobility and citizenry (the two upper ranks of Venetian society), are displaced by the fictional school of the Saturnyne matriarch Rosanna Calvierri, where no religion is acknowledged and it is implied that the girls come from low-status families. This development dramatizes the feared corruption of the political body of Venice covered in Mary Leven's study of late Renaissance Venetian convents *Virgins of Venice*.[18] A movement for reformation of manners, co-dependent with the Roman Catholic Counter-Reformation, encouraged nuns to live in greater isolation from the city where they had previously played a large role in elite social life: like the girls taken by the Saturnynes, they had to 'Forget [their] people, and [their] father's home'.[19] The presentation of Rosanna Calvierri and her school also bears comparison with another confined female community in sixteenth-century Venice, that of the prostitute. A proclamation of the Venetian government in 1543 claimed that elite women were unable to tell luxuriantly dressed prostitutes apart from their own rank.[20] In *Doctor Who* the 'perception filter' is an electronic device, but the effect is similar. However, while these historical allusions are present they are secondary to the influence of horror-genre conventions. 'The Vampires of Venice' dines à la carte on history; its relation to the Venice of 1580 is supportive to its manipulation of twentieth-century genre conventions.

'The Vampires of Venice' refashions the history of both its fictional and real-world settings into a watery pastiche of the generic Mitteleuropa of Hammer's cinematic horror cycle. Set in a hyperbolised Gothic palace, the refugee Saturnynes posing as 'vampires' are alien predators not only seeking to feed, but to change members of the native society into their own kind, like Dracula in nineteenth-century London. The girls of Rosanna's school wear nightgowns reminiscent of those worn by the pupils of the girls' school in the film *Lust for a Vampire* (1971), part of Hammer's 'lesbian vampire' sequence, while the incestuous undertones of the relationship between Rosanna and Francesco borrow from that of the vampire Baron Meinster and his mother in *Brides of Dracula* (1960). These associations remove *Doctor Who* from the urban, global, female-friendly contemporary signature of Russell T Davies and instead root the programme in an older form of British fantasy drama, preoccupied with threats to masculinity and racial or species integrity. The effect is to emphasise the postmodern knowledge of the regulars, who deconstruct the conventions of Gothic period horror as they go, as well as draw attention to *Doctor Who*'s early years. Matt Smith's Doctor produces a library card showing William Hartnell's face. While *Doctor Who* in the Hartnell period did not display the overtly Gothic trappings which the series did in the mid-1970s, 'Journey into Terror', an episode of 'The Chase' (1965), reveals a castle inhabited by Dracula and Frankenstein's Monster to be an artificial construction, a robotic attraction at the 1996 World's Fair.

The 'Vampires of Venice' themselves are likewise not what they seem; but where the 1965 episode reinforced the series' rationalism with a technological explanation, the assimilation of several more genres and conventions in the intervening years allows the 2010 episode to contrast different modes of fantasy. This fantasy enables the programme to explore different themes.

For example, 'Venice' amalgamates concepts drawn from cultural representations of the 'other' and the 'East'. Some production decisions are historically aware. The casting of black actors in prominent roles might be understood primarily in terms of the multi-ethnic modern Britain projected into the legendary past seen in other BBC 'family' series such as *Robin Hood* (2006–09) and *Merlin* (2008–). But it also indicates to modern audiences that Venice included 'ethnic minority' communities within its metropolitan population, implying its status as an imperial power with extensive trade links in Europe, the Middle East and North Africa. This portrayal of ethnic diversity has been found troublesome: Frank Collins finds 'The Vampires of Venice' 'morally conflicted in its themes of speciesism and racism'.[21] Moreover, Venice is visited in 1580 because the Doctor dare not risk the eighteenth century and an encounter with Casanova. Adult viewers are encouraged to remember Russell T Davies's *Casanova* for the BBC (2005) where the eponymous memoirist was played by David Tennant. Memories of Davies's portrayal of a Venice thriving upon conspicuous consumption and casual sex are contrasted with the new series' upholding of monogamous commitment (which will be discussed further in Dee Amy-Chinn's chapter, following). At the same time, the episode teases the prospect of Matt Smith clashing with his predecessor. Attention is also drawn to the cultural heritage of the Doctor's touristic 'romantic' reading of Venice and the pas de deux of sexuality and possession which drives the plot.

Series six's headline approach to history was its willingness to include historical figures notorious for misdeeds. 'The Impossible Astronaut' and 'Day of the Moon' portray Richard Nixon's paranoia as magnified by exposure to the Doctor's working methods and their shared awareness of the Silence's threat. On the one hand, the programme offers signposts to historical integrity. First is the Doctor's exchange with River where River proposes that Nixon did some good as president. The second comes at the Doctor's parting from Nixon. Having asked whether he will be

DOCTOR WHO, *THE ELEVENTH HOUR*

remembered, Nixon can only receive the Doctor's evasive invocation of Nixon's 'Tricky Dicky' sobriquet, and is told 'Say hi to David Frost for me'. This points towards the interview in which Richard Nixon implicated himself in the Watergate affair before a television audience.[22] On the other hand, the story takes priority over the representation of history: a historical appreciation of Nixon's presidency is subverted by the Doctor's appropriation of Nixon's authority for his own investigations. The televised historical event which the Doctor uses to apparently end the domination of Earth by the Silence is Neil Armstrong's first walk on the Moon in July 1969. The received historical meanings of the event are undermined. Not only was humanity's 'race to the moon' inspired by alien intelligences, the importance of the landing's televising was principally to render Earth inhospitable to the Silence through interpolating into the broadcast the Silence's invitation to kill them.

In 'The Curse of the Black Spot', Henry Avery continues the turn in the presentation of contentious figures from history. The anchor for Avery's story in 'The Curse of the Black Spot' is a historical event – the theft by Avery and his crew of the treasure carried by a convoy of ships from the Moghul emperor of India making the Hajj to Mecca. In the first online 'preview' (a short video prequel to the episode) Avery's ship is given the same name as its historical counterpart, the *Fancy*.[23] The story's depiction of Avery follows some cues from recent historical writing. Documentary research has characterised Avery as a family man who sent money home to his wife in Wapping.[24] This need not be taken as an example of especially devoted behaviour, given that many mariners would have remitted money back to their spouses in their home countries. Nevertheless, it might be the foundation for the introduction of Avery's (historically unattested) son, implausibly concealed on board, which raises audience awareness of the domestic life of the seventeenth-century mariner. Avery's career as depicted in 'The Curse of the Black Spot', however, owes as much to the mythology of his deeds and disappearance established in popular literature of the early eighteenth century. The Doctor is visiting a criminal hero of early modern fable rather than the enigmatic but documented felon, self-consciously adding to a historical process begun during Avery's lifetime.[25] The mariner of documentary sources and informational reportage is superseded by the pirate constructed by broadside-writers and balladeers. Historically the ship *Fancy* itself did not disappear with Avery, having been broken up beforehand, but as *Doctor Who* features a representation of Avery drawn from historical fable, the *Fancy* appears as one of Avery's accoutrements just as King Arthur might appear with his sword Excalibur. Hills notes that 'the guiding parameters seem...to be pastiche' and refers to Moffat's assertion in *Doctor Who Confidential* that 'you want certain things in a pirate story: a storm, swashbuckling, a stowaway child, and so on'.[26] Indeed, in the pre-credit sequence, the Doctor mimics the pirate's 'Ho, ho, ho' and then asks whether no one says that anymore. Furthermore, the crew of the *Fancy* are lured by a Siren, like the Venetian vampires given a pseudoscientific explanation, but placed in the history of the mythology of sailors seduced by sea-maidens (see Homer's *The Odyssey* as the main example of this).

For all the contributions of the historical Henry Avery to the character seen on television, the historical story gives way to a fantasy and the story is not there to make a historical point but one complementary to the character themes of the series. Hills writes that this offering by Steve Thompson

> is surely a script marked by choice Moffatisms. Automated technology carrying on, saving humanity whilst being misinterpreted as evil – that's textbook Moffat, right out of 'The Empty Child'/'The Doctor Dances'. Moving from a historical setting to a futuristic spaceship...say hello to 'The Girl in the Fireplace'.[27]

In addition to Hills' points, the Avery of 'The Curse of the Black Spot' is analogous to the Doctor. Neither have homes to go to except their ships. It is a teasing parallel for the Doctor to be compared to a pirate one episode before 'The Doctor's Wife', where the Doctor is addressed by the personified TARDIS matrix as 'my thief'. 'The Curse of the Black Spot' also deals with loss and parent–child affection, themes that will be picked up on several episodes later in 'A Good Man Goes to War' where Amy Pond is both separated from her baby Melody, yet also (re)united with Melody in her form of River Song.

The announcement that Hitler would appear in the eighth episode of the 2011 series of *Doctor Who* was received with some apprehension. In the event, the consignment of Hitler to a cupboard serves to underline the marginality of Hitler to the story in an episode titled 'Let's Kill Hitler'; though he provokes Mels's regeneration by accidentally shooting her, his regime serves as an environment to provide a parallel for River Song's programming by the Silence. 'Nazi' is inaccurately coded as synonymous with uniform, while the episode distances itself from engagement with Germany under Nazi rule by not exploring the environment further than the privileged setting of the dining room of the Hotel Adlon. As Hills has put it:

> the conventions of the Davies-esque celebrity historical are firmly deconstructed. Adolf's not the point of the story, aligned with some evil, alien force as might be expected, because Hitler's shut in the cupboard, ridiculed and regulated to the sidelines. Storywise, it's all about the arc, not the Reich ... Moffat's ... free to tell the story he's really interested in – 'The Beginning of River Song'.[28]

In the pre-credits sequence, when Mels points her gun at the Doctor and delivers the title of the episode in dialogue, she invokes the debate within *Doctor Who* on moral responsibility in time travel.[29] The crew of the Teselecta in 'Let's Kill Hitler' navigate through history by mining their database and applying rigid protocols. The Teselecta's 'justice department' is not identified further; their source of authority is uncertain. 'Let's Kill Hitler' exposes the absurdities of the historian, when empowered with time travel, dispensing clumsy justice as a 'hanging judge'.[30] Hans Zimmerman is dismissed as a 'loyal member of the Nazi party' and liquidated because he is guilty of 'category three hate crimes' and because his removal in 1938 has a limited (but not null) effect on causality. Hitler cannot be punished because the crimes for which the Teselecta crew are pursuing him have for the most part not yet occurred.

Series seven continues the pattern of history being cast in a fantasy way. The dinosaurs in Chris Chibnall's 'Dinosaurs on a Spaceship' are not the feathered proto-birds of some recent research but the giant lizards of the *One Million B.C.* (1940) tradition. Queen Nefertiti may well have been a figure whom Amy learnt about in school from textbooks, but here her sexuality and desire for the Doctor casts her in a comic role while her ancient status forms part of Solomon's plot to collect now-extinct species or individuals. Her inclusion brings with it vague associations of H. Rider Haggard's *She* (1886–7), another tale of a lost civilization.

Whithouse's 'A Town Called Mercy', meanwhile, combines preoccupations of the classical Western with some self-aware historical contextualisation, while telling a fantasy story. The town of Mercy draws on a cultural commentator's view of the Western as America's nation-building device. Set five years after the American Civil War, it encapsulates the new America of the frontier as seeking to break from past divisions (e.g. the town's preacher is African-American). Religious belief is also important to the episode as a whole. Into this utopia comes the Gunslinger, a powerful image of American dystopias, with debts to *RoboCop* (1987) and *The Terminator* (1984) as well as to Yul Brynner's *Westworld* (1973) and Clint Eastwood's Man with No Name from the 1960s *Dollars* trilogy. There is also commentary on the Doctor's role. Rather than being the lone stranger of Western myth, he is accompanied by Amy and Rory, but he is certainly an ambiguous hero figure not sure of the right course of action.

Thematising the Notion of a '*Doctor Who* History'

During his era, Moffat also intriguingly thematises the very notion of an alternative *Doctor Who* history. This is apparent through the idea of royal succession in 'The Beast Below'. Liz Ten's suggestion of a sexual relationship between the Doctor and Elizabeth I converts a frivolous allusion in 'The End of Time' Part One (2009) into a placement of the Doctor at the conception of English-British Protestant patriotism. Through the debunking of the 'Virgin Queen' nickname, the mystical monarchical strand of British patriotism is undermined; but within the fiction of the series, the Doctor's activities are interwoven with that same strand. The programme replaces the royal historical myth with a self-conscious fiction.

'The Pandorica Opens' and 'The Big Bang', comprising the final narrative of Moffat's first series, use genre portrayals of history to fit in with Moffat's story arc. The Doctor and his companions believe they are engaging with real Roman soldiers and (within the fiction of *Doctor Who*) the historical problem of the

DOCTOR WHO, *THE ELEVENTH HOUR*

origin and function of the Pandorica; but the soldiers are Nestene facsimiles – as if actors playing parts in historical theatre – based upon Amy's memories of studying Roman history at school. Even the Pandorica is drawn from a version of the Pandora's Box story once read by Amy. The Roman Britain of 'The Pandorica Opens' is explicitly dependent upon a picture-book of the kind published by Dorling Kindersley or Usborne. The Doctor is deceived within the narrative because he is used to being in history.

All these events centre around Stonehenge. Stonehenge is already associated with interference in history within *Doctor Who*. In 'The Time Meddler' (1965), the Doctor's fellow Time Lord the Meddling Monk says that he assisted 'the ancient Britons' to build Stonehenge with an anti-gravitational lift. Stonehenge as a signifier of 'Mysterious Britain' is a cliché of cinema and television, stretching back at least to the film *Knights of the Round Table* (1953). In the legendarium of Geoffrey of Monmouth, Stonehenge is erected by Merlin at the bidding of Aurelius Ambrosius, the heroic defender of post-Roman Britain against the Saxons, and uncle of King Arthur. It becomes Aurelius's burial site.[31] Geoffrey's British mythology was drawn upon in the construction of the Elizabethan myth co-opted and mocked in 'The Beast Below'. The burial of the Doctor in the Pandorica under Stonehenge thus associates the Doctor with the Galfridian tradition and renews the association with royal succession made in the earlier episode.

Stonehenge represents the undocumented – a crack in time itself, where time is understood through material relics of human experience – while also acting as a cornerstone of British or English identity.[32] Despite reminders that Stonehenge had a lost meaning to its builders made by general works such as Norman Davies's *The Isles* (1999) and more specific accounts such as Mike Pitts's *Hengeworld* (2000), its strength as a symbol derives in part from successive societies having attributed meaning to it. In Steven Moffat's scheme, Stonehenge's mystery is transmitted to the Pandorica. Thus all the TARDIS travellers become Galfridian buried warriors – first the Doctor and then Amy in the Pandorica, with (extending the metaphor) Rory as the Pandorica's guardian, while River is entombed within the TARDIS in stone.

The wallchart of the Pandorica's history seen in 'The Big Bang' illustrates a British history where events familiar to viewers are distorted around the Pandorica. The Blitz (recalling 'Victory of the Daleks') is among the chronological landmarks, where the 'lone centurion' who has waited by the Pandorica for centuries is depicted in a painting. This recalls and reinforces the use the opening sequence of 'The Pandorica Opens' makes of characters from three earlier stories: Vincent van Gogh from 'Vincent and the Doctor'; Churchill and Bracewell from 'Victory of the Daleks'; and Liz Ten from 'The Beast Below'. Van Gogh creates a fictional painting of the TARDIS exploding which is passed down through thousands of years to Churchill and Bracewell to Liz Ten, and then collected by River Song. Both paintings are interpretations of what prove to be unfolding historical events as well as prophecies of the end of the universe. But Moffat's concern with plots involving time sees 'The Big Bang' make the Doctor the first cause of a refashioned universe.

In the following season, the mystery of the Doctor's apparent death at the hands of River Song thematises a 'Doctor Who history' and becomes a parable about the verification of historical events. As a sequel to a chain of representations of history which in one way or another deconstruct perceptions of historical narratives to emphasise aspects which serve the purpose of storytelling, 'The Wedding of River Song' depicts the Doctor as interrogating his own storyline to establish 'what exactly happened'. His investigations enable him to manage the event concerned without removing the record of his death at Lake Silencio. River goes to prison to support the widely perceived but incomplete history that the Doctor has been killed. Similarly, the television viewer has seen the Doctor 'die' in 'The Impossible Astronaut', but this perception is reversed at the end of 'The Wedding of River Song'.

As a result of River Song's refusal to 'kill' the Doctor, history is distorted but is put back into place at the end of the episode. Ian McNeice's Winston Churchill returns, but time has been all rolled into one moment as a result of River's refusing to shoot the Doctor. Churchill is presented as a Holy Roman Emperor, and surrounded by icons of the classical Roman Empire rather than its medieval western European successor. He reigns from a Buckingham Palace called 'Buckingham Senate' and is still dressed in his World War II attire. Once the Doctor has been captured by Amy, references widen: Egypt, ancient (pyramids), classical (Cleopatra) and medieval and modern (Cairo), and another United States president (Kennedy).

Conclusion

Doctor Who's treatment of history has often reflected the programme's status as a British television institution. The aspiration of the founders of *Doctor Who* – that stories set in the past should be 'based on the best factual information of situations in time' available – has long been set aside.[33] However, *Doctor Who* is still historically literate, and in 'Vincent and the Doctor', demonstrates that it is capable of making polemical drama. This was the first time in the programme's 50-year history that viewers were directed to a Helpline during the end credits, as the issue addressed is relevant today. Otherwise the programme's awareness of its own long duration as a storytelling device has shaped *Doctor Who's* perception of history. After the first few of years of the 'classic' series, history was used as a backdrop to tell science-fiction stories and both Davies's and Moffat's *Who* belong largely to this lineage. Coupled with that, the form of new *Who* also allows Moffat to subordinate history to his story arcs.

Notes

1. Matt Hills, *Triumph of a Time Lord: Regenerating Doctor Who in the Twenty-First Century* (London, 2010).
2. Howard Brenton, *Never So Good* (London, 2008).
3. Michael Billington, *Guardian*, 27 March 2008.
4. Charles Spencer, *Daily Telegraph*, 28 March 2008.
5. Alice Jones, *Independent*, 28 March 2008.
6. Benjamin Cook, 'Who on Earth Is ... Ian McNeice', *Doctor Who Magazine* 420 (2010), p. 66.
7. For *Doctor Who* as 'quality television' see Hills, *Triumph of a Time Lord*, esp. Chapter 5.
8. Stephen James Walker, *Cracks in Time* (Prestatyn, 2012), p. 122.
9. For example, 'KBO' for 'Keep Buggering On' is recorded in a letter of 11 December 1941.
10. Walker, *Cracks in Time*, p. 123.
11. My thanks to Melissa Beattie for this observation.
12. Evert van Uitert, 'Gough, Vincent van' in *Grove Art Online*. Available at www.oxfordartonline.com/subscriber/article/grove/art/T033020 (accessed 22 May 2012). Also see Belinda Thomson, 'Gough, Vincent Willem van' in *The Oxford Companion to Western Art*, Hugh Brigstocke (ed.), Oxford Art Online. Available at www.oxfordartonline.com/subscriber/article/opr/t118/e1080 (accessed 22 May 2012).
13. BBC Editorial Guidelines 17.4.21 Helplines and Online Support Services. Available at www.bbc.co.uk/editorialguidelines/page/guidelines-interact-

ing-telephone-services/#helplines-and-online-support-services (accessed 14 July 2012).

14. BBC Editorial Guidelines 5. Available at www.bbc.co.uk/editorialguidelines/ page/guidelines-harm-suicide/ (accessed 14 July 2012).

15. For a short study of this period, see Lez Cooke, *British Television Drama: A History* (London, 2003), Chapter 3.

16. For more on the BBC as Public Service Broadcaster in the 1960s, see Matthew Kilburn, 'Bargains of necessity? *Doctor Who*, *Culloden* and fictionalising history at the BBC in the 1960s', in David Butler (ed.), *Time and Relative Dissertations in Space* (Manchester, 2007), pp. 68–85.

17. John Julius Norwich, *A History of Venice* (London, 1982), p. 494.

18. Mary Laven, *Virgins of Venice: Enclosed Lives and Broken Vows in the Renaissance Convent* (London, 2003 [2002]).

19. Laven, *Virgins of Venice*, p. 23, citing *Psalms* 45:10.

20. Richard Sennett, *Flesh and Stone: The Body and the City in Western Civilization* (New York, 1996), p. 237.

21. Frank Collins, *The Pandorica Opens: Exploring the Worlds of the Eleventh Doctor* (Cambridge, 2010), p. 100.

22. See the film *Frost/Nixon* (2008), based on Peter Morgan's stage play of the same name (2006).

23. Available at www.bbc.co.uk/programmes/p00gqrv7 (accessed 1 June 2012).

24. Joel Baer, ' "Captain John Avery" and the Anatomy of a Mutiny', *Eighteenth-Century Life* 18:1 (1994) pp. 1–26.

25. See Joel Baer, *Pirates of the British Isles* (Stroud, 2005), Chapter 4. Also see Joel Baer (ed.) *British Piracy in the Golden Age*, London 4: pp. 342–70.

26. Matt Hills, 'Steve Thompson's Steven Moffat's *Doctor Who*: A Pirate Copy?', 9 May 2011. Available at http://blog.commarts.wisc.edu/2011/05/09/steve-thompsons-steven-moffats-doctor-who-a-pirate-copy/ (accessed 7 June 2012).

27. Ibid.

28. Matt Hills, '*Doctor Who* Let's Kill Hitler Review 2', 27 August 2011. Available at http://reviews.doctorwhonews.net/search?updated-max=2011-10-02T04:8:00%2B01:00&max-results=15 (accessed 2 June 2012).

29. See David Whitaker, *Doctor Who and the Crusaders* (London, 2011 [1965]).

30. David Knowles, *The Historian and Character* (Cambridge, 1955), p. 19 cited Richard J. Evans, *In Defence of History* (London, 2000), p. 49.

31. Geoffrey of Monmouth, *The History of the Kings of Britain*, Lewis Thorpe (ed.) (Harmondsworth, 1966), p. 202.

32. See 'Stonehenge/English Heritage'. Available at www.english-heritage.org.uk/daysout/properties/Stonehenge/ (accessed 1 June 2012).

33. BBC Written Archives Centre, T5/647/1, '*Doctor Who* – General Notes on Background and Approach for an Exciting Adventure-Science Fiction Serial for Children's Saturday Viewing', 1963.

4

AMY'S BOYS, RIVER'S MAN

Generation, Gender and Sexuality in the Moffat Whoniverse

Dee Amy-Chinn

S teven Moffat took over the helm of *Doctor Who* with an impressive and intriguing track record in the representation of gender and sexuality. Having authored episodes that introduced omnisexual Captain Jack Harkness ('The Empty Child'/'The Doctor Dances'), Madame de Pompadour ('The Girl in the Fireplace'), Sally Sparrow ('Blink') and, of course, River Song ('Silence in the Library'/'Forest of the Dead'), the new Executive Producer and lead writer had a lot to live up to. Superficially he more than met the challenge in series five, six and the first part of seven, particularly with regard to gender, placing at the heart of the series some of the strongest women to emerge in the history of the show, women who appear to embody the twenty-first-century New Girl Order in which feminism is no longer in tension with femininity. He also created male leads that move beyond traditional representations of hegemonic masculinity and combine heroism with vulnerability – the hallmark of hybrid and unstable twenty-first-century masculinit*ies*.[1] This is consistent with an era in which the white male action hero is increasingly depicted as under all manner of assault.[2]

But can it be that straightforward? One of the distinguishing features of new *Who* has been the extent to which it is seen as an authored text, with Alec Charles describing how Russell T Davies was given unprecedented control over the show.[3] In the Moffat era this is taken further, with the introduction of longer and more complex story arcs. This not only creates the cliff-hangers ensuring the audience returns for the next episode – it also encourages revisiting past episodes in the light of new information, maximising rewatchability and epitomising what Jason Mittell argues is the complex narrative structure that distinguishes the best contemporary television.[4] And by putting the main characters at the centre of the reveals and reversals, the programme plays a game with the audience around generation and gender, where nothing is quite what it seems. Underpinning the narrative is an equally complex *ideological* structure that illustrates what Frederic Jameson saw as the tension between reification and utopia in mass culture. According to Jameson, popular culture

> cannot be ideological without at one and the same time being implicitly or explicitly Utopian as well: they cannot manipulate unless they offer some genuine shred of content as a fantasy bribe to the public about to be so manipulated.[5]

Thus textual analysis – a technique that has been at the heart of media and cultural studies since its inception – must employ 'a method capable of doing justice to both the ideological and the Utopian or transcendent functions of mass culture simultaneously'.[6] Clearly such a method much eschew a simplistic reading of any text as either progressive *or* regressive in favour of an approach that recognises the co-existence of fantasies of gender and sexual empowerment and equality, with the legitimation of the existing social order. Drawing on what Angela McRobbie has described as 'double entanglement',[7] I will argue that although the show promotes an agenda of liberalisation with regard to choice and diversity in domestic, sexual and kinship relations, this is paralleled by a neo-conservative agenda in relation to gender, sexuality and family life – the latter aligning directly with the target audience for the show.

The Family Pond

Doctor Who has always represented the paradigm of multi-generational television, and in recent years the BBC Saturday

evening schedule has become 'a nostalgic enshrinement of traditional family viewing'.[8] This was reflected in the themes that
recurred throughout the first four series of new *Who*, in which all
the companions were located within earth-bound family structures that were apart from, but integral to, the action – and to
which they were able to return. Charles quotes Mark Bould's
contention that the programme's storylines have focused on
'the drive to reunite the nuclear family'[9] – seeing this as a radical departure from the classic era, which was notable for the
'orphan' status of companions.[10]

Series five appeared, initially, to return its new companion to
this isolated status. When the TARDIS lands outside the home of
seven-year-old Amelia Pond, she is alone in the house. Although
the explanation for this state of affairs becomes clear at the end
of the series, which sees the restoration of her family, this does
not lead to her family members subsequently having a role in
the show. Yet ultimately, Moffat's *Who* is more than ever about
family – a very queer family where gender roles are (sometimes)
reversed, the parents are (for the most part) younger than the
daughter, and the raggedy man who eventually returns to save
a child from the crack in her wall may turn out to be her future
son-in-law. While this queer family is at the heart of the overarching story arc, more traditional families feature prominently
in a number of stand-alone episodes including 'The Hungry
Earth'/'Cold Blood', 'The Curse of the Black Spot', and (as examined by Frank Collins) 'Night Terrors' and 'Closing Time'. All these
episodes share the core message of the importance of the family,
and the power of unconditional love of parents for children to
overcome the darkest forces of the universe. The family values
agenda could not be more explicit.

In her highly influential work on post-feminism and popular culture, Diane Negra argues that one of the key tropes now
dominating the fictional representation of women is that of
retreatism and the return to family, in particular the importance
of marriage and motherhood. But whereas both were once
viewed as problematic for the position of women, they are now
de-politicised and repositioned as *choices* rather than inevitable
outcomes – recasting traditionalism as innovation.[11] Linked to
this are what Negra describes as the heightened cultural profile
for mother–daughter relationships, in particular creative formulas

that promote a cultural and ideological rapprochement between the generations.[12] In keeping with the zeitgeist, Moffat plays with these themes while giving them a twist that sets *Doctor Who* apart from shows whose focus is the geographical stability and the co-consuming status that enable the women to bond – and which Negra roundly critiques for their conservatism. I have argued elsewhere[13] that Russell T Davies failed to deliver on his promise that new *Who* would deliver a 'Buffy-style female sidekick... a modern action heroine'.[14] Certainly the companions from the Davies era – Rose, Martha and Donna – were all more central to the action than their predecessors from the classic era although, as Noah McLaughlin has argued, ultimately the show contains, and even erases, their challenge to the Doctor's masculine authority.[15] But even in this pantheon, Amelia/Amy Pond is special. Where earlier companions in new *Who* were ordinary women who went on extraordinary adventures, Amy is herself extraordinary, having grown up with a crack in her wall that allowed the Universe to seep through, making her part of something big and significant. And while previous companions were central to the resolution of key story arcs, Amy *is* the story arc – although not necessarily in the same unequivocally positive manner as her predecessors, all of whom came straightforwardly to the Doctor's rescue at a time of crisis. In contrast, Amy's childhood imagination provides the scenario through which the Doctor's enemies attempt to trap him in the Pandorica, and her daughter is kidnapped at birth and brainwashed to become the weapon by which he is expected to meet his death. Amy thus embodies the potential danger posed by women – and the fact that she does so unwittingly offers a sub-textual agenda of female passivity at odds with a more straightforward reading that puts focus on her agency.

When Moffat's appointment was announced, tabloid attention focused on rumours that he was to create the sexiest companion ever. Not surprisingly, this sent the right-wing British press into something of a spin, coming as it did in the midst of a moral panic about the sexualisation of mainstream culture and concern over the appropriateness of some media content aimed at a family audience.[16] Writing in the *Mail Online* on 25 March 2010, Allison Pearson expressed outrage at 'Doctor Whooarr' – claiming that Doctor Who's 'assistant' (a more demeaning role than companion) was meant to be 'one of the boys' and wondering if it was too much to ask that family TV remain the one universe yet to be invaded by *Nuts* magazine.[17] This coverage set the scene for Amy's debut, which did not disappoint. When the audience and the newly regenerated Doctor first encounter the adult Amy, she is dressed as a 'policewoman' – but one who wears a very short skirt and seamed tights. And far from being in awe of the Doctor, she knocks him out with a cricket bat and chains him to a radiator. More explicitly than any previous companion, Amy embodies the post-feminist discourse as presented in the popular press, where feminism is taken for granted to the extent that women no longer have to decide between pursuing equality and performing femininity. Yet many feminist scholars[18] seek to draw attention to the complexity and contradiction inherent in the way women are currently represented in popular culture because, as Kat Banyard has noted, equality between the sexes remains an illusion.[19] Speaking to the *Radio Times* in June 2010, Karen Gillan (the actress who played Amy Pond) illustrated the attitudes that contemporary scholarship would like to see, viewed through a more critical lens. In the interview she claims that 'Feminism is not the issue any more', and that both she and her character take 'equality as the absolute baseline', having never experienced any situation in which sexism has been an issue.[20] In line with Ros Gill's argument that young women no longer see sexualised self-presentation as problematic, Gillan claims that she didn't see anything unusual in Amy's suggestive costumes or behaviour towards the Doctor.[21] She goes on to describe Amy as 'just a strong girl, woman, whatever' (settling on the term 'female') and positions Amy's default attitude to the Doctor as 'Come on, impress me'.[22]

The word most associated with Amy is 'feisty'. Even at the age of seven, Amelia is courageous, praying to Santa to send someone to save her from the crack in her wall, then investigating when she hears a crash outside her window. Despite being alone, she is unfazed by the man who emerges from a blue box and demands food. Further evidence of Amelia's resourcefulness is given in 'The Big Bang' when she follows the Doctor's trail of instructions (despite not knowing where they've come form) in order to restore and free her future self from the Pandorica. Waiting 12 years for her 'hero' to return, she has reason to be sceptical on his reappearance – hence the cricket bat and handcuffs. So from the outset she is less deferential and more independently minded than her predecessors, as well as being smart and combative. Her first adventure on board the TARDIS ('The Beast Below') sees her make connections that no one else does, enabling her to save not only the Star Whale but to prevent the Doctor from acting contrary to his nature. Similarly, in 'Victory of the Daleks', Amy is instrumental in defusing the bomb by encouraging Bracewell to concentrate on his emotional memories. Her actions in these episodes demonstrate Amy's emotional intelligence – a trait associated with women rather than men, to the extent that a key trope in the history of Western philosophy has been the way in which women's presumed emotionality excluded them from consideration as rational beings.[23] But while emotional intuition is viewed positively in these and subsequent episodes, I would argue that, overall, *Doctor Who* remains equivocal about the value of basing judgment on emotion and intuition. After all it is Amy herself who, in 'The Doctor's Wife', warns the Doctor that he should not get emotional – as this is when he makes mistakes. And it is River's 'emotional' decision not to kill the Doctor at Lake Silencio that subsequently leads to the collapse of time. Amy's early adventures with the Doctor may not present her as the new Buffy, but – as we see perhaps most clearly in 'The Girl Who Waited' – her potential as a kick-ass heroine has been there all along. This episode, which sees Amy trapped alone for 36 years in a time stream, showcases her resourcefulness and ability to develop both technical competence (constructing her own 'sonic probe' and reprogramming the handbots) and impressive self-defence skills. In the accompanying *Confidential,* Steven Moffat notes that Amy has always possessed the capacity to be dangerous and deadly, suggesting that she has a 'James Bond thing' going on – an allusion picked up in the Moffat-authored series six finale when Amy, heading a contingent of soldiers, introduces herself to the Doctor as 'Pond, Amelia Pond'. So at various points across the series we see numerous examples of her ability to think independently, and willingness to take whatever action is needed to protect both herself and her 'boys'.

This use of the diminutive in reference to both the Doctor and Rory serves to situate Amy as the girl/woman on top – confident and assertive in her relationships with men. Her initial presentation to the audience in the guise of a hyper-sexualised policewoman has already been noted. Her occupation as a kissogram places her on the very edge of the sex industry in a way that is both consistent with the pre-watershed broadcast environment and reflective of Negra's argument that traditional stigma attached to sex work is being eradicated.[24] Yet – highlighting the ambivalence that still exists around explicit displays of active female sexuality – her attempt to seduce the Doctor into a one-night-stand at the end of 'Flesh and Stone' caused ructions in the conservative press and prompted 43 complaints to the BBC message board.[25] Frank Collins also views Amy's behaviour at this point as highly problematic, and as playing into fan criticism that she was too sexualised and sluttish.[26] Contra the post-feminist position that women's sexual assertiveness is no longer problematic as long as it is chosen freely, Collins argues that the sexual worldliness Amy displays contributes to the audiences' sense of estrangement from the character, and that the Doctor's response to her overtures shows his moral disapproval of her actions.

But consistent with the family-oriented atmosphere of the show, and the double-entanglement argument that liberalism and neo-conservatism now co-exist within the same discourse, Amy's virtue is soon recuperated and her moral compass reinstated. Childhood sweetheart Rory is brought on board as a fellow-traveller and suitable object for her affection, and she soon realises that he is the most important person in her life. In 'Amy's Choice' she comes to recognise that she would rather not live at all than live without him – a choice she makes again at the end of 'The Girl Who Waited' when, realising that her chance of being rescued and reunited with him has passed, she allows herself to be 'helped' (i.e. killed) by the handbots of the plague-ridden world on which she is trapped. And, in her final adventure, Amy allows herself to be transported back in time by the Weeping Angels because *any* future together is more important that a life apart. Rory's presence not only reinstates a conventional heteronormative, and generationally appropriate, romance – leading to marriage and motherhood – at the centre of the action, it inaugurates a story arc that focuses on the male role as protector of women and children. By the time of 'A Good Man Goes to War', Amy is able to tell her new-born daughter Melody that she is going to have to be 'very, very, brave'; that however scared she is, she will never be alone, for there is a man who will never let her down, one who is the last of his kind, and who – although looking young – has lived for hundreds of years. This man is her father – and lest the audience fears that Amy has already betrayed her husband, it is almost immediately made clear that the reference is to Rory. Indeed, by the mid-point of series six, and throughout series seven (a), it is difficult to tell from Amy's descriptions which of her 'boys' she is referring to, as she not only reflects on her love for Rory – but also accords him a level of respect that seemed inconceivable in their early adventures together.

Although in the dream-world of 'Amy's Choice' Rory is a Doctor, in the diegetic world of the show he occupies the less prestigious position of nurse. His occupation as a member of one of the key caring professions serves to feminise him, as does his emotional dependence on Amy and his desire to marry and settle down. It is he, not Amy, who is seeking the stability of family life – reflected in his Leadworth fantasy which has the two of them not only married, but with Amy pregnant, baking, and living in a cottage that (quite literally) has roses around the door. There could be no more conservative image of the family. Rory's desire for a family life returns as a theme in the first episode of series seven, 'Asylum of the Daleks', which opens with the shocking revelation that Amy and Rory are to divorce. Towards the end of the episode it transpires that the reason behind the crisis in their marriage is Amy's inability to have more children following the medical procedures carried out on her at Demon's Run. Amy confesses that she is sacrificing her own happiness to allow Rory the opportunity to start over with someone new – an offer he rejects in favour of them remaining a couple.

Rory's dream of a traditional family life is never going to come to pass, but he does become the father-protector in ways that reinforce a traditional reading of gender relationships. At the time of their wedding, the Doctor has no hesitation in referring to Rory as Mr Pond – an appellation that Rory is forced to acknowledge. And in the *Confidential* that accompanied 'The Rebel Flesh', there was much discussion of Rory's vulnerability to being exploited by someone who appeared to need his protection, and the need for Rory to 'prove himself' and 'man up'. But throughout the sixth series, the Rory who stood guard by the Pandorica for 2,000 years is never far from the surface, so by the time he and the Doctor have infiltrated Demon's Run to save Amy and Melody, Rory's new-found status gives him the confidence to address Amy as Mrs Williams – even if their child does not take his name. In 'Vampires of Venice', Rory's small torch is no match for the Doctor's huge UV portable light – prompting the inevitable 'yours is bigger than mine' line that puts the two men in competition for Amy's affection. But by the time of the final battle in 'Good Man', Rory stands alongside his fellow warriors, a huge sword in one hand and a pulse pistol in the other while Amy takes refuge with (what she believes to be) their daughter. The Doctor – as befits his image as a man who solves problems through brain not brawn[27] – remains apart from the physical fighting. Despite the new martial attributes that signify Rory's transformation into a more traditional hero able to demonstrate both a physicality and an aptitude with weapons and technology,[28] his caring side never deserts him. Throughout his adventures with the Doctor, he cares for the sick and wounded, and shows compassion to the dying. It is this combination of qualities that exemplifies Moffat's representation of the gender order in which all men struggle to situate themselves in reference to a hegemonic masculinity in respect of which they always fall short.[29]

Another Ripple on the Pond: The Doctor's Wife?

Despite Rory's growing status as a warrior, he is far from the most phallic character in Moffat's Whoniverse. This attribution must attach to Dr/Professor River Song. From her first appearance in series four, we have known that River is to be an important part of the Doctor's life. And although neither we, nor he, yet know the full extent of the role she is to play, we do know that she has a sophisticated understanding of the working of time, has the technical skills to fix a teleport, and can fly the TARDIS better than the Doctor. But while she shares all these characteristics with the Doctor, one thing sets her apart: her willingness to carry a gun – and use it. Weaponry is rarely a feature of the 'white hats' of the Whoniverse, but River is more than happy to resort to gunning down her enemies, whether a resurrected Dalek in 'The Big Bang' or a host of Silents in 'Day of the Moon'.

Eve Kosofsky Sedgwick has defined 'queer' as applying to anyone whose (sexuality and/or) gender fails to signify monolithically,[30] and the hallucinogenic-lipstick-wearing, gun-toting intergalactic archaeologist fits the definition. Appearance-wise nowhere is this clearer than at the start of 'The Time of Angels' as she moves from the hyper-femininity of evening dress with toweringly high red patent leather stiletto heels (with all the phallic signifiers this entails) to the masculine functionality of combat dress – looking equally at ease in both. Indeed, her seeming ability to play whatever role is required of her keeps both the audience and the Doctor off balance, and enables the air of mystery that is key to her function in the narrative. Furthering my argument that one of the hallmarks of the Moffat era is that it places women at the heart of the action, the centrality of Amy is matched by the audience's desire to know answers to the question who – and what – is River Song? The revelation in the series six mid-season finale that River Song is Melody Pond – the daughter of Amy and Rory – was designed to raise more questions than it answered. It also queers the mother–daughter relationship between River and Amy. Until that point, River has occupied a maternal role as both she and the Doctor act in *loco parentis* to Amy and Rory. Suddenly that relationship is turned on its head as the Doctor/Amy/Rory triumvirate attempts to protect the new-born child and as – later on – a precocious Melody seeks out her birth parents in order to grow up alongside them as their wayward and impetuous best friend, constantly needing their help negotiating encounters with authority.

As noted above, marriage is an important trope in the Moffat Whoniverse. Series five plays out the relationship between Amy and Rory that starts with her running away from her wedding – only to embrace her destiny at the climax of the series' story arc. Running parallel is the possibility that, somewhere in time, River is already the Doctor's wife. This theme starts in the Davies-era, but Moffat-penned, 'Silence in the Library'/'Forest of the Dead' – the narrative structure of which appears to see both the Doctor and Donna finding, and losing, their perfect partners. Speculation continues in 'The Time of Angels', with Amy asking both River and the Doctor about their relationship, and the Doctor himself exploring the issue in 'The Big Bang'. The audience is teased further with the title of the final episode of series six – 'The Wedding of River Song'. But despite River's constant reference to the Doctor as her husband in 'The Angels Take Manhattan', the enigma of the Doctor/River relationship remains unresolved – for while a wedding has taken place, what River married was the Doctor's Teselecta double. The real wedding – if it is to ever take place – would appear to remain in the future. Regardless of their formal relationship, from the outset the relationship between River and the Doctor is playful and highly spirited, with verbal exchanges reminiscent of the very best Hollywood screwball comedies that could well be described as post-feminist *avant la lettre*, and which play out a battle-of-the-sexes theme with independent women who are more than a match for their male 'adversaries'. These exchanges also foreground the sexiness of the character. 'The Pandorica Opens' toyed with the idea of River as Cleopatra, one of the leading femme fatales of the ancient world. And improvising code names for his companions in 'The Impossible Astronaut' the Doctor chooses to call River 'Mrs Robinson', a character described by Steven Moffat in the accompanying *Confidential* as 'the icon of all sexiness'. This reference is reinforced both visually and verbally in 'Let's Kill Hitler'. Yet while it seems reasonable to assume that the Cleopatra and Mrs Robinson references are *intended* to be read positively in that they acknowledge the sexual allure of older women, it should also be recognised that these characters carry negative connotations as both used their sexuality to manipulate men in ways that ultimately work to those men's disadvantage. Similarly River's appearance as a film-noir femme fatale in 'The Angels Take Manhattan', in which she is described (albeit by her future self) as having her 'stocking seams straight', her 'lipstick combat ready' and 'packing cleavage that could fell an ox at 20 feet', is open to more than one interpretation. Such references support the idea that – whatever their age – women's power rests primarily in their attractiveness and sexuality rather than their in intelligence. This is reinforced by the first reaction of the newly regenerated Melody – a desire to weigh herself, and a 'joke' (on noticing her newly acquired curves) that her strategy will be to wear a lot of jumpers. It is also impossible to ignore the fact that even for the gun-toting River, her most potent weapon is a kiss – abetted by the use of hallucinogenic, or poison-impregnated, lipstick.

The Doctor's relationship with River has an edge of discomfort to it, both because there is so much that he does not know about her that he finds it difficult to trust her, and because it is unusual for him to be in any situation where someone knows more than he does about what is going on. Hence, the only truly comfortable relationship he has is with the TARDIS. The Doctor's affection for his 'old girl' has never been in doubt, and the erotic edge to their interaction was noted by Sarah-Jane Smith and Rose Tyler in 'School Reunion' (2006) when they shared a joke over the Doctor's habit of stroking the TARDIS' console. But in 'The Doctor's Wife', there is finally the opportunity to foreground and explore a friendship that has existed for 700 years. In keeping with the gendered pronoun used by the Doctor over the years (and to suit a pre-watershed family show) the soul of the TARDIS is transferred into the body of a woman (Idris). Anyone inclined to disappointment that the episode does not reveal more of the Doctor's relationship to River is rewarded with a relationship that shares the same degree of playful familiarity and banter.

Can it Get any Queerer?

Wit and verbal dexterity have been a hallmark of all previous Doctors – both classic and new. But in a post-2005 framework, a useful way of distinguishing what is different about the Eleventh Doctor is to assess his performance of masculinity against the character traits of the most recent Doctors as identified by Marc Shuster and Tom Powers;[31] for while he remains a Favourite Uncle, Teacher and to some extent a Cult Leader, possibly even a Metrosexual, in his new incarnation he is far from being a Mid-Lifer or a Player. Whereas Doctors Nine and Ten were self-confident, sexy and flirtatious – with Shimpach noting that they were sexualised in a way that was inconceivable in the classic era,[32] and Piers Britton arguing that both presented an unprecedentedly sexualised straight identity[33] – the Eleventh Doctor reverts to a less overtly sexual, and more unstable, self-presentation. But although he seeks to distance himself from any explicit knowledge of sex (for example he clearly does not want to consider in any detail the circumstances of Melody's conception) it is clear through his banter with River that he is not 'beyond sex'[34] in the same way as the first seven Doctors. In a further reflection of the classic Doctors, the new incarnation also embodies Nicholas Cull's contention that the character incorporates a number of British types, including H. G. Wells' time traveller, Sherlock Holmes, Van Helsing and 'the ever resourceful back room boffins' responsible for British victory in World War Two'.[35] Even in terms of dress, the tweed jacket, braces and bow-tie reflect the 'retro' costuming that Cull argues 'gave the whole programme a flavour of projecting something from a better past into an uncertain future'.[36] This sense of history is picked up by the Doctor himself who, in 'The Lodger', presents himself to his potential landlord as 'less young professional and more ancient amateur', in an episode that embodies the Doctor's 'Heath Robinson' qualities as he assembles a scanner to detect alien activity from a range of everyday items including a garden hoe, a rake, a broom, an oar and a lampshade.[37]

The narrative premise of 'The Lodger' – which requires that the Doctor attempt to pass as 'normal' – showcases the difference between the Eleventh Doctor and his two previous incarnations, neither of whom seem likely to have found this task a challenge. But my interpretation of this episode (building on Frank Collins' chapter) is to see it as showcasing the Doctor's (albeit rather clumsy) attempt to facilitate heterosexual courtship. Craig and Sophie function as a more normal parallel to Amy and Rory – both couples failing to realise their importance to one another until their encounter with the Doctor creates a crisis to which the resolution requires a recognition and declaration of love. There is a further parallel between the two couples in that both Rory and Craig subsequently perform masculinity at its most hegemonic in defence of their children – Rory as he seeks to defend the new-born Melody, and Craig as his paternal instinct to save his son Alfie enables him to overcome the attempt to assimilate him as the new Cyber-Controller. 'The Lodger' highlights the hybrid nature of contemporary masculinity and the role of homosocial bonding – themes picked up in 'Closing Time' which sees the Doctor and Craig reunited for a second adventure. But while this later episode seeks to reflect the growing normalisation of both same-sex couples and same-sex parenting (with shop assistant Val reading them repeatedly as a gay couple), what the episode once again demonstrates most successfully is the power of parental love, and the Doctor's status as outsider.

Matt Hills has described the sexual landscape of the Russell T Davies era as making sexuality unremarkable through a 'casual candidness' that incorporated gay identities in a matter-of-fact manner.[38] This quotidian approach seemed to be missing from Moffat's first series in charge, although it returned at key moments in series six and seven. While the new era has yet to offer anything comparable to the post-queer pansexuality of 'Gridlock' (2007), in the opening of series six we find out that the reason for Clayton Delaware's dismissal from the FBI is his desire to marry a black man, and in 'A Good Man Goes to War' we have 'thin fat gay married Anglican marines', supreme authority vested in the papal mainframe *her*self, and a hint at lesbian visibility in the relationship between Jennie and Madame Vastra. This resurfaces in series seven with Oswin's references to Nina in 'Asylum of the Daleks', and the invitation to Amy to be a bridesmaid at a lesbian wedding in 'The Power of Three'. Returning to the theme of double-entanglement, one of the hallmarks of these representations is that they walk a fine line between transgression and conservatism. By adding miscegenation to the mix with Clayton, Moffat is able to denote the Doctor's support of both same-sex and inter-racial relationships, even if the Eleventh Doctor's own apparent sexual naivety means no gay flirting. Yet these relationships are located within a recuperative framework that allies homosexuality with the conservative institutions of marriage and the military/security service. Both of these reflect the rising tide of gay neoliberalism that Lisa Duggan has argued seeks to emphasise the conformity and compatibility of same-sex relationships to the current political order while at the same time confounding the stereotype that conflates gender and sexuality through the linking of homosexuality, promiscuity and effeminacy.[39] This double-edged sword – promoting tolerance subject to conformity to Steven Seidman's definition of the 'good gay' as someone who is gender conventional – links sex to love and a marriage-like relationship, defends family values, personifies economic individualism and displays national pride.[40] This returns us to Jameson's contention that the role of popular culture is to offer both a reification of the existing social order alongside a genuine bribe of a better future.

Conclusion

If we accept Jameson's argument that any text of mass popular culture must be, at one and the same time, both ideological and utopian – and combine this with John Fiske's assertion that the producerly text 'treats its readers as members of a semiotic democracy, already equipped with the discursive competencies to make meanings and motivated by pleasure to want to participate in the process'[41] – then it is clear that the representation of gender and sexuality in series five, six, and seven is indeed complex and polysemic. Those who wish to focus on the reification/ideological aspects of the text will draw attention to the taming of female sexual licence, the assertion of heteronormativity and traditional family values, the tolerance of homosexual identities provided that they function in the service of both state and family, and the continued dominance of patriarchal authority. Those who wish to promote the utopian dimension will focus on Amy as a young woman who is feisty, assertive and in control, River as a powerful, sexy, witty, older woman, and the Doctor and Rory as showcasing masculinities that can be simultaneously heroic, caring and compassionate. They will also note that the series offers a vision of a world in which sexual diversity is taken for granted – even in those institutions (notably the Church and military) which, to date, have seemed the most resistant to the gay agenda. It is the nature of the postmodern text that it is impossible to privilege either of these readings. Which the viewer chooses to adopt will depend on his or her personal view of the future.

Notes

1. John Beynon, *Masculinities and Culture* (Maidenhead, 2002).
2. Shawn Shimpach, *Television in Transition: The Life and Afterlife of the Narrative Action Hero* (Oxford, 2010), p. 31.
3. Alec Charles, 'War Without End? Utopia, the Family and the Post-9/11 World in Russell T Davies's *Doctor Who*', *Science Fiction Studies* 35 (2008), pp. 450–64.

4. Jason Mittell, 'Narrative Complexity in Contemporary American Television', *Velvet Light Trap* 58 (2006), pp. 29–40.
5. Frederic Jameson, 'Reification and Utopia in Mass Culture', *Social Text* 1 (1979), p. 144.
6. Ibid.
7. Angela McRobbie, *The Aftermath of Feminism* (London, 2009).
8. Charles, 'War Without End?', p. 459.
9. Ibid.
10. Kim Newman, *Doctor Who* (London, 2005), p. 44.
11. Diane Negra, *What a Girl Wants? Fantasizing the Reclamation of Self in Postfeminism* (London, 2009), p. 50.
12. Negra, *What a Girl Wants?*, pp. 31–2.
13. Dee Amy-Chinn, 'Rose Tyler: The Ethics of Care and the Limits of Agency', *Science Fiction Film and Television* 1/2 (2008), pp. 231–47.
14. Davies quoted in Shaun Lyon, *Back to the Vortex* (Tolworth, 2005), p. 72.
15. Noel McLaughlin, 'Gender Redux: *Bionic Woman, Doctor Who* and *Battlestar Galactica*', in Christopher J. Hansen (ed.) *Ruminations, Peregrinations and Regenerations: A Critical Approach to Doctor Who* (Newcastle upon Tyne, 2010), p. 124.
16. Linda Papadopoulos, *The Sexualisation of Young People Review* (London, 2010); Reg Bailey, *Letting Children Be Children* (London, 2011).
17. Allison Pearson, 'A New Sexy Doctor Who? Exterminate', *Mail Online*, 25 March 2010. Available at www.dailymail.co.uk/femail/article-1260206/ ALLISON-PEARSON-Warning-Just-dont-dare-middle-class.html (accessed 30 July 2011).
18. Rosalind Gill, 'Postfeminist Media Culture: Elements of a Sensibility', *European Journal of Cultural Studies* 10/2 (2007), pp. 147–66; Amanda Lotz, 'Postfeminist Television Criticism: Rehabilitating Critical Terms and Identifying Postfeminist Attributes', *Feminist Media Studies* 1/1 (2001), pp. 105–21; Angela Mc Robbie, 'Post-Feminism and Popular Culture', *Feminist Media Studies* 4/3 (2004), pp. 255–64; Sarah Projansky, *Watching Rape: Film and Television in Postfeminist Culture* (New York, 2001).
19. Kat Baynard, *The Equality Illusion: The Truth about Men and Women Today* (London, 2010).
20. Karen Gillan, '12 Weeks that Changed My Life: Interview with E. Jane Dickson', *Radio Times*, 19–25 June 2010, pp. 21–24.
21. Ibid.
22. Ibid.
23. Geneviere Lloyd, *The Man of Reason: 'Male' and 'Female' in Western Philosophy* (London, 1984).
24. Negra, *What a Girl Wants?*, p. 99.
25. Catriona Wightman, 'BBC Receives Complaints Over Sexy "Who"', *Digital Spy*, 5 May 2010, Available at www.digitalspy.co.uk/tv/s7/doctor-who/news/ a218242/bbc-receives-complaints-over-sexy-who.html (accessed 23 March 2012).
26. Frank Collins, *The Pandorica Opens: Exploring the Worlds of the Eleventh Doctor* (Cambridge, 2010), p. 78.
27. Nicholas Cull, '"Bigger on the Inside ...": Doctor Who as British Cultural History' in Graham Roberts and Philip M. Taylor (eds) *The Historian, Television and Television History* (Luton, 2001), pp. 95–111.

28. Shimpach, *Television in Transition*, p. 44.
29. Robert Connell, *The Men & The Boys* (Cambridge, 2000), p. 11; Lynne Segal, 'Back to the Boys? Temptations of the Good Gender Theorist', *Textual Practice* 15/2 (2001), pp. 231–50.
30. Eve Kosofsky Sedgwick, *Tendencies* (London, 1994), p. 8.
31. Marc Schuster and Tom Powers, *The Greatest Show in the Galaxy* (NC, 2007), pp. 54–6.
32. Shimpach, *Television in Transition*, p. 175.
33. Piers D. Britton, *TARDISBound: Navigating the Universes of Doctor Who* (London, 2011), p. 85.
34. Cull, 'Bigger on the Inside', p. 106.
35. Ibid., p. 100.
36. Ibid.
37. Referencing the English cartoonist and illustrator William Heath Robinson (famous for his drawings of eccentric machines), the term 'Heath Robinson' is used as a shorthand description of any unnecessarily complex and implausible contraption.
38. Matt Hills, *Triumph of a Time Lord: Regenerating Doctor Who in the Twenty-First Century* (London, 2010), p. 34.
39. Lisa Duggan, *The Twilight of Equality? Neoliberalism, Cultural Politics, and the Attack on Democracy* (Boston, 2003).
40. Steven Seidman, *Beyond the Closet* (New York, 2004), p. 133.
41. John Fiske, *Television Culture* (London, 1987), p. 95.

PART TWO

WIDER BROADCASTING CONTEXTS

5

'HALFWAY OUT OF THE DARK'

Steven Moffat's *Doctor Who* Christmas Specials

David Budgen

In 2005 *Doctor Who* returned as a regular series after a gap of 16 years. Overseen by series producer Russell T Davies, it quickly established itself as one of the BBC's greatest assets, drawing huge audiences and rewarding the corporation through merchandising and overseas sales. The possibility of a *Doctor Who* Christmas special was first mooted long before the new series had been broadcast, and was confirmed in March 2005.[1] 'The Christmas Invasion' was broadcast on Christmas Day 2005, and introduced David Tennant as the new Doctor, Christopher Eccleston having decided to exit the role after only one series. It was the first time *Doctor Who* had been shown on Christmas Day since 'The Feast of Steven', the seventh episode of 'The Daleks' Master Plan' in 1965. 'The Christmas Invasion' attracted a peak audience of 9.8 million, and was the second most watched programme on Christmas Day; only *EastEnders* achieved a higher audience.[2] Within a relatively short period of time, *Doctor Who* had become a 'beloved institution' of the BBC's Christmas schedule, with further specials appearing every subsequent year.[3] This chapter seeks to examine the Christmas specials produced under the stewardship of Steven Moffat, who replaced Davies as series producer in 2010, introducing

Matt Smith as Tennant's replacement. It will begin by placing the Christmas specials in context, establishing the nature and history of Christmas television and its audiences. It will then focus upon Moffat's first two specials in detail, addressing such issues as Moffat's authorial voice, the difference between the *Doctor Who* Christmas specials and main series episodes, and the ways in which these episodes fit the genre of Christmas television.

Christmas on Television

Christmas is the peak of a television year punctuated by events and festivals. Paddy Scannell has suggested that 'the calendrical role of broadcasting' has allowed the BBC to become 'perhaps *the* central agent of the national culture',[4] a point reiterated by John Ellis:

> Television in Britain owes a lot to the ceremonial: it was the televised coronation of Queen Elizabeth in 1953 that convinced a generation that they really needed a television set. And public service television has been repaying the debt ever since. Television became the keeper of the national calendar, marking the season by a ritualistic round of sporting events and commemorations. ... Beyond this lay the patterns of annual holidays (midsummer for northern Europe, August for the Mediterranean countries), secular celebrations and religious holidays. Christmas demanded weeks of special editions of popular programmes (often recorded during the summer months), and in different countries [television] adapted its scheduling routine to the annual cycle of religious festivals.[5]

Of these festivals, Christmas is the highlight of the television year, its programmes markedly different from anything shown throughout the preceding 11 months. For a fortnight in December, regular viewing is overturned in favour of new dramas, classic adaptations, special individual episodes of favourite programmes, hundreds of films and hours of repeats. It is at once a fertile place for special televisual 'treats' and a dumping ground for schedule fillers. Such traditions stretch back further than the age of television.

In his 1843 preface to *A Christmas Carol*, Charles Dickens described his tale as a 'Ghostly little book, to raise the Ghost of an

Idea, which shall not put my readers out of humour with them-selves, with each other, with the season, or with me'.[6] In many ways, this introduction aptly conveys the nature of Christmas television. It is often frivolous, appealing to a broad audience, conveying a warm sense of nostalgia rather than cutting-edge entertainment. The most popular programmes of the year are given the honour of a Christmas special, often with a festive theme to justify their singling out for special treatment. They are usually small and inti-mate productions, as opposed to big cinematic extravaganzas. Ellis has regarded the establishment of television as a 'domestic rather than public medium', establishing an intimacy with its audience in a way that cinema could not.[7] Christmas specials often reflect the audiences watching them. As Robert J. Thompson has suggested, Christmas specials have an obsession 'with a nostalgic reverence for the idea of home and the family', and Ellis' understanding of television as a domestic object correlates with the nature of the season as a celebration surrounding hearth and home.[8] Indeed, Davies-era *Doctor Who* was strongly focused on family, with com-panions' parents and grandparents integral throughout his ten-ure. In this sense, the Davies Christmas specials expanded upon ideas prevalent in the main series.

In a preview for 2005's 'The Christmas Invasion', Russell T Davies remarked that, 'I hate those specials where it's Christmas but they bugger off to Spain or Prague or Fuengirola, without a sprig of holly to be seen. Honestly, it's not rocket science – a Christmas Special should be both Christmassy, and special.'[9] 'The Christmas Invasion' fulfilled this remit, with murderous robotic Santas, an exploding Christmas tree and the Doctor sharing Christmas din-ner with the Tyler family, an act 'suggesting', as James Chapman has remarked, 'that he has been accepted into their community'.[10] This became an ongoing trend throughout the Christmas specials. The Doctor's refusal to dine with Donna Noble and her family, for example, re-established him as an outsider after the loss of Rose Tyler. However, in 'The Next Doctor' the Doctor goes off to share Christmas with Jackson Lake. These scenes emphasised the bond between the Doctor and the audience. The *Radio Times*, in December 2011, published interviews with Matt Smith and Maurice Cole, one of the child stars of 'The Doctor, the Widow and the Wardrobe'. Both pronounced that they would be watch-ing the Christmas special with their families, taking part in the new tradition and challenging the miserable family gatherings which dominate the plots of soap operas on Christmas Day.[11]

Christmas Day television, particularly on the BBC, can be seen as the extension of those Reithian values which underpinned the organisation at its founding, and have continued to influence its direction to a greater or lesser extent throughout its history. Paddy Scannell has described Christmas as the 'supreme family festival', and noted Reith's role in persuading the King to broadcast to the nation in 1932:

> The royal broadcast quickly became part of the ritual of the British Christmas. ... It set a crowning seal on the role of broadcasting in binding the nation together, giving it a particular form and content: the family audience, the royal family, the nation as family.[12]

Christmas television is very much about ritual and family. The schedule of BBC1 is similar each year; family movies throughout the morning and early afternoon – inessential viewing that occupies those in the household not involved in preparing the Christmas dinner – interrupted only by the Queen's speech at 3 o'clock. Other programmes in the Christmas Day line-up are often one-off light entertainment programmes. In 2010, for example, 'A Christmas Carol' was bookended by *The One Ronnie*, a sketch show with Ronnie Corbett, and the *Strictly Come Dancing* Christmas special. Christmas television is supposed to be comforting and warmly nostalgic, and in framing their Christmas Day schedule around Corbett, *Doctor Who* and Bruce Forsyth, the BBC reached back into the annals of television history to bring viewers programmes and entertainers that had stood the test of time, and were comforting in their familiarity. Christmas television is aimed at families, rather than individuals, and as such is generally not edgy or contentious.

This need to stay away from controversy manifests itself in various ways. For a religious holiday, the Christmas Day schedules are remarkably secular. In 2010, BBC1 showed a mere 65 minutes of religious programming, while ITV could only manage a 25-minute carol service. Indeed, while Christmas television celebrates morality and generosity, the spirit of the season, it also reinforces the forces of consumerism and capitalism. Thompson has suggested that 'most [American] Christmas television demonstrates that kids like toys, and lots of them, and that we should plan our shopping strategies accordingly'.[13] Like the 'classic' series, *Doctor Who* has developed a strong merchandising element since its re-launch in 2005. DVD box sets are released in time for Christmas, along with books, calendars and action figures. In 2008, a voice-changing Dalek helmet was one of the most popular toys of the year.[14] The London toy store Hamleys predicted in June 2011 that one of the best-selling toys for Christmas would be a £200 inflatable sit-in Dalek.[15] The *Doctor Who* Christmas special is just one ingredient in the Time Lord's influence on Christmas; some children will spend the day playing with their new *Doctor Who* toys, before watching the real thing on BBC 1. In 2005, 'The Christmas Invasion' was introduced by the BBC announcer with the words, 'And now the present you've all been waiting for ...'.

The absence of Christianity does not necessarily mean that Christmas television is devoid of values. As Thompson has noted of American television:

> Many of the songs, images, and stories of Christmas are now safely secular, and many Christmas television shows choose to stick with these. The indictments of Scrooge, the Grinch, Rudolph's exclusionary reindeer pals ... communicate warm values associated with Christmas without the gravity of obvious religious belief.[16]

Much the same could be said of British television. Indeed, many of the films shown on Christmas Day are American films depicting an American Christmas. Such films, however, are an important part of the schedules. Some have little to do with the festive season, having become associated with Christmas through repeated showings each year. In 2007, Russell T Davies told *Doctor Who Magazine* that "The *Doctor Who* specials will always be Christmassy, at least while I'm around".[17] Yet the special he was promoting, 'Voyage of the Damned', was openly acknowledged as a homage to 1970s Hollywood disaster movies, with particular reference to Ronald Neame's *The Poseidon Adventure* (1972). Davies described it as 'a sci-fi-murder-mystery-Christmas-disaster-movie-epic! With echoes of *The Poseidon Adventure*, *The Robots of Death*, and Kylie's 2001 *On a Night Like This* tour!'[18] The festive season is constantly assimilating new works of popular culture into its traditions, and certain films have become part of this process in the last few decades. The establishment of *Doctor Who* as a festive favourite is evidence of this. Moreover, older traditions flourish.

Christmas television may be a relatively recent development, but the tradition of storytelling during the festive season stretches back much further. During the mid-nineteenth century, these oral traditions were seized upon by publishers.[19] Charles Dickens' *A Christmas Carol* was first published in 1843, and was the first of his five Christmas stories published yearly until 1848.[20] Dickens fulfilled a role similar to that of Davies and Moffat when he edited the Christmas editions of the popular journals *Household Words* and *All the Year Round*, a role he maintained for 17 years. Like *Doctor Who*, these works were widely read throughout the year, but attracted a greater audience at Christmas.[21] Dickens was not the only writer to address the subject of storytelling at Christmas. Henry James' novella *The Turn of the Screw* (1898) begins with party guests telling each other ghost stories. James describes one of the stories as having 'held us, round the fire, sufficiently breathless, but except the obvious remark that it was gruesome, as on Christmas Eve in an old house a strange tale should essentially be, I remember no comment uttered'.[22] An ITV adaptation of *The Turn of the Screw*, starring Jodhi May, Colin Firth and Pam Ferris, was shown on Boxing Day 1999, while the BBC screened a 1920s-set version on 30 December 2009. The tradition of Christmas ghost stories has moved from oral and literary traditions to become an integral part of the festive schedules.

Between 1971 and 1978, the BBC strengthened the link between the festive season and supernatural tales. In *A Ghost Story for Christmas*, several of the works of M.R. James were adapted for television, including *The Stalls of Barchester* and *A Warning to the Curious*, as well as an interpretation of Dickens' *The Signalman*. James' stories had been intended for consumption at Christmas; many were written to be read aloud to his friends and fellow academics on Christmas Eve each year. The tradition of the Christmas ghost story has gained further momentum in recent years, with *Doctor Who* writer Mark Gatiss's *Crooked House* broadcast over the period 22–24 December 2008, and a new version of James' *Whistle and I'll Come to You* shown on Christmas Eve 2010. Ellis has commented upon the difference between cinema and television, noting the 'small and luminous' nature of the small screen.[23] To some extent this argument may have been superseded by the development of large-screen television sets and high-definition transmissions; nevertheless, the glowing television screen telling stories can be seen as a natural progression from tales told around the glowing fireplace. These ghost stories are part of a wider tradition of classic-novel adaptations over the Christmas period. Sarah Cardwell has examined the role these dramatisations play at Christmas:

> Classic-novel adaptations are portrayed as distinct from other television programmes, characterised in terms of a 'haven' within the televisual. Over Christmas 1999, viewers were treated to two serialised Dickens adaptations: *Oliver Twist* (ITV) in December, and *David Copperfield* (BBC) on Christmas Day and Boxing Day; they were also offered an adaptation of Henry James's *The Turn of the Screw* (ITV) and Mrs Gaskell's *Wives and Daughters* (BBC). The television schedules thus depend upon 'heritage' pieces, in terms both of the programmes' content and of their links with long-standing televisual traditions: the traditional Christmas Dickens adaptation, the Christmas ghost story, and other quality family viewing.[24]

So it can be seen that, in using Dickens and C.S. Lewis for inspiration, Moffat's specials were located within a framework of pre-existing Christmas traditions which audiences would already be familiar with.

'A Christmas Carol'

'A Christmas Carol' saw a move away from the science-fiction extravaganzas of the Davies years to a complex fantasy incorporating elements of Dickens, *Mary Poppins* and *Peter Pan*, in keeping with Moffat's wider interest in investing the series with a story-book atmosphere. The Doctor, inspired by Dickens' *A Christmas Carol*, uses time travel to rewrite the past of a misanthropic miser, undoing the unhappy childhood that had made him so malevolent so that he will save a seemingly doomed intergalactic cruise-ship, aboard which Amy and Rory are honeymooning. The opening of 'A Christmas Carol' plays with audience expectations. The spaceship Amy and Rory are trapped on

DOCTOR WHO, *THE ELEVENTH HOUR*

is wholly modern, white and clinical; the crew are dressed in uniforms both futuristic and familiar. Indeed, the opening has been seen by some as a nod to *Star Trek*.[25] This introduction takes place before the opening credits and theme music, and almost seems like part of a separate story. Upon the end of the title sequence, we are introduced to a street scene of purest Victoriana, complete with street performers, chirpy newspaper vendors and urchins. The science-fiction trappings of *Doctor Who*, which could alienate a broader audience, are put to one side, while a setting familiar to anyone with a cursory knowledge of festive stories moves into prominence. 'A Christmas Carol' seems to start as a science-fiction disaster movie, and is then diverted into a fantasy character-piece emphasising the virtues of home, family and the spirit of the season.

Family, as in all good Christmas stories, is vital to 'A Christmas Carol'. The character Abigail (Katherine Jenkins) has been taken as 'security' for money loaned to her family by Elliot Sardick (Michael Gambon). We are first introduced to his son, Kazran (also Gambon), as the now aged family plead for her to be unfrozen for Christmas Day. Furthermore, we learn that Kazran became a misanthrope because of the lack of paternal love in his childhood. Later in the episode, as has become a custom in the Christmas specials, the Doctor enjoys a Christmas dinner with Abigail, her family and young Kazran (Danny Horn), the episode holding up a mirror to its audience. The *Doctor Who* Christmas special is broadcast in the early evening, after the traditional Christmas meal-time. Watching the Doctor engage in this ritual creates an indelible link between the Time Lord and the audience through their shared experience. The use of Christmas meals and gatherings to create a sense of unity has a long tradition. After Scrooge's redemption in Dickens' *A Christmas Carol*, he joins his nephew for Christmas dinner: 'Wonderful party, wonderful games, wonderful *unanimity*, wond-der-ful happiness!'[26] Similarly, at the height of World War II in 1942, Noel Coward's *In Which We Serve* used three separate Christmas meals to establish what Jeffrey Richards and Anthony Aldgate have described as a 'mutuality of interest' between the film's protagonists.[27] Separated by the class system and the hierarchy of the Royal Navy, these men were, like Britain itself, united by shared values and traditions exemplified by their celebration of the Christmas season. Science fiction has not traditionally been a prominent feature of the Christmas Day schedules, so 'A Christmas Carol' establishes a bond between the Doctor and non-fans by showing that even a 900-year-old alien's hearts can be warmed by the festivities.[28]

Other techniques are used to draw in the Christmas audience. *Doctor Who Magazine* noted that the script went 'to some lengths to highlight the traveller's ownership of this time of year, from that fireside entrance, to ... the manic building of the snowmen at the end'.[29] At key moments in the episode, characters address the audience directly, forging a new link which had not been present in the Davies era. Before the title sequence, when asked the meaning of a message from the Doctor, Amy Pond looks directly at the camera: 'It's Christmas!' Later, the Doctor speaks directly to camera, metaphorically winking at the audience as he plans to use Dickens' tale to save the 4003 people aboard the spaceship: 'So that ship needs to land, but it can't land unless a very bad man suddenly decides to turn nice just in time for Christmas Day.' Moffat approaches the source material in a respectful manner; it is not mocking *A Christmas Carol* or its values, but reinforcing them. This is crucial given the need to appeal to a wider Christmas audience. Moreover, it acknowledges *Doctor Who* lore. As Moffat remarked:

> The greatest Christmas Story is *A Christmas Carol* ... and there's no point trying to beat it. Because we all know that Charles Dickens is a personal friend of the Doctor's, so he obviously couldn't find himself re-enacting his mate's biggest hit, without noticing.[30]

Another way in which the *Doctor Who* Christmas specials appeal to a wider festive audience is through the use of guest stars. This trend began with the second Christmas episode, 'The Runaway Bride' (2006), in which the comedian and actress Catherine Tate made her first appearance as Donna Noble. In 2007, Kylie Minogue played Astrid Peth in 'Voyage of the Damned', while in 2008, David Morrissey guest-starred as Jackson Lake. These guest appearances fulfilled a vital role. Recognisable figures from other fields of popular culture would provide non-fans with a way into the episode, a familiar face amongst the in-jokes and science fiction techno-babble. As Greg Smith has noted, 'a guest character can create a serious conflict and then depart, thus satisfying the series' need for drama without requiring a full commitment of the show's "resources"'.[31] Moreover, their plotlines can be 'of vital importance ... without burdening the serial with a continuing narrative obligation'.[32] This is of particular relevance to the *Doctor Who* Christmas specials. Irregular viewers are able to enjoy the episode as a unique narrative. Furthermore, the Christmas specials made between 2006 and 2008 all used guest stars to temporarily replace the Doctor's companions (Rose, Martha and Donna) who had departed at the end of each previous series. Permanent replacements would not be found until the series proper.

In this sense, 'A Christmas Carol' is left with a dilemma. The Christmas episodes now have a tradition of guest companions, yet Amy and Rory had not left at the end of Matt Smith's first series. Indeed, 'A Christmas Carol' marks Rory's elevation to the role of companion, being the first episode in which Arthur Darvill's name appears in the opening credits. Instead, they are left stranded for most of the episode, while guests take their place. Unlike most of the classic *Doctor Who* serials both Davies and Moffat tended to construct their series around a larger narrative arc. This could be alienating to a wider, unknowing audience, so the introduction of guest characters brings all viewers back to the same starting point. The viewer who only watches on Christmas Day is able to engage with a story in which pre-established relationships between the main characters are largely sidelined. In addition, the appearance of a popular classical singer and the actor who played Dumbledore in the *Harry Potter* films would bring other significant fan-bases into the *Doctor Who* audience, as Moffat noted: 'Michael Gambon is as distinguished an actor as I can imagine and the fact that he was Dumbledore means that he is already known to millions of children.'[33]

Moffat uses other techniques to allow the extra Christmas viewers to feel included. The Dickens-inspired source material is highly familiar for modern audiences on both sides of the Atlantic, and 2010 was the first year in which *Doctor Who* was broadcast on Christmas Day by BBC America. In the United States, *A Christmas Carol* has provided the inspiration for special episodes of series ranging from *Family Ties* and *WKRP in Cincinnati*, to *Quantum Leap* and *Xena: The Warrior Princess*.[34] In 1988, Rowan Atkinson starred in Richard Curtis and Ben Elton's *Blackadder's Christmas Carol*. Reversing the conventions of the novel, James Chapman sees it as showing 'how the *Carol* itself remains a highly promi-nent point of reference in the cultural construction of Christmas in our society'.[35] It should also be noted that Moffat includes various references within the script to appeal to the episode's different audiences. Sardick's atmosphere-controlling machine has isomorphic controls, an allusion to the 1975 Tom Baker serial 'Pyramids of Mars', while a mention of *Mary Poppins* (1964) con-jures images of some of the non-Christmassy films which are indelibly linked to the festive season. Amy and Rory appear in costumes from earlier in the series, a kissogram policewoman's uniform worn throughout 'The Eleventh Hour', and a Roman sol-dier's uniform from 'The Pandorica Opens'. These are also remi-niscent of Rodney and Cassandra Trotter's costumes in the 2001 Christmas special of *Only Fools and Horses*, the most watched single television episode of the decade.[36] In 2006, *Doctor Who Magazine* remarked upon the excitement surrounding the first *Doctor Who* Christmas special by declaring 'move over Del Boy!' Emphasising the association of the festive season with the antics of the Trotter family, this anticipated the new status of the Time Lord at the centrepiece of the Christmas schedule.[37]

'The Doctor, the Widow and the Wardrobe'

Just as 'A Christmas Carol' had opened with a homage to *Star Trek*, 'The Doctor, the Widow and the Wardrobe' begins with a direct reference to *Star Wars* (1977), with a gigantic spaceship looming into view in the opening shot. Again, Moffat immedi-ately moves away from US science-fiction references to a quin-tessentially British (or, more accurately, English) setting, where a 1938 housewife (Claire Skinner) comes to the Doctor's aid. The main story, set three years later, follows the Doctor's attempts to repay her kindness. When compared with the twisting, elab-orate plotting and general cleverness of 'A Christmas Carol', 'The Doctor, the Widow and the Wardrobe' is much more con-ventional. Series six of *Doctor Who* had been controversial with its time-jumping narrative arc revealing the origins of the char-acter River Song (Alex Kingston). Critics complained it was too complicated, prompting defensive responses from the writers. 'I don't think the problem is that *Doctor Who* has become more complicated', Toby Whithouse retorted. 'Surely it's the fact that the rest of television has become more simplistic.' He wrote 'The themes and plots of New Who are no more complex than some classic Who stories. The only difference is, Tom Baker's Doctor wasn't jostling in the schedules against *Red or Black*.'[38] Yet, as we have seen, a Christmas special needs to appeal to wider audience. Indeed, of the 2011 special Nick Setchfield of *SFX* noted that 'Moffat dials down the time-scrambling maziness that's so characterised the last 12 months of *Doctor Who*.'[39]

'The Doctor, the Widow and the Wardrobe' may begin with an exploding spaceship, but this situation is resolved before the opening credits. There is no pervading danger to instigate the Doctor's actions, only the desire to reward Madge's kindness. Davies-era Christmas specials had all involved the Earth in peril, as had many of the episodes within the main series. Andrew Billen of the *The Times* lamented in 2010, 'The days when he would merely help to separate warring stone-age tribes or exterminate the Daleks on their home planet are long gone'.[40] Moffat's specials took place on a smaller scale; the Doctor became an alternative Father Christmas, rather than an action hero. Writing in the *Radio Times*, Moffat remarked, 'When I was little, the Doctor and Father Christmas lived in the same place in my head – kind, funny lunatics, who looked like grown-ups but definitely weren't'.[41] In a separate interview, Matt Smith re-emphasised this: 'The spirit of the Doctor and the spirit of Christmas are entwined somewhere. ... He just loves it because it's everything about the human spirit that he likes, at its best.'[42] A clear departure could be seen from what Billen had described as the 'Messiah Complex' of Davies and Tennant's Time Lord.[43]

The role of guest stars has become vital to the festive *Doctor Who* tales, yet in 2011 the use of such actors would be slightly different. An announcement in September 2011 revealed that the Doctor would be joined by Bill Bailey, Claire Skinner, Alexander Armstrong and Arabella Weir for the Christmas special, with particular focus on Bailey's role.[44] All four were strongly associated with comedy. In the actual episode, Bailey and Weir's parts were ultimately peripheral, their characters being largely forgotten. Furthermore, Skinner and Armstrong's characters were oddly reminiscent of other roles they were strongly associated with. Skinner was best known as the frazzled mum in the BBC sitcom *Outnumbered* (2007–) while Armstrong played a teen-speak spouting Battle of Britain pilot in recurring sketches on the *Armstrong and Miller Show* (2007–). Their characters in *Doctor Who* represented alternate versions of their previous roles. Armstrong remarked upon this in a *Radio Times* interview, emphasising the differences while jokily acknowledging that he was being type-cast as a World War II aviator.[45] The *Independent* made a similar connection.[46] The *Radio Times* explicitly coupled Skinner's two roles by recommending the *Outnumbered* Christmas special on Christmas Eve to those who were looking forward to *Doctor Who*.

Again, the usual companions were sidelined for the Christmas special, ensuring that the story did not get mired in a self-referential tirade of in-jokes alienating the wider Christmas audience. Director Farren Blackburn noted that 'The Christmas special appeals to a really broad audience, from the kids right up to the grandparents'.[47] At the same time, the Christmas special attempted to appease the core audience. In the *SFX* review of 'A Christmas Carol', it was noted that 'there will be some who mourn the passing of *Who* as hardcore SF', and a section of fans had indeed been vociferous in their criticism. The finale of 'The Doctor, the Widow and the Wardrobe', in which the Doctor re-establishes contact with Amy and Rory, seems to be aimed squarely at regular viewers. Its dialogue – that River told them the Doctor was still alive – is not self-explanatory, relying upon prior audience knowledge of the previous season for its meaning.

Both Christmas specials incorporated elements of adaptation as a focal point for the audience, although to different extents. The title and some of the settings were evocative of C.S. Lewis' *The Lion, the Witch and the Wardrobe* (1950). Promotional material and, indeed, the BBC schedulers, focused upon this. The *Radio Times* explicitly linked the *Doctor Who* Christmas special to the Christmas Eve screening of *The Chronicles of Narnia: The Lion, the Witch and the Wardrobe* (2005) and a radio dramatisation of the same tale on BBC Radio 4 Extra on 23 December. 'A Christmas Carol' was knowingly partaking in a reworking of the Dickens story. In 2011, however, actual references to Lewis' work were few and far between. Instead, as many reviewers pointed out, there were more allusions to Tolkien's *The Lord of the Rings*, James Cameron's *Aliens* (1986) and *Star Wars*, as well as a reference to the Davison-era *Doctor Who* serial 'The Caves of Androzani'

(1984). Yet in linking *Doctor Who* to the works of Lewis, Moffat was taking the series back to its origins. Cecil Edwin Webber's original suggestion was that a 'good old Magic Door' as a means of transport would become the TARDIS and Gary Gillatt has noted the similarities between the Doctor's time machine and the wardrobe which leads the Pevensie children into Narnia.[48]

The Christmas specials also continue trends from previous Moffat-written episodes. Time progresses in a non-linear manner in both episodes: in 'A Christmas Carol' the Doctor jumps between the past and the present, using his knowledge to rewrite Sardick's life, while in 'The Doctor, the Widow and the Wardrobe', time moves faster in the snow-covered forest than on Earth. Yet, given the Lewis connection, there was no reference to time being kept on hold. In *The Lion, the Witch and the Wardrobe*, Mr Tumnus reveals the plight of Narnia to Lucy: 'Always winter and never Christmas; think of that!'[49] It could be argued that such a sentiment was more relevant to the 2010 special, in which Abigail could enjoy a series of Christmas Eves but never reach Christmas Day. In Moffat's 'The Doctor Dances', the Doctor saved the people of London, proclaiming, 'Just this once, everybody lives!' This notion recurred throughout future Moffat-penned episodes, and the ending of 'A Christmas Carol' was no exception with the spaceship able to dock successfully and its passengers celebrating Christmas in Sardicktown. Similarly, the 2011 special ends with the reappearance of Reg, who had been shot down on a flying mission. Madge's adventures with the Doctor culminated in a shimmering white light used by Reg to guide his crew home. Again, the festive special eschewed the misery and tragedy of the Christmas soap operas, ending positively with a celebration of family and domesticity, and a sense of hope for the future.

Conclusion

The Christmas specials are different from the main series. As both Davies and Moffat have emphasised, they must be Christmassy. *SFX* remarked upon Moffat's efforts to get into the Christmas mood when writing the special in the summer: 'Tomorrow he will close the blinds against the leafy London summer, crank up the Slade and the sleighbells and endeavour to summon page one of this year's *Doctor Who* Christmas special.'[50] Most importantly, the Christmas specials have a different audience. Viewers who watch *Doctor Who* with their families only at Christmas must be catered to. Therefore, the Christmas specials must ensure that prior knowledge of story arcs or *Who*-history is unnecessary. In his first two Christmas specials, Moffat achieves this in a number of ways. The removal of the companions allows guest stars to take central roles; they are introduced to non-regular viewers and fans at the same time. No one need worry about keeping up. Moreover, particularly famous guest stars will bring their own fans to the episodes, expanding the audience further.

The use of adaptation has also been fundamental to the success of Moffat's Christmas episodes, with explicit connections drawn between *Doctor Who* and classic Christmas tales. Widespread familiarity with the source material again gave non-regular audiences easy access to the series and, in the case of 'A Christmas Carol', an established knowledge which allowed them to keep up with the 'wibbly-wobbly, timey-wimey stuff'.[51] In 2005, TV critic Sam Wollaston established the crux of the problem:

> *Doctor Who* used to be a bit like a garden shed, a place where geeky males and Dalek enthusiasts hid. But 'The Christmas Invasion' is one for the whole family, a good old-fashioned tale of good versus evil with the entire future of the world at stake.[52]

Moffat continued this tradition, creating episodes that were both inventive and inclusive.

Notes

1. Benjamin Cook, 'Doctor Who Christmas Preview: 2005 Christmas Special The Christmas Invasion', *Doctor Who Magazine* 364 (2006), p. 22.
2. 'BBC wins Christmas TV Ratings War'. Available at http://news.bbc.co.uk/1/hi/entertainment/4560594.stm (accessed 1 July 2012).
3. Mark Aldridge and Andy Murray, *T is for Television: The Small Screen Adventures of Russell T Davies* (London, 2008), p. 197.
4. Paddy Scannell, 'Radio Times: The Temporal Arrangements of Broadcasting in the Modern World', in Phillip Drummond and Richard Paterson (eds) *Television and Its Audience: International Research Perspectives* (London, 1988), pp. 17–18.
5. John Ellis, *Seeing Things: Television in the Age of Uncertainty* (London, 2002), p. 44.

DOCTOR WHO, *THE ELEVENTH HOUR*

33. Ben Dowell, 'Katherine Jenkins to Star in Doctor Who Christmas Special', *Guardian* 12 July 2010. Available at www.guardian.co.uk/media/2010/ jul/12/doctor-who-christmas-special (accessed July 1 2012).

34. Diane Werts, *Christmas on Television* (Westport, CT, 2005), pp. 145–57.

35. James Chapman, ' "God Bless Us Everyone": Movie Adaptations of *A Christmas Carol*' in Mark Connelly (ed.) *Christmas at the Movies: Images of Christmas in American, British and European Cinema* (London, 2000), pp. 32–3.

36. Paul Revoir, 'Christmas TV Backlash: BBC Hit by Ratings Slump as Viewers Complain of Repetitive Scheduling', *Daily Mail*, 29 December 2009. Available at www.dailymail.co.uk/news/article-1238999/BBC-hit-ratings-slump-viewers-complain-repetitive-scheduling.html (accessed 1 July 2012). The first *Only Fools and Horses* Christmas special was shown in 1981. Between 1983 and 1993, it was shown every 25 December on BBC1. More specials appeared sporadically afterwards.

37. Cook, 'Doctor Who Christmas Preview', p. 22.

38. Dan Martin, 'Has *Doctor Who* Got Too Complicated?', *Guardian*, 20 September 2011. Available at www.guardian.co.uk/tv-and-radio/tvandradioblog/2011/sep/20/doctor-who-too-complicated?INTCMP=SRCH (accessed 1 July 2012). *Red or Black* (2011) is an ITV game show in which contestants bet on the outcome of various competitions, with a 50/50 chance of progressing.

39. Nick Setchfield, '*Doctor Who* "The Doctor, the Widow and the Wardrobe" TV review', *SFX*, 25 December 2011. Available at www.sfx.co.uk/2011/12/25/ doctor-who-the-doctor-the-widow-and-the-wardrobe%E2%80%9D-tv-review/ (accessed 1 July 2012).

40. Andrew Billen, *The Times*, 2 April 2010, p. 26.

41. Steven Moffat, *Radio Times*, 17–30 December 2011, p. 35.

42. Matt Smith quoted in *Radio Times*, 11–17 December 2010, p. 18.

43. Billen, *The Times*, p. 26.

44. 'Bill Bailey Lands Role in Doctor Who Christmas Special'. Available at www.bbc.co.uk/news/entertainment-arts-15005076 (accessed 1 July 2012).

45. Claire Webb, 'Matt Smith and the *Doctor Who* Stars Preview the 2011 Christmas Special', 20 December 2011. Available at www.radiotimes.com/ news/2011-12-20/matt-smith-and-the-doctor-who-stars-preview-the-2011-christmas-special (accessed 1 July 2012).

46. Neela Debnath, 'Review of *Doctor Who* 'The Doctor, the Widow and t he Wardrobe', *Independent*. Available at http://blogs.independent. co.uk/2011/12/25/review-of-doctor-who-%E2%80%98the-doctor-the-widow-and-the-wardrobe%E2%80%99/ (accessed 1 July 2012).

47. Dave Golder, 'Stocking Thriller', *SFX* 217 (2012), p. 63.

48. Gary Gillatt, *Doctor Who from A–Z* (London, 1998), pp. 14–15.

49. C.S. Lewis, *The Lion, the Witch and the Wardrobe* (London, 1986 [1950]), p. 23.

50. Nick Setchfield, 'Who Do You Think You Are Killing – Mr Hitler?', *SFX* 213 (2011), p. 55.

51. Ibid.

52. Sam Wollaston, 'Christmas TV', 23 December 2005. Available at www. guardian.co.uk/media/2005/dec/23/broadcasting.tvandradio (accessed 1 July 2012).

6

THE TRANSATLANTIC DIMENSIONS OF THE TIME LORD

Doctor Who and the Relationships between British and North American Television

Simone Knox

Through the history of critical literature on *Doctor Who* runs an interest in the Britishness of the programme. Despite the fact that the programme's central protagonist is technically a humanoid from a different planet, this is hardly surprising, given the place this long-running series has in the history of British television, its preoccupation with British history, culture and society, and the enduring interest from its domestic audience. As John Tulloch and Manuel Alvarado note, this programme has 'become something of an institution within British cultural life'.[1] What interests me for this chapter is that considerations of the Britishness of *Doctor Who* also – inevitably – encounter and take account of the programme's relationship to US television. I say 'inevitably', because of both the historical inter relationship between US and British television programming across time, and the conceptual relationship between British television and US television as its structuring 'other', whereby the two function to give each other definition and meaning.

Within the existing scholarship on *Doctor Who*, it is possible to detect somewhat of a diachronic shift, from writing that explores the Britishness of the series and touches on the links to US television, to writing that is more explicitly focused on the series' transnational relationships.[2] This critical shift towards the programme's transatlantic dimensions is connected to the recent turn within Television Studies towards the transnational. Pooling together the previously parallel interests in distinct national television cultures and globalisation/cultural imperialism, the discipline in the last decade has understood the relationships between US and UK television as marked by connection and distinction, influence and resistance. What this present chapter will do is build on this turn towards the transnational, and explore some of the textual specificity of the Steven Moffat/Matt Smith *Doctor Who*, in relation to its specific positioning within the current transatlantic television landscape. The chapter will develop further the existing scholarship on *Doctor Who*, by both offering a critical assessment of the transatlantic dimensions of the current version, and by challenging some of the existing critical arguments about *Doctor Who*'s transatlantic dimensions.

Doctor Who in the Age of US Quality Television Drama

The already noted shift in scholarly attention on *Doctor Who* towards the programme's transatlantic dimensions clearly responds to, and recognises, the changes in the institutional context and their impact on the text after its 16-year absence. When *Doctor Who* was rebooted in 2005, it found itself in a noticeably different broadcasting landscape, one marked by deregulation and an opening up of the international television market, in which, due to growing commercial pressures, securing overseas funding and sales had acquired crucial significance, including for public service broadcasters such as the BBC. As Matthew Jones has noted, '[m]uch has been made of the BBC's desire to export [*Doctor Who*] to foreign markets since its 2005 return'.[3] Indeed, this desire was a necessity, given that, as both Jones and Barbara Selznick have observed, the programme's rebirth was underpinned by development funding from the Canadian Broadcasting

Corporation, and then secured further support through eventual sales success with the US Sci Fi (now Syfy) channel.[4]

The impact of this contextual need for overseas exportability on the production of the rebooted *Doctor Who* has certainly received due critical attention. Selznick notes the special significance of the reboot's higher production values *vis-à-vis* the long-standing connotations of *Doctor Who* with US audiences 'as a campy, low-budget sci-fi program for geeks',[5] as part of her discussion of how the programme has mobilised different brands of Britishness and shifted from 'heritage' and 'eccentric' towards 'cool'. I will return to her argument, but for now it suffices to note that the youthful cast of the reboot is also important in this shift towards the cool. Interested in the series' longevity, James Chapman understands the reboot of *Doctor Who* in the wider context of the influence of US quality television drama on British television production.[6] The significance of this influence is reflected by the 1996 television movie *Doctor Who*, which was co-produced by the BBC and Universal Television for the Fox network: Selznick argues that the television movie crucially lacked the televisuality and narrative complexity of contemporary US television drama, and that its lack of success in the USA prevented the development of a new series in the 1990s.[7] This lack of success was also due to the movie's being steeped in continuity to appeal to long-term fans at the same time as echoing American science fiction to appeal to a US audience.[8] By 2005, lessons had evidently been learned, and the reboot featured high production values, a narrative structure compatible with US broadcasting conventions in its complex mixing of episodic narratives within episodes of 45 minutes and larger season arcs, less emphasis on continuity, faster pacing and the use of dynamic action sequences. Furthermore, the reboot used pre-credit sequences, cast names in the opening titles and 'Next Time' trailers. This influence by US quality television drama production has been specifically understood via the presence of Russell T Davies, the main creative force behind the reboot, and his oft-stated personal influence by the work of US showrunner Joss Whedon. Indeed, it has been through Davies's involvement in *Doctor Who* that the US-based term 'showrunner' has gained prominence in scholarly, press and public discourses on contemporary television drama production in Britain.

While these observations and arguments were made in relation to the Christopher Eccleston- and David Tennant-era *Doctor Who*, they are still relevant to the current version. Indeed, with Matt Smith the youngest actor to play the Doctor (he was cast at the age of 26) and fewer recurring older characters (Alex Kingston's increased presence notwithstanding), the youthfulness of the cast is even more pronounced in the current version. Moreover, Alex Kingston's presence explicitly grounds the links to US quality television drama via her previous role on *ER*; season six's Wild West iconography and series seven's film noir quality in 'The Angels Take Manhattan' are the result of location shooting in the USA; and with Davies having been replaced by Steven Moffat, the showrunner figure is still very much in place. What is noticeable is that the high-budget spectacularity of the Russell T Davies *Doctor Who* is comparatively lessened. I will consider some aspects of the textual specificity of the current version in relation to the changes in the series' current transatlantic broadcasting context later; at this point in the chapter, it should certainly be uncontentious to note that since its reboot, and continuing into the Moffat era, *Doctor Who* is influenced by US quality television drama and considerations for its overseas exportability on an aesthetic, narrative and production level.

Howdy Doctor: Historiography, *Doctor Who* and Transatlantic Dialogue

This US influence duly noted, it may be tempting to understand the post-2005 *Doctor Who* as bearing out a trajectory of increasing Americanisation, to think of it as a(nother) British institution having become Americanised. However, the historiographical picture is, of course, more nuanced, and *Doctor Who* has always had complex transatlantic connections, as existing scholarship has noted. In his perceptive exploration of how the relationship between *Doctor Who* and Britain is 'far more complex than much of the discourse that surrounds the programme allows for',[9] Jones notes that the classic series 'made occasional concessions to its international audience',[10] with an Australian companion (Tegan Jovanka) from 1981 to 1984 and an American companion (Peri Brown) from 1984 to 1986,[11] as well as a temporary move towards a 45-minute episode length in 1985. Furthermore, during the 1970s – a decade that saw *Doctor Who* become more widely available on US television and featured in Tom Baker its then-youngest doctor – the programme was beginning to show, as Chapman argues, signs of a response to US science fiction (such as *Star Wars* and *Battlestar Galactica*) and its expensive special effects, not by matching these, but instead by stressing 'its "quirky" characteristics'.[12]

So, as the historiographical scholarship on the series bears out, the production of *Doctor Who* is historically marked by a careful consideration of US television. Some of this consideration has fed into a lessening of the programme's difference to US television, thereby reducing the text's cultural discount;[13] some has helped to work towards a heightening of its difference to US television, thereby producing product differentiation. Both the lessening and heightening of the text's difference can work as part of a strategy to appeal to US audiences, the strategy of product differentiation having compatibility with the targeting of niche audiences that US cable television strives for. With both attempts to reduce the cultural discount and investment into product differentiation across the history of *Doctor Who*, there is certainly a diachronic transatlantic dialogue here that complicates any argument concerning a recent Americanisation of the text.

Turning to the 1960s and the very beginning of the series, *Doctor Who* at its point of creation is usually understood in terms of the text's difference to US television. Reasons for this include the design of the Doctor as a 'paternalistic and intelligent hero rather than the sexualized and action-oriented stars of US based science fiction shows',[14] the programme's darker outlook on science and technology that again contrasted with its US counterparts, the pedagogical discourse concerned with informing and educating the child audience, fitting in with the BBC's public-service remit, as well as the lower production values, the 25-minute episode length, and the fact that the switch in 1970 to colour production was contemporaneous with BBC1's move to colour transmission. This difference has been understood as located within the context of British television, and the particular state of the BBC at the time. Given the success of competitor ITV, the creation of *Doctor Who* – overseen by Sydney Newman, recently arrived from ITV – can be 'understood as part of the BBC's campaign to claw back its diminishing audience share through the commissioning of different programme forms and genres'.[15] As Peter Gregg suggests, the product differentiation in place here was focused on distinguishing *Doctor Who* from US imports and US-influenced ITV programmes for British audiences.[16]

However, although its origins are clearly strongly located within the British context, they, too, are marked by transatlantic dimensions: as Nicholas Cull has carefully traced, BBC creative personnel were taking close account of US science fiction when *Doctor Who* was being commissioned.[17] And there is a further transatlantic dimension of the text's origins to which less attention has been paid so far: Canadian expatriate Newman had previously been head of programming for CBC where he oversaw *Howdy Doody* (1954–9). A Canadian spin-off of the US series of the same name, this puppet show for children early in its run featured a character called Mr. X who, following an educational remit, travelled through time and space in a device called the Whatsis Box. The connection between these two Sydney Newman programmes is noteworthy,[18] and online fan discourses have picked up on this.

What is surprising is the lack of mention this connection has received in critical literature on *Doctor Who*. Such a transatlantic connection adds interesting complexity to a range of discourses, including those concerned with the BBC's role as a public-service broadcaster and children's television, as well as discourses on *Doctor Who* (including BBC self-discourses) that have emphasised the Britishness of its origins by stressing that the initial format was conceived by the BBC's Script Department member Cecil Edwin (C. E.) Webber and bears strong links with British children's literature (including C. S. Lewis' Narnia books and Lewis Carroll's *Alice's Adventures in Wonderland*).[19] Certainly, a complex transatlantic dialogue drawing on the television cultures of North America runs through the history and very core of this British institution.

'Bow ties are cool!': The Britishness of Matt Smith's Doctor in *Doctor Who*'s Current Transatlantic Dialogue

I will now consider the textual specificity of the current *Doctor Who* and explore this in relation to the text's transatlantic broadcasting

landscape, which has changed in important ways since the programme was rebooted in 2005. Certainly, the influence of US quality television notwithstanding, the current *Doctor Who* is marked
by signifiers of Britishness in a number of ways, including the use
of British actors and dialects (especially companion Amy Pond's
Scottish accent) that continue to stress regional identity,[20] the playful drawing on British iconography, such as Matt Smith's bow tie
and tweed jacket, and the shorter series run associated with British
television production. Moreover, a continued interest in British settings, culture and history features strongly in episodes like 'The
Beast Below' and 'Victory of the Daleks' (as discussed earlier in this
collection). Whilst all of these make for interesting objects of analysis, I will focus my attention on the central figure of the Doctor.

On the basis that the Britishness of a text can be a useful
strategy for exportability and product differentiation for an
overseas audience, my exploration of the current Doctor will
draw on Selznick's thoughtful work on the Britishness of *Doctor
Who*. Selznick suggests that 'there are three familiar "brands
of Britishness" in the US that are frequently attached to British
media: heritage, cool, and eccentric'.[21] To briefly sketch out: heritage is connected to nostalgia, tradition, a preoccupation with a
certain past (or pastness) that often involves issues of class, privilege and (cultural) elitism. The cool brand moves away from heritage via youthful rebelliousness, a thematic focus on the working
class and/or issues of realism. Overlapping with heritage to some
extent, the eccentric brand concerns quirky unconventionality,
often rendered via character stereotypes. With the classic *Doctor
Who* combining elements of heritage (patriarchy and chivalry),
coolness (the anti-establishment stance) and eccentricity, but
the eccentric coming to shape the connotations of *Doctor Who*
for US audiences, Selznick argues that the 2005 reboot moved
away from heritage and the eccentric and towards the cool, and
that this contributed to its success in the USA.

Building on Selznick's argument, there is much to be said about
Matt Smith as the Eleventh Doctor. Tall, with a lanky frame, a bony
face with prominent cheekbones and a strong jawline, his accent
close to Received Pronunciation (RP), and a costume that includes
bow tie, tweed jacket, braces and ankle boots, he is infused with
signifiers of Britishness, reflecting a noticeable development of the
Doctor since 2005. A noticeable audio-visual trajectory between

the Ninth, Tenth and Eleventh Doctors sees Eccleston's close crop, leather jacket and northern accent (as he commented, 'lots of planets have a North') giving way to Tennant's Doctor's spiky hair, pinstripe suit and Estuary accent, giving way to the current Doctor's quiff, elbow-patched Harris tweed jacket and RP-inflected accent. Smith's Doctor shifts to the heritage and eccentric – indeed, his old-fashioned-ness of dress is in itself eccentric, never more so than when he dons retro aviator goggles while repairing the TARDIS. In his bowtie-wearing and fish fingers and custard-cooking ways, Smith's Eleventh Doctor is more closely connected to Tom Baker's unorthodox, scarf-wearing and jelly-babies-eating Fourth Doctor than he is to his reboot brethren.

There are, for example, significant differences between Eccleston's and Smith's Doctors in terms of their physicality, costume and performance. Citing Eccleston's Doctor as a factor in the shift towards cool, Selznick argues that the 2005 *Doctor Who* 'moves away from the stereotype of the British gentleman and closer to the image of the angry young man'.[22] However, as the youngest actor to play the Doctor – he was 26 when cast, Eccleston was 40 – Smith is *actually* a young man, but as the Doctor certainly much more closely aligned to the traditional British gentleman than the angry young man. It is interesting to note here the links that have been made in promotional and press discourses between *Doctor Who*'s Smith and *Sherlock*'s Benedict Cumberbatch, both actors recently gathering acclaim for their roles in high-profile BBC1 series overseen by Steven Moffat. However, while Cumberbatch's Holmes prefers contemporary designer wear (the iconic deerstalker appears in *Sherlock* only as part of a knowing in-joke), Smith's Doctor dresses comparatively closer to what one might associate with the Victorian figure of Sherlock Holmes. So, as Eccleston's Doctor, striding through urban London in a contemporary, pared back costume, worked 'as a metaphor for modern Britain...disassociating itself from the colonialism and exploitation that had been the hallmark of its historical reputation',[23] it is tempting to understand the Smith-era *Doctor Who* as falling back onto the heritage brand in its rendering of Britishness. It does, however, do something more complex than that, as I will now argue.

First, the notion of heritage is as much re-established as it is complicated by Smith's Doctor. Moffat has expressed that the casting team was looking for an older actor to replace Tennant, but chose Smith, partly because he is 'like a young man built by old men from memory'[24] and that 'it takes a very special actor to play [the Doctor]. You need to be old and young at the same time ... a cheeky schoolboy and the wise old man of the universe.'[25] Vicenarian Smith as the Doctor certainly embodies a tension of the young and old, with a youthful, childlike energy to his perform-ance whilst dressed in old-fashioned garb. In 'The Eleventh Hour' – although still dressed in the Tenth Doctor's costume – he strides through a village green with a smartphone in his hand. Especially significant here is his face, which has been aptly referred to as a 'young/old face' in online fan discourse. Despite his strong bone structure, Smith's face has been repeatedly described as a 'baby face', perhaps because of his fresh complexion – one press article has described him as 'look[ing] a good decade off shaving'.[26] That his face has been called old seems perhaps puzzling, given his biological age, and I am tempted to explain this by calling his a 'classic English face'.[27] Whilst this is, of course, a highly problem-atic term, I am inclined to use it because it seems to capture the sense of pastness and heritage that I find marking Smith's features (and which makes the idea that Smith chose his Doctor's costume, on the grounds that he felt comfortable with it, only more fasci-nating). Reminiscent of British actors of the 1920s and 1930s such as Alec Guinness or Michael Redgrave (Smith has been explicitly linked to the latter in online fan discourse), he is the kind of actor easily imagined cast in British costume drama, and indeed, his roles have included parts in several period dramas – the adapta-tions of *The Ruby in the Smoke* (BBC, 2006) and *The Shadow in the North* (BBC, 2007), set in Victorian London, *Christopher and His Kind* (BBC, 2011), set in 1930s Berlin, and most recently, the 1948 London Olympics drama *Bert & Dickie* (BBC, 2012).[28] Smith's young/old Doctor interestingly complicates Britishness as herit-age, perhaps metaphorically reflecting the complexity of identity of his text and contemporary Britain, both of which, ultimately and inevitably, bear a tension of the old and the new.

Second, the current *Doctor Who* brings together the heritage and eccentric brand with the cool noticeably differently to the classic series, which, as Selznick argues, experienced problems with US audiences because of how it was managing the brands at different points in time. For example, that *Doctor Who*'s cool themes did not appeal to US viewers during the early decades was furthered by the fact that 'they were *wrapped up* in a heritage style text'.[29] Contrary to Piers Britton's reading (based on various media reports) that the Eleventh Doctor's first costume is not cool,[30] I would argue that the current version does not so much wrap up its cool themes in heritage, but very explicitly reclaims and reconfigures heritage as cool. This reclaiming is part of a wider cultural trend where items previously deemed old-fashioned become retro-chic; Harris tweed is an interesting choice of material for the Doctor, as it itself has strong heritage connotations and over time acquired a somewhat 'fusty' reputation, but has in recent years been 'rediscovered' by fashion designers such as Vivienne Westwood. Indeed, during late 2011, I was fascinated to discover that a picture of Matt Smith as the Doctor – tag-lined 'He chose Harris Tweed. Why don't you?' – was used in Reading town centre in a window display by family-owned department store Jacksons (Figure 6.1). *Doctor Who*'s explicit linking of heritage and cool is here tapped into by a shop that, with its still functioning pneumatic tube system and blog, is itself negotiating these two brands. Importantly, there are repeated instances in which, when mocked for his sartorial choices, Smith's Doctor confidently asserts that 'bow ties are cool!', and even though these moments are framed through the programme's comedy mode, the Doctor is not being seriously undercut. While Selznick already sees much fluidity between the brands of Britishness through which she discusses the pre-Matt Smith *Doctor Who*, the current version arguably goes a step further in that it deliberately reclaims and rebrands these brands.

This particular engagement with Britishness links in several ways to the programme's broadcasting context, which itself has changed since its return in 2005. The emphasis on Britishness and heritage within one of the BBC's flagship programmes can do no disservice to this public-service broadcaster at a time when its perennial need to justify the licence fee is particularly pronounced. With a six-year freeze and additional liabilities imposed on the licence fee by the coalition government in 2010, and intense debates about the future of the BBC, it is significant that *Doctor Who* supports the BBC's claim that, in an age of multi-platform consumption, it facilitates families and the nation coming together to watch – close to seven million viewers watched the BBC broadcast of season five's finale on 26 June 2010 – and to watch a 'very British' text at that.

6.1 Window display for Harris tweed, Reading, 2011

The emphasis on Britishness as heritage is also beneficial for its broadcasting context in the USA, where BBC America, a channel owned and operated by BBC Worldwide, has bought the rights to premier the programme. Whilst this furthers the brand consolidation essential for the BBC's ambitions as a global brand, it also means that *Doctor Who* is now more closely integrated into an Anglophiliac environment, whose pre-delivered audiences are specifically interested in British programming. That *Doctor Who*'s Britishness is not straightforwardly heritage, but a heritage-as-cool Britishness, is especially useful for BBC America, which has striven to raise the BBC brand with a younger audience by offering British programmes 'closer to the *new Beetle* than to the Jaguar'.[31] Indeed, the series' multiple textuality, as a mix of the young and old, US-influence and signifiers of Britishness, affords much flexibility for its transatlantic broadcasters, who can draw on this textuality according to their branding strategies; for example, while the BBC's website during season five gave prominence to the 26–06–2010 base code of the universe/UK transmission date,[32] BBC America's website has made much of season six's Wild West/US iconography.

The current *Doctor Who*'s rendering of Britishness has seen transatlantic success, with particular noteworthy growth in the USA, especially in DVD and iTunes sales. This achievement is made more significant by the fact that the current *Doctor Who* has also been subject to production budget cuts as part of the BBC's wider 'efficiency' drive, cuts that are reflected in the comparatively lessened high-budget spectacularity. Here, the shift to heritage can be understood as a compensatory strategy of product differentiation, echoing the already mentioned shift to the quirky in the 1970s. However, this budget cut raises the role of commercial distributor BBC Worldwide, for whose considerable global revenues *Doctor Who* has been a linchpin, and which states itself that 'BBC Worldwide's role in driving growth for the wider UK creative industries and reinvesting money back into the BBC is more important than ever in a tough financial climate'.[33] At the present time, *Doctor Who* is a multi-million pound franchise competing, and for the time being successfully so, on a reduced production budget in the age of US quality television drama, on both sides of the Atlantic.

Concluding Reflections on another Transatlantic Time Lord: Showrunner Moffat

I will conclude by briefly reflecting on how the transatlantic dialogue of *Doctor Who* has been channelled and negotiated through its current showrunner Steven Moffat. As mentioned, the term 'showrunner' has gained, via *Doctor Who*, wider currency in British discourses on television, with the exception, interestingly enough, of the BBC, which on its website refers to Moffat as the programme's 'lead writer and executive producer'. It seems that, despite the links it has to the British tradition of the writer-producer and historical antecedents in creative personnel like *Doctor Who*'s own Sydney Newman and Verity Lambert, the BBC is not comfortable with this term, doubtless because of its roots in US/commercial television production culture and its 'brassy, circusy feel'.[34] However, a ringmaster is precisely what *Doctor Who* needs in its efforts to manage the diverse discourses on the series. Continuing Davies's function, Moffat produces not just the programme itself, but also a performative discourse of authorship that includes regular appearances at events such as Comic-Con and statements seeking to manage transatlantic online audience buzz.

For example, when news of the budget cuts were circulating in the British press, Moffat referred to the tradition of British ingenuity in the face of adversity when denying any negative effects on the programme, pointing to the TARDIS exterior as a creative reuse of a prop from *Dixon of Dock Green* (BBC, 1955–76).[35] It is important here that the lessened spectacularity can also be understood via the auteurial imprint of Moffat, who is known for creatively responding to budgetary and other restrictions – he wrote the acclaimed Doctor-lite 'Blink' – and shifted the programme from Davies's London-based urban realism towards a fairy-tale quality that emphasises the magical power of storytelling. The shift from urban London to the sleepy hamlet of Leadworth as a recurring setting in series five and the numerous fairy-tale tropes – orphaned Amelia/Amy Pond grows up in a haunted house, runs away at night and in 'Flesh and Stone' finds herself in a scary forest wearing a red hood(ie) – saw Moffat's *Doctor Who* balance its heritage-inflected Britishness with a sense of universality that aids the text's accessibility for overseas audiences; the latter of which is especially timely in an age of unprecedented pressures on the series.

While the programme's particular emphasis on the importance of storytelling is less dependent on expensive action-spectacle and thus suits the reduced budget, befitting Moffat's authorial reputation as *Doctor Who*'s puzzlemeister, and is suitable for transmedia branding, *Doctor Who* has recently attracted criticism in British press and public discourses that its intricate narratives are too difficult for child audiences. Moffat has dismissed this criticism, arguing that '[y]ou have to sit down and focus, and a child audience certainly does that'.[36] However, it appears that the combination of popular Saturday tea-time family viewing in Britain and aspirations to authored, US-influenced, narratively complex quality drama is not without its tensions, and it remains to be seen how the programme's pronounced narrative complexity will affect its repeatability within broadcasting schedules and might develop should the noted alienation of some viewers refuse to desist. Certainly, as the BBC develops its brand further in a global television landscape, Moffat – until the point when he himself is regenerated – remains a significant figure in *Doctor Who*'s negotiation of the discourses of connection and distinction, influence and resistance that have shaped it since its very beginning. Steered by the showrunner, this British institution is set to continue its travels through transatlantic time and space.

Notes

1. John Tulloch and Manuel Alvarado, *Doctor Who: The Unfolding Text* (London, 1983), p. 1.
2. See especially James Chapman, *Inside the Tardis: The Worlds of Doctor Who* (London, 2006); Nicholas J. Cull, 'Tardis at the OK Corral: *Doctor Who* and the USA' in John R. Cook (ed.), *British Science Fiction Television: A Hitchhiker's Guide* (London, 2006); Barbara Selznick, 'Rebooting and Re-Branding: The Changing Brands of *Doctor Who*'s Britishness' in Christopher J. Hansen (ed.), *Ruminations, Peregrinations, and Regenerations: A Critical Approach to Doctor Who* (Newcastle, 2010); and Matthew Jones, 'Aliens of London: (Re)Reading National Identity in *Doctor Who*' in Christopher J. Hansen (ed.), *Ruminations, Peregrinations, and Regenerations*.
3. Jones, 'Aliens of London', p. 95.
4. The complexity of the international television trade is encapsulated by the fact that, while *Doctor Who* received a regular scheduling slot on this cable channel, 'something that had eluded the BBC during the series' earlier manifestation' (Jones, 'Aliens of London', p. 95), the same channel had initially rejected the reboot because it considered it 'too British' (Cull, 'Tardis at the OK Corral', p. 67).
5. Selznick, 'Rebooting and Re-Branding', p. 68.
6. Chapman, *Inside the Tardis*, pp. 184–201.
7. Selznick, 'Rebooting and Re-Branding'.
8. Peter Wright, 'Expatriate! Expatriate!: *Doctor Who: The Movie* and Commercial Negotiation of a Multiple Text', in Tobias Hochscherf and James Leggott (eds) *British Science Fiction Film and Television: Critical Essays* (Jefferson, 2011), pp. 128–42. Wright has argued that 'the film's producers seemed to settle on strategies they believed capable of attracting as many viewers as possible' with 'no-one...considering how the film might be tailored for certain audiences'. ('Expatriate! Expatriate', p.131). So, for example, as part of an attempt to draw in viewers of US science fiction, the opening titles are intertextually linked to *Star Trek's* and the Doctor, like Spock, is half-human, allowing sexualisation of the character.
9. Jones, 'Aliens of London', p. 86.
10. Ibid., p. 95.
11. Actor Nicola Bryant who played Peri was, however, born in Britain.
12. Chapman, *Inside the Tardis*, p. 75.
13. This term has been defined as follows: 'A particular programme rooted in one culture, and thus attractive in that environment, will have a diminished appeal elsewhere as viewers find it difficult to identify with the style, values, beliefs, institutions and behavioural patterns of the material in question.' Colin Hoskins and Rolf Mirus, 'Reasons for the US Dominance of the International Trade in Television Programmes', *Media, Culture & Society* 10/4 (1988), p. 500.
14. Selznick, 'Rebooting and Re-Branding', p. 72.
15. Chapman, *Inside the Tardis*, p. 14.

16. Peter B. Gregg, 'England Looks to the Future: The Cultural Forum Model and *Doctor Who*', *Journal of Popular Culture* 37/4 (2004), p. 656.
17. Cull, 'Tardis at the OK Corral', pp. 52–70.
18. In a further connection to television SF, *Star Trek*'s William Shatner and James Doohan were among the voice actors cast for the Canadian *Howdy Doody*.
19. See, for example, Gary Gillatt, *Doctor Who: From A to Z* (London, 1998).
20. For a discussion of the relationship between the rebooted *Doctor Who* (a BBC Wales production) and Wales and Welshness, see Matt Hills, *Triumph of a Timelord: Regenerating Doctor Who in the Twenty-First Century* (London, 2010).
21. Selznick, 'Rebooting and Re-Branding', p. 69.
22. Ibid., p. 81.
23. Jones, 'Aliens of London', p. 97.
24. Moffat at the 2010 Edinburgh International Television Festival. 29 August 2010. Available at www.guardian.co.uk/media/video/2010/aug/29/doctor-who-casting-video (accessed 31 August 2010).
25. Moffat in BBC press release, 'Matt Smith is the New Doctor', 3 January 2009. Available at www.bbc.co.uk/pressoffice/pressreleases/stories/2009/01_january/03/who.shtml (accessed 5 January 2009).
26. Simon Hattenstone, 'Meet Matt Smith: Star of the New *Doctor Who*'. *Guardian*, 6 March 2010.
27. I am here indebted to my friend and colleague Michael Stevenson.
28. Although the focus of my argument lies elsewhere, it touches here on the issue of a class-based habitus whereby Smith's features are arguably readable to audiences as connoting upper- or middle-class identity. With Smith's 'classic English face' corresponding to the cultural and symbolic dominance of specifically *classed* bodies and physionogmies, I wish to make this issue – made more complex still by the fact that Smith has played working-class characters in the Philip Pullman adaptations and *Bert & Dickie* – available for further discussion.
29. Selznick, 'Rebooting and Re-Branding', p. 74; emphasis added.
30. Piers D. Britton, *TARDISbound: Navigating the Universes of Doctor Who* (London, 2011), p. 104.
31. Paul Lee, then-BBC America's chief operating officer, cited in James Poniewozik, 'Anarchy from the U.K.', *Time Magazine*, 5 June 2000, p. 65; emphasis added.
32. The date of broadcast on BBC and BBC America has since been synchronised in order to address online piracy.
33. BBC Worldwide press release, 'Record Profits Driven by Rising International Creative Exports', 12 July 2011. Available at www.bbc.co.uk/pressoffice/bbc-worldwide/worldwidestories/pressreleases/2011/07_july/annual_review.shtml (accessed 31 July 2011).
34. Emily Nussbaum, 'Emily Nussbaum on the New Interactive Showrunner', *New York*, 15 May 2011. Available at http://nymag.com/arts/tv/upfronts/2011/emily-nussbaum-interactive-showrunner-2011–5/ (accessed 31 May 2011).
35. Tim Masters, '*Doctor Who* Boss Not Worried by Budget Squeeze', BBC News website, 23 March 2010. Available at http://news.bbc.co.uk/1/hi/entertainment/8580299.stm (accessed 31 March 2010).
36. Moffat in Rosie Millard, 'Best Job in the Universe', *Radio Times*, 4–10 June 2011, p. 19.

PART THREE

SIGHTS AND SOUNDS

7

THE LOOK

Style, Technology and Televisuality in the New *Who*

Jonathan Bignell[1]

This chapter explores the distinctive qualities of the Steven Moffat/Matt Smith era of *Doctor Who* by discussing how dramatic emphases are connected with emphases on visual style, and how this depends on the technologies and production methods used to make the episodes. The US television theorist Horace Newcombe argued that television is intimate, continuous and immediate, and thus most suited to verisimilitude and a focus on character and story. Visual stylishness, on the other hand, was associated with cinema rather than television.[2] But the technologies used to produce television programmes, and also to watch them, have eroded this distinction. *Doctor Who* was first made in the 1960s era of live, studio-based, multi-camera television with monochrome pictures. However, as technical innovations like colour filming, stereo sound, CGI (computer-generated imagery) and post-production effects technology have been routinely introduced into the programme, and now high-definition (HD) cameras, they have given *Doctor Who*'s creators new ways of making visually distinctive narratives. Indeed, it has been argued that since the 1980s television drama has become increasingly like cinema in its production methods and aesthetic aims.[3] In relation to the reception of programmes, viewers' ability to watch *Doctor Who* on high-specification TV sets, and to record and repeat episodes using digital media, also encourage attention to visual style in television as much as in cinema. In 2009, 'Planet of the Dead' was the first *Doctor Who* story to be shot in HD and released on Blu-ray disc, and this new higher-specification format is designed to provide yet greater visual clarity and detail. The chapter evaluates how these new circumstances of production and reception have affected *Doctor Who* under the supervision of showrunner Steven Moffat.

The chapter engages with arguments that visual style has been allowed to override characterisation and story in the current *Doctor Who*. The argument in this chapter is that contemporary technologies and production methods are used in different ways, and do not in themselves lead to a certain aesthetic style. For example, visual spectacle using green-screen and computer-generated imagery (CGI) can function as a set-piece (at the opening or ending of an episode) but the same technologies can also be used 'invisibly' to add digital elements that might scarcely be noticed in a scene and which enhance the drama. Moments of visual spectacle in episodes under Moffat's leadership connect back to Russell T Davies's concern to show off the BBC's investment in the series, and Moffat's desire to extend the capability of *Doctor Who* to make an impact visually. But Moffat's *Who* also references British traditions of intimate character-focused drama that were evident in 'classic' *Doctor Who* of earlier decades. This chapter will also build on Simone Knox's previous offering on the transnational dimensions of the new *Who* by arguing that the visually spectacular nature of the Russell T Davies era typical of American telefantasy is greatly reduced for budgetary reasons.

New Contexts of Production and Reception

Doctor Who needs to provide a satisfying experience for the wide range of viewers and viewing contexts. This is because television has become an aspect of media convergence culture in the developed world, where production technologies, programme texts and fictional genres cross back and forth from one viewing platform to another. The programme must work on large screen HD TV sets as well as smaller conventional ones, since *Doctor*

Who is broadcast on the BBC's dedicated HD channel simultaneously with its first run screening on BBC1. It must be satisfactory
when seen with the restricted resolution and colour consistency
of computer monitors as a download or an iPlayer stream. It must
also be possible to enjoy the programme on the tiny screen of
a mobile phone. *Doctor Who* has been leading the BBC's extension of its programmes beyond conventional broadcasting, both
to reinforce the programme's powerful brand and to demonstrate the BBC's commitment to convergent technologies. Using
Doctor Who, the BBC has previously pioneered spin-offs and
paratexts such as SMS feeds and 'mobisodes', and now games.
BBC Worldwide now plans to market *Doctor Who* on Facebook,
and episodes will be available on Facebook in Europe, the USA,
Canada, Australia and New Zealand for a two-day viewing window.[4] *Doctor Who* needs to be made with these new viewing
contexts in mind, and it is a vehicle for bringing the BBC as a
brand into the consciousness of the mainly young people who
use these new media technologies. These factors affect what
Doctor Who episodes look like.

The production values of television drama are perpetually
increasing[5] and digital technologies have increased the sharpness
and complexity of both images and sound. Television is made in
very much the same ways as cinema and animation, because of
the convergence of television's digital production systems with
the technologies used by specialist visual effects companies who
work in several media. All original BBC dramas are now shot in
HD, and edited and post-produced digitally. The all-digital work-
flow in production, which can integrate inputs from a range of
sources at different stages of production, has been used to drive
consumer demand for digital reception technologies like wide-
screen and HD television sets, projectors and surround-sound.
This emphasis on visual quality stimulates television makers to
exploit its capabilities.

'Quality' drama can be defined in part by how it recruits
involved and active viewers by offering aesthetically challenging programmes that combine visual spectacle with dramatic
complexity.[6] When Moffat took over the showrunner role for
Doctor Who, the tone and visual style of the series was deliberately altered to emphasise a fantasy or fairy-tale quality, not only
in the writing but also in the visual look of the episodes. The HD

cameras, lenses and the directors of photography that were used to shoot the episodes, according to the producer Piers Wenger, 'have all been chosen with that aim, with the aim of giving a series a sense of childlike wonderment'.[7] This was understood by the production team as a way of making television that has a lot in common with cinema. Wenger explained that

> those cameras, they are movie cameras. They aren't as portable and they are more expensive, but they strike a really good balance between this being a mainstream, Saturday-night, all-embracing family drama series and having a new atmosphere, doing credit to Steven's writing and vision.[8]

The Moffat era of the series has aimed for visual distinctiveness, by integrating technologies from cinema into television at the level of image definition (which is the primary advantage of HD, hence its name) but linked this hyperrealism of image detail to a palette of generic narrative tropes from fantasy.

Foregrounded and Embedded Spectacle

Moffat's new series declared an interest in the visual set-piece from the beginning, where the TARDIS crashes to Earth in London at the start of 'The Eleventh Hour'. Hurtling over London at the height of several hundred feet, with the doors of the TARDIS hanging open and the Doctor dangling out, the TARDIS crashes into Amy Pond's garden. The pace and changing point of view in the sequence seem calculated to encourage the sense of wonder that is one of the ways of characterising telefantasy as a genre. The sequence contributes little to the plot or to the exploration of character, but it encourages a sense of awe and admiration of its expertise, and in this respect it is comparable to the opening 'hook' sequences of blockbuster action movies, where the cinema viewer is quickly rewarded with an exciting opening. The philosophical concept of the sublime[9] has been used to explore spectacular US cinema science fiction where narrative pace and a distanced point of view allow time to contemplate special effects, such as in the lengthy effects sequences of the film *Star Trek: The Motion Picture* (1979). But the effects sequences of

Doctor Who are too rapidly cut and point of view is too mobile to produce a sublime feeling. Instead, the sequences recall the space opera of US telefantasy of the 1950s–1970s, where effects were designed to thrill, shock and energise the viewer.[10] In the opening TARDIS flight of 'The Eleventh Hour', the rapid movement is effectively exciting and is a visual tour de force in itself. It is a helicopter shot that has been digitally overlaid with studio-shot green-screen sequences of the Doctor dangling from the TARDIS, and it is the roller-coaster pace of the editing of the sequence that is responsible for its impact as much as the visual content of any particular shot. Similarly, there is a space battle in 'Victory of the Daleks' that uses extreme wide shot and depth of field to emulate the awe-inspiring scenes of cinemascope fantasy films like *Star Wars*, where numerous spacecraft fill the screen in rapidly moving combat scenes. As Frank Collins has noted, the space battle sequences of *Star Wars* (1977) were planned by George Lucas with reference to aerial dogfights in World War II films such as *The Battle of Britain* (1969) and bomber attacks in *The Dam Busters* (1955). The visual realisation of the action sequences in 'Victory of the Daleks' re-works a tradition that is itself composed of re-workings of earlier set-pieces.[11] But the duration of individual shots is short, and much of the impact of the set-pieces in 'Victory of the Daleks' also derives from inventive editing. While the post-2005 *Doctor Who* certainly references cinema, and the epic science-fiction blockbuster especially, the realisation of set-pieces is different from what might be expected from the epic sublime. These spectacular action sequences can give way to a fairy tale atmosphere, as seen in 'The Eleventh Hour'.

CGI is often used in 'invisible' ways to enhance the drama rather than to draw attention to itself. For example, in the shooting of the season finale 'The Pandorica Opens' and 'The Big Bang', the director Toby Haynes reported[12] that the effects team from The Mill had specially sent a camera crew to Kew Gardens in London to shoot the leaves of tropical plants so that these detailed shots could be merged into the digitally created jungle of the Planet 1 environment for close-ups. Here, CGI and specially shot frames were knitted together so that the CGI sequences appeared equally as realistic as the shots made in the studio using 'practical' (physically constructed) props and sets.

An exception, in Moffat's opening episode 'The Eleventh Hour', is a stop-frame sequence replaying what the Doctor perceived at Leadworth village green when the Atraxi broadcast a universal message. The jerky sequence is marked out by its visual difference from the surrounding footage, to show that it is a recapitulation of the Doctor's vision as he tries to recall what had just happened. In other words, visual distinctiveness is motivated by an interest in character, where the viewer is aligned with the Doctor as puzzle-solver.

The current production system, while much more open to the use of effects sequences, also leads to an aesthetic of confinement and interior dialogue-based sequences that counterpoint the scale and epic ambitions of the new *Who*. The result is to place greater weight on performance by the actors. The producers have described the series as like a series of films, with a budget for film-like effects. This affects the way that the regular actors work, since as Karen Gillan commented in an interview, 'We're making mini feature films, in the space of two weeks! ... We have to get through a lot in a day.'[13] Moffat's 'Return of the Weeping Angels' blog expresses this in terms of Matt Smith's combination of action hero and quirky comic character: 'Both Chris [Eccleston] and David [Tennant] were quite cool Doctors, and while Matt certainly isn't short on cool, he has an amazing clumsiness. He's halfway between Indiana Jones and Stan Laurel.'[14] The reference to Stan Laurel here alludes to the silent movie star's physicality of performance, which was marked by ineptitude and unease with his own body (characteristics noted earlier in this volume). Developing on the earlier discussion of performance, however, these characteristics require the camera to dwell on Smith's performance in extended sequences at close range, rather than the movement in long shots that action sequences (like those of the Indiana Jones films) require.

Spatial strategies for epic scale versus character interaction, and for exterior spectacle versus interior constraint, are aspects of larger patterns of visual style and performance in Moffat's seasons. There are set pieces of physical action in 'Amy's Choice' when Amy and Rory are chased by alien-infested elderly people, and later their house is virtually demolished, for example. In 'Vincent and the Doctor', a skulking alien creature emerges from the shadows of an empty church, contrasting with the sunny

flower-filled fields around van Gogh's house. But in each of these episodes, it is the interactions between the characters that determine how the narrative will progress, and thus the actors' performances that are foregrounded. In 'The Lodger', too, the focus is on the interaction between the characters of the Doctor and Craig and the performances of Matt Smith and James Corden in those roles. Although moments of visual revelation with the uncanny presence upstairs in Craig's house are significant to the narrative, its dramatic core is a domestic interior (shot in the studio) in which lively dialogue is exchanged and the comedic performance styles of Smith and Corden are centre stage. Similarly, in its sequel from series six, 'Closing Time', the invading Cybermen remain in the background and there are mostly interior scenes of the Doctor and Craig who form 'a double act with elements of classic comedy partnerships'.[15] Other episodes from series six and seven such as 'Night Terrors', 'The Girl Who Waited', 'The God Complex' and 'Asylum of the Daleks' (which presents a Parliament of CGI Daleks) also make extensive use of interior filming and focus on small groups of characters.[16]

Furthermore, in his first season Moffat developed the spatially restricted and psychological focus of 'Blink' into the two-part return of the Weeping Angels, 'The Time of Angels' and 'Flesh and Stone'. In an interview with *Doctor Who Magazine*[17] he described the story as a 'highly coloured, loud action-movie one', comparing the relationship between 'Blink' and the two-parter to the spatially constricted haunted house motif of the film *Alien* (1979) versus the spatially expansive sequel *Aliens* (1986). This expansiveness is foregrounded at the start of 'The Time of Angels' when the Doctor, Amy and River Song arrive on a broad open beach, bordered by high cliffs. The remains of a huge crashed spacecraft add to the sense of scale in the scene. But characteristically, the constraints of the production schedule required Moffat to rewrite part of the episode, since most of a day of location filming was dogged by heavy rain. As a result, Moffat's ambitions to place more of the action in the open location setting had to be abandoned, and replaced with scenes inside the TARDIS that were shot in the studio. The result is that in some ways Moffat's *Doctor Who* returns to the production systems and thus also to the aesthetic strategies of 1960s *Doctor Who*, where interiors predominated and the drama had to make the most out of spatial restriction. The constraints of budget and time for outside filming meant that the 'classic' *Who* had to place greater emphasis on character interaction in restricted studio spaces.

Graham Sleight has further pointed out a sense of scale in post-2005 Russell T Davies *Doctor Who* in terms of story arcs.[18] Davies reshaped the *Doctor Who* format by planning lengthy story arcs that comprise both set-piece action sequences and moments of high-budget spectacle. Davies's work can be seen as an attempt to transcend the perceived limitations of visual style in the *Doctor Who* format. In an interview with *Doctor Who Magazine*, Davies said that 'the thing that enticed me to do *Doctor Who* [was] – big pictures. Television doesn't do that enough; most television is people sitting there talking.'[19] Davies's story arcs typically concluded in two-part season finales. The penultimate episode of Moffat's first season 'The Pandorica Opens' promises a large-scale set-piece ending, with the appearance of a whole range of monsters at the end (Daleks, Cybermen, Sontarans, Judoon, etc.), but the second part, 'The Big Bang', confounds viewer expectations by doing something rather different. 'The Big Bang' is organised around a temporal paradox centred on the four main characters of the season (the Doctor, Amy, Rory and River Song), and its tone therefore feels quite different from, for example, 'The Parting of the Ways' (the final episode of Davies's first season) and the climactic sequences of massed Daleks in battle. Series six differs in that it does not conclude with a two-parter but rather with the episode 'The Wedding of River Song'. However, while the episode features a visual rendering of the way time has been distorted, the episode features one (very short) scene of an incapacitated Dalek lying on its side and the episode's focus is again on these four central characters.

Places and Spaces

The spaces where production takes place, and the technologies of shooting, have significant effects on the resulting programme. As the series production company, BBC Wales has been the base for the shooting of *Doctor Who* and also its accompanying *Confidential* making-of series and the spin-offs *Torchwood*

and *Torchwood Declassified* for adults, and *Totally Doctor Who* and *The Sarah Jane Adventures* for children. With so many hours of drama to make, BBC Wales leased the Upper Boat complex near Cardiff in 2006, where a dedicated studio was built for the programmes.[20] Standing sets for the TARDIS and for *Torchwood* interiors were housed there, along with open interior stages where sets for specific episodes were constructed. In Pontypool, not far from the production base, a disused factory on the Mamhilad Industrial Park was also used as a soundstage, initially for sets constructed for 'The Impossible Planet' and 'The Satan Pit' (2006). On the large sound-stages, green screens can be erected to allow the insertion of CGI sequences in post-production (discussed above). Green-screen sequences themselves are shot at the production base, usually in subsequent shooting blocks from the main recording of scenes for the episode in which they will appear. The separate shooting of effects sequences was always part of the 'classic' *Doctor Who*, where any sequences that required models, explosions, or other specially constructed effects were carried out at the BBC's Ealing Film Unit. This was because the studios in BBC Television Centre where the bulk of the programme was shot were equipped for multi-camera video recording that was done in long tranches as-if-live, so that the performers could be used most economically over a short run of shooting days. Brief effects sequences were shot on cinema film using single cameras, and these shots were inserted into the previously shot video episodes. This produced a different visual look in the video versus the filmed sequences. Since filmed inserts were significantly more expensive to make than as-if-live video, they were used sparingly and could appear comparatively more prominent.

One of the distinctions between post-2005 *Doctor Who* and its predecessor series is the privileging of location shooting and the use of a single technology (HD video) for interior and exterior scenes, including effects shots. Not only does this make the interior, exterior and effects shots share the same visual look as dialogue scenes, it also means that that they are shot in broadly the same way. One distinguishing feature of multi-camera video production in 'classic' *Doctor Who* was the shooting of the same action from different simultaneous points of view, where the director in the studio gallery was, in effect, editing the sequence

DOCTOR WHO, *THE ELEVENTH HOUR*

live by choosing when to cut from one camera to another. The other distinctive feature was the duration of performance, since the actors would perform scenes of several minutes' duration while being shot by the three cameras. In post-2005 *Doctor Who*, the use of a single camera means that all editing takes place in post-production, when the actors are absent. Moreover, each shot is recorded in a separate take, and the adoption of a different camera position requires the re-setting of lights, props or any other element that needs to appear the same in two takes. While *Doctor Who*'s action is frequently placed in other-worldly and fantastical settings, the consistency of the look and texture of its visual images enhances the programme's ability to denote a coherent fictional world (or worlds) that engages the viewer.

The second distinction between pre- and post-2005 shooting practices concerns the performer. Although scenes might be rehearsed and performed in fairly lengthy tranches, the single-camera shooting method means that actors may often perform very short sequences of a few or even one line of dialogue. Production planning privileges the camera, since it is organised around single takes, whereas multi-camera shooting privileges the performer (and performer interactions with each other). Extreme examples of this include the elaborate green-screen sequences of wire-work in 'The Eleventh Hour', where individual shots of Matt Smith suspended from the ceiling of the Upper Boat studio against a green screen were required as raw material for the post-production edit. Hours could be spent perfecting single shots of one actor. In CGI sequences where the actor is not close to the camera, digitally generated avatars of the main characters are created from reference photographs, but the actors are not otherwise required at all.

Locations have been significant in both Davies's and Moffat's seasons, but in different ways. 'Daleks in Manhattan' and 'Evolution of the Daleks' (2007) were shot partly in New York, 'The Fires of Pompeii' (2008) in Rome and 'Planet of the Dead' (2009) in Dubai. In Moffat's second Eleventh Doctor season, 'The Impossible Astronaut' and 'Day of the Moon' were shot partly in the USA, as was his third season episode 'The Angels Take Manhattan'. But in Moffat's seasons, the use of ambitiously distant and unfamiliar locations combines with narratives that emphasise psychological drama and character exploration.

Sleight has argued that strategies to increase the global reach of *Doctor Who* narratives were often unsuccessfully present during Davies's tenure as showrunner:

> A further aspect to the issue of scale is the series' attempts to take the Earthbound action outside the UK. ... [These episodes] are ... carefully rationed in how much they use their overseas locales ... [also] are the series' attempts, especially in its series finales, to show that the whole of Earth is under attack, not just the UK ... [there is] that old standby, news reports from around the globe.[21]

When Moffat invited Toby Whithouse to offer the story that eventually became 'Vampires of Venice', the brief to produce a 'big, bold, funny, romantic' episode[22] led to Whithouse suggesting Venice as a location because of its romantic associations. Budget restrictions and the impossibility of shooting in a tourist destination led to the idea of going to Venice being excluded from planning, and instead Dubrovnik in Croatia was chosen because both 'Vampires of Venice' and 'Vincent and the Doctor' (set in Provence) could be made there. A local production company, Embassy Films, was engaged to provide crew and art-department staff at favourable rates compared to the costs of UK production. Similarly, the series seven episode 'A Town Called Mercy' saw Spain as standing in for the Wild West. Actual place is less important than the dramatic significance of the fictional space that can be created there.

Most of the shooting locations are in the UK, however, where the decisions of the production team show that they seek either extreme familiarity of place or exoticism. The modern city is usually represented by London, from where the companions Rose Tyler, Martha Jones and Donna Noble originate and thus where numerous stories return for their settings. The headlong flight over London in 'The Eleventh Hour' signals the importance of place by including landmarks such as the Palace of Westminster, the Tower of London, Buckingham Palace and 'The Gherkin' (the Swiss Re building). But the important issue is these places' significance in the fictional world. As Sleight has noted, Davies used specific London settings to reference known places and thus to threaten the British political and cultural establishment in 'Aliens of London' and 'World War Three' (2005).[23] In this respect, the showrunners and writers of post-2005 *Doctor Who* continued a tradition, since 'The Dalek Invasion of Earth' (1964), most famously, had established the motif of alien invasion and destruction of London landmarks and continued it in the cinema film *Daleks – Invasion Earth 2150 AD* (1966). Existing real places are used but their characteristics are enhanced in order to make them conform to readily recognised emblematic or even stereotypical spaces.

Collins sees Moffat's locations across his episodes in relation to the UK Government's 'Icons of England' project (which began in 2006) in which the public nominated representative images of Englishness.[24] Of these visual signifiers of national identity, Moffat has used many, including Stonehenge, the Spitfire fighter aircraft (discussed earlier in this collection) and the novel *Alice in Wonderland*. It is not only places that signify Englishness, but also a range of cultural symbols and texts that derive from various time periods. The small village of Leadworth where Amy Pond grew up and to which she and the Doctor frequently return is a significant contrast to London. What links these spaces is their emblematic role as images of Englishness, despite Leadworth being created around the cathedral green in the town of Llandaff which is in Wales. The production team fabricated the village duck-pond, dressed houses to represent the 'typical' English pub the Traveller's Rest and surrounding cottages and brought in an old-fashioned red telephone box. Leadworth's idyllic representation also enabled the meeting of the Doctor and the young Amy to have (what Simone Knox has called a universal) fairytale uncanniness that the director of 'The Eleventh Hour', Adam Smith, planned visually by referencing Tim Burton's cinema work and the down-to-earth encounter of a child with an alien being in *E.T. – The Extra Terrestrial* (1982).[25]

The fairy-tale quality of spaces was further exploited in 'Flesh and Stone', which was filmed on location at Puzzlewood in the Forest of Dean, Gloucestershire. The night-time shoot made much of the deep gullies and dramatic rock formations of the wooded 14-acre park, which was dressed with extensive smoke and shot in low light. The forest attraction had already been used by the BBC for location filming for the Arthurian fantasy series *Merlin* and, according to Puzzlewood's manager, Helen

O'Kane, the production team chose the location after seeing it in *Merlin*.[26] The setting did not fit the script, but they showed photographs of the location to Moffat who adjusted the episode to enable filming there. The tonal significance of this fantasy place was important enough to Moffat for him to rewrite parts of his script, demonstrating how the aesthetic resources offered by a specific location can impact on the completed programme.

Special Effects and Limited Budgets

Texts in the wider *Doctor Who* franchise include behind-the-scenes commentary on how special-effects work is achieved, for example in the *Confidential* series, box set DVDs extras and in interactive media outlets that expand the narrative. When 'The Eleventh Hour' was advertised in late March 2010 before its first screening on BBC1 on 3 April, Moffat's opening sequence of the TARDIS over London was made available on the BBC website and the interactive 'red button' digital television service. It is significant that it was this high-speed effects sequence that was chosen as the teaser for the series, to showcase its visual appeal. Moreover, a series of short videos was added to the website and red button feed, about the making of the effects sequence. The pre-visualisation artist Dan May explained how he constructed the CGI animation from a storyboard, and James Swanson, director of photography for the helicopter sequence, described the experience of making it. Similar contextual material forms part of the output of niche channels like Syfy and has helped to define telefantasy as generically associated with effects production. Effects sequences are expensive to make, but so also are the location-shot sequences where cast and crew need to be transported to distant places for filming. This means that while, in theory, new media channels allow the space for innovative, inexpensive programmes that can afford to have small audiences, in fact telefantasy programmes still need large audiences to support their continued existence.[27] BBC still wants *Doctor Who* to be a mainstream network programme for a mass audience, just as it was in the duopolistic era where there were only two main terrestrial channels, BBC and ITV. Moffat's role is to continue to keep faith with expert niche audiences, while exposing *Doctor Who* more and more to mass audiences both in the UK and internationally by means of many different media products and texts.

Picking up on Simone Knox's previous chapter, as James Chapman has shown, the revitalised *Doctor Who* has continuities with a specifically national aesthetic but like other contemporary telefantasy series such as *Spooks* (BBC, 2002–11) and *Hustle* (BBC, 2004–12) it also seeks to accommodate itself to American norms of production and generic expectation.[28] Writing about recent US television drama, Peter Dunne argues that 'technological excellence is the determining factor today. For this reason the dramatic dynamic has changed over that time from stories about people and purpose, to stories capitalising on visual feats.'[29] The presence of set-piece effects spectacles in *Doctor Who* can be seen as an acceptance of perceived preferences in the American market for telefantasy that draws on the hardware and software developed by the Hollywood companies who make television drama but were founded to make cinema. These companies work across convergent media on franchises like *Star Trek* that exist in several different forms.[30] Speaking in an interview with *Doctor Who Magazine* about their work with special effects company The Mill, the executive producer Piers Wenger commented in relation to *Doctor Who* that 'Our aspiration is always to make it as good as the viewers' favourite American show or their favourite genre movie'.[31] However, the revitalised *Doctor Who* is restrained by a limited budget.

Across the BBC as a whole, Director-General Mark Thompson's 'Putting Quality First' policy accepted a 20 per cent budget cut agreed with the government as a response to the economic downturn, so that *Doctor Who* was required to produce episodes with fewer resources. While Moffat commented that 'We could do with a budget like *Avatar*'s for every episode',[32] he recognised that reductions in specially made CGI sequences could have dramatic advantages. Whereas the previous showrunner and series creator Russell T Davies had a penchant for epic set-piece sequences at the ends of seasons, providing a sense of scale and spectacle at the resolution of storylines, Moffat has more often integrated CGI into episode storylines as a means of embedding uncanny, monstrous and frightening visual sequences into narratives based around puzzles and character revelation. These are the aspects of telefantasy that are most effective at retaining loyal fan audiences and sustaining niche or cult status,[33] since they provide opportunities for immersion in an extended fictional world. Production technologies, visual style and narrative form work together in Moffat's seasons to generate distinctive experiences for viewers that aim to maintain the tone of the programme and broaden its audiences.

Conclusion

The forces discussed in this chapter that impact on Moffat's *Doctor Who* are dynamic and often contradictory. Emergent technologies of production and reception like shooting in HD or watching on Blu-ray have made it possible for a long-running series programme like *Doctor Who* to emulate what Moffat and other members of the production team perceive as 'cinematic' visual style. What they mean by this encompasses several aspects of the production. It is partly the greater level of visual detail that can be captured by the camera, and this leads to greater attention to the details of make-up, costume, set dressing and lighting than was required in the 'classic' era when the programme was shot predominantly on video. Cinematic style also refers to the integration of special effects into episodes, and although many effects are still created by models, prosthetics or props, the notion of the cinematic predominantly means post-production effects created by CGI. Related to this, the ambition for television to be cinematic implies a sense of visual scale that is most clearly seen in set-piece action sequences, often at the beginnings or ends of episodes. The visual set-pieces, however, are integrated differently in *Doctor Who* than in a cinema film because they are ambivalently related to the format of the programme, and its deployment of pace and dramatic beats within episodes, stories and seasons. Hybrids mixing episodic plotlines of the drama series with multi-episode arcs of soap opera and the mini-series have become increasingly common in television drama,[34] and the closure offered in one free-standing episode plot co-exists with the continuation of others. This means that set-pieces are used as teasers in trailers, and are explained in making-of featurettes, so that they appear very prominently in the BBC's address to potential viewers. But they do not easily contribute to the ongoing story arcs of Moffat's seasons, and they do not easily offer the character development and space for bravura performance that Moffat has also wanted to achieve in *Doctor Who*.

The tensions discussed here are familiar in the genre of tele-fantasy,[35] which is inhabited by an emulation of cinema in visual spectacle and effects technology, at the same time as the mobilisation of episode storylines and character trajectories that characterise the ongoing serial flow of television. Telefantasy can make mobility across space and time a key aspect of a programme format (it is obviously the case for *Doctor Who*), yet Moffat's *Doctor Who* is much more spatially restricted than it might appear. Within the fictional world that telefantasy creates, the details of a fictional place, a shooting location or a studio set-up energise the ways that scripts are realised and performances are created. Television, and some of the devices supplementing the television set as the place where *Doctor Who* can be viewed, is a domestic medium, but telefantasy encompasses the familiar and homely but also the alien and uncanny. Visual resources are clearly vital to this dynamic interplay in the genre, and Moffat's work on *Doctor Who* has sought to activate the potential of each of them. Moffat has consistently aimed for a fantastical, child-like feeling of wonder in the series, and although this has been constructed partly by the use of sophisticated production technologies, it has also been a property of the physical locations where episodes have been shot, and the relatively inexpensive studio settings where green-screen sequences and built sets (like the TARDIS itself) have been made. Physical locations have been chosen to suggest both exoticism and also familiarity of place. Moffat's episodes have moved across space and time, from the various alien worlds to the exotic in Earth's past and present as represented by Venice, or Death Valley. But some of these locations were actually somewhere else, where one place masqueraded as another for budgetary reasons. Moreover, *Doctor Who*'s paradigmatic Britishness meant locating stories in characteristically English locations, though many of those were actually simulated in Wales on location or in the studio. Moffat's aim for an expansive, large-scale, visually sumptuous look for *Doctor Who* has had to be realised inventively with restricted budgets, and this has often brought benefits in adapting storylines to available spatial resources and strengthening the attention to character that has always been central to the format.

Notes

1. This chapter is one of the publications arising from the AHRC-funded research project 'Spaces of Television: Production, Site and Style', based at the University of Reading from 2010 to 2014 and led by Professor Jonathan Bignell.
2. Horace Newcombe, *TV: The Most Popular Art* (New York, 1974).
3. Noel Carroll, 'TV and Film: A Philosophical Perspective', *Journal of Aesthetic Education* 35/1 (2001), pp. 15–29.
4. BBC Worldwide, Annual Review and Accounts 2010–11. Available at www.bbcworldwide.com/annual-review/annual-review-2011.aspx.
5. Robin Nelson, 'Quality TV Drama', in Janet McCabe and Kim Akass (eds) *Quality TV: Contemporary American Television and Beyond* (London, 2007), pp. 38–51.
6. Jonathan Bignell, 'The Police Series', in John Gibbs and Douglas Pye (eds) *Close-Up 03* (London, 2009), pp. 1–66.
7. Unknown interviewer, 'Journey into Time and Space', *Doctor Who Magazine* 419 (2010), pp. 18–23.
8. Ibid.
9. Scott Bukatman, 'The Artificial Infinite: On Special Effects and the Sublime', in Annette Kuhn (ed.) *Alien Zone II: The Spaces of Science Fiction Cinema* (London, 1999), pp. 249–75.
10. Oscar Le Los Santos, 'Irwin Allen's Recycled Monsters and Escapist Voyages', in Lincoln Geraghty (ed.) *Channeling the Future: Essays on Science Fiction and Fantasy Television* (Lanham, 2009), pp. 25–40; Wheeler Winston Dixon, 'Tomorrowland TV: The Space Opera and Early Science Fiction Television', in J.P. Telotte (ed.) *The Essential Science Fiction Television Reader* (Lexington, 2008), pp. 93–110; J.P. Telotte, 'Introduction: The Trajectory of Science Fiction Television', in J.P. Telotte (ed.) *The Essential Science Fiction Television Reader*, pp. 1–34.
11. Frank Collins, *The Pandorica Opens: Exploring the Worlds of the Eleventh Doctor* (Cambridge, 2010), p. 49.
12. Tom Spilsbury, 'Shooting Stars', *Doctor Who Magazine* 426 (2010), p. 30.
13. Jason Arnopp, 'Chasing Amy!' *Doctor Who Magazine* 421 (2010), p. 28.
14. Steven Moffat, 'The Return of the Weeping Angels' blog entry. Available. at www.bbc.co.uk/blogs/tv/2010/04/doctor-who-the-return-of-the-w.shtml.
15. Andrew Pixley, *The Doctor Who Companion: The Eleventh Doctor Volume 5* (2012), p. 24.
16. See, for example, Andrew Pixley, *The Doctor Who Companion: The Eleventh Hour, Volume 4* (2011) and Pixley, *The Doctor Who Companion, Volume 5*.
17. Andrew Pixley, *The Doctor Who Companion: The Eleventh Doctor, Volume 1* (2010), pp. 69–78.
18. Graham Sleight, 'The Big Picture Show: Russell T Davies's writing for *Doctor Who*', in Simon Bradshaw, Antony Keen and Graham Sleight (eds) *The Unsilent Library: Essays on the Russell T Davies Era of the New Doctor Who* (London, 2011), pp. 15–28.
19. Benjamin Cook, 'Tooth and Claw: the Russell T Davies Interview', *Doctor Who Magazine* 360 (2005), p. 13, quoted in Sleight, 'The Big Picture Show', p. 15.

20. TARDIS Index File: BBC Wales. Available at http://tardis.wikia.com/wiki/BBC_Wales.

21. Sleight, 'The Big Picture Show', pp. 24–5.

22. Pixley, *The Doctor Who Companion Volume 1*, pp. 86–9.

23. Sleight, 'The Big Picture Show', p. 23.

24. Collins, *The Pandorica Opens*, pp. 7–8.

25. Pixley, *The Doctor Who Companion Volume 1*, pp. 19–41.

26. BBC Gloucestershire News, '*Doctor Who* films at Puzzlewood'. Available at http://news.bbc.co.uk/go/pr/fr/-/local/gloucestershire/hi/people_and_places/arts_and_culture/newsid_8635000/8635073.stm.

27. Barbara Selznick, 'Branding the Future: Syfy in the Post-Network Era', *Journal of Science Fiction Film and Television* 2/2 (2009), pp. 177–204.

28. James Chapman, *Inside the TARDIS: The Worlds of Doctor Who* (London, 2006), pp. 184–5.

29. Peter Dunne, 'Inside American Television Drama', in Janet McCabe and Kim Akass (eds) *Quality TV: Contemporary American Television and Beyond* (New York, 2007), p. 101.

30. Noel Carroll, 'TV and Film: A Philosophical Perspective', *Journal of Aesthetic Education* 35:1 (2001), pp. 15–29.

31. Unknown interviewer, 'Journey into Time and Space'.

32. Ben Dowell, 'How Will the Doctor Get Out of This One?', *Guardian*, Media section, 12 July 2010, p. 5.

33. Matt Hills, *Fan Cultures* (London, 2002).

34. Michael Z. Newman, 'From Beats to Arcs: Towards a Poetics of Television Narrative', *The Velvet Light Trap* 58 (2006), p. 16.

35. Catherine Johnson, *Telefantasy* (London, 2005).

8

'IT'S ALL-NEW DOCTOR WHO'

Authorising New Design and Redesign in the Steven Moffat era

Piers Britton[1]

As its title indicates, this book is founded on a presumption of difference – a presumption that there is something idiosyncratic about Steven Moffat's tenure as showrunner (or 'head writer') and Matt Smith's as lead in *Doctor Who*, distinguishing all episodes since 'The Eleventh Hour' from what went before. As regards design – costumes and make-up, settings and props both real and virtual, and graphics – this presumption needs to be tested with special care. This is by no means to deny that there has been significant visual change since the beginning of the 2010 season (series five). Matt Smith's arrival was attended by conspicuous and highly publicised reworking of designs which are central to *Doctor Who*'s brand identity, including the show's title sequence and logo, the TARDIS and the Daleks. Stimulus for some of the design regeneration in series five is directly attributed to Steven Moffat within *Doctor Who*'s intertextual relay (which is to say, the discourses of publicity, marketing and reception which envelop the primary text).[2] And as I shall discuss below, statements by Moffat himself might well be adduced in support of claims for an aesthetic of difference in his 'era'.

All such suggestive data notwithstanding, I am ultimately going to argue in this chapter against a straightforwardly dependent model of the relationship between design-function and author-function in *Doctor Who*. Contrary to a recent tendency explicitly or implicitly to exalt showrunners as auteurs and thus to envisage their control as extending to every aspect of the *mise en scène*, the assumption that all design is always either immediately or ultimately authored by a writer-producer is not sustainable. Nor is the matter resolved by simply reassigning authorial power from the showrunner to another 'creative' figure, such as the credited production designer (or for that matter to someone who wields other kinds of institutional power over a series and its reception, such as a brand manager). As I shall discuss in relation to key, sometimes controversial, design choices in the Moffat era, design eludes straightforward authorship, especially single authorship. My main purpose in this chapter is to tease out some of the complexities of the authorisation process, and also to examine some of the consequences of *not* placing authorial or other legitimating weight behind a given design.

Television Design and Authorising Statements

In order to gain perspective on what is at stake in authorship debates around design for *Doctor Who*, it is useful first to draw back from industrial, production and reception issues, and consider how design operates structurally as a unit within a series narrative. Roland Barthes distinguished between two main classes of narrative unit, *functions* and *indices*; the former operate at the level of doing, the latter at the level of being. In other words, indices are unlike functions in that they do not relate to consequential acts but refer to 'a personality trait, a feeling, or an atmosphere (e.g. suspicion), a philosophy'.[3] Design has a primarily indicial status in the television-series narrative, even though designed places and things may also operate as functions. Take that most useful of narrative devices, the TARDIS. Travel in the TARDIS is always a *cardinal function* of the *Doctor Who* narrative, since without the ship, or some substitute for it (such as Jack Harkness's and River Song's 'vortex manipulator' bracelets), the time-and-space-travel premise of the series could not be sustained. On the other hand, the actual design of the ship at any given moment, within and without, is *indicial*, establishing mood and ethos rather than organising the flow of events or narration. For example, in the TARDIS interior designs by Richard Hudolin (1996) and Edward Thomas (2005, 2010), the central control console serves to index the maverick, unpredictable character of the Doctor and the ethos of his adventures through its increasingly eccentric, lo-tech appearance and its madcap incorporation of found objects.

Because indices never advance narrative per se, but serve to articulate some aspect of character, circumstance or mood, a number of indices may point to the same signified. Whereas functions correlate with one another in a linear, teleological fashion, indices cluster around a signified like iron filings around a magnetic pole.[4] Their purpose is to create patterns of enrichment, to qualify and ultimately to clarify. This traditionally applies to design imagery: a character's clothing and domicile, for example, are supposed to complement and usually harmonise with what we learn of this character in the scripted narrative. Nevertheless, there are important distinctions between the index as an overall class of unit within narrative and the design-index as a unit within the more particular context of a television-series narrative.

In a novel, the operation of indices is relatively clear-cut, since the wording of the text controls and limits what as readers we 'see', and the order in which we 'see' it. The same constraints do not exist for the audience of screen fiction, for all that the design imagery is always quite literally framed for us. The inherent polysemy of the visual image applies with special force in the case of design for film and television, for as C. S. Tashiro and others have noted, sets and locales, costumes and props may trigger associations which have nothing to do with the narrative.[5] Even where there is a scripted gloss, or where there are clearly defined anchors for significance (as with police or nursing uniforms), identifying conventional or specified meaning for an item of clothing does not exhaust that item of its connotative charge. Part of the reason for this is that on screen we do not see design elements in isolation but en masse and in juxtaposition, as part of a series of moving pictures. Thus the polysemy of clothing, objects and settings is compounded by the unpredictable ways in which their various associations may collectively interact in the mind of any given viewer.

In a series narrative, and especially in a long-running television series, there are further vagaries in the operation of the design-index. One likely consequence of a series' success is the increased tendency – and in terms of brand logic the *need* – for design imagery to 'bleed' potential meaning beyond the frame of the narrative. Where this is not carefully managed, it may complicate the indicial role of the design. Moreover, certain settings, props or sartorial images in a series, seen repeatedly over a period of years, may acquire overarching significance: some even come to serve as synecdoches for the series itself, their discursive field thereby transcending the series and its intertextual relay to permeate larger cultural narratives.[6] The TARDIS police box and the Daleks in *Doctor Who* fall into this category, for both are now icons of British television. Any significant revision to such designs obviously represents a very deliberate kind of intervention.

By extension, where a new regular character is introduced into a series, costume can become a site for debate on the effectiveness of that character in relation to both internal precedent and external benchmarks. In the case of a new companion in *Doctor Who*, such as Amy Pond, this may lead to costume's becoming the subject of various meta-narratives, such as those pertaining to gender ideology or sexuality (as I discuss at length below).

One way of summarising the above points is to say that designs in television series are more likely to generate ongoing *talk* than any film design, however iconic. A high-profile, long-running series such as *Doctor Who* is calculated to produce iterative dialogical responses, in the press, blogs, online forums, social networking and so on. Those people with a platform for engaging in this talk authoritatively, such as a director, producer, 'expert' analyst or even self-appointed moral arbiter, can restrict design's meaning by what they say, authorising it into discourse, anchoring it there and implicitly excluding the kinds of meaning that are not important to the speaker. This restrictive positioning of design clearly has special significance when the speaker can claim creative power over the design image in question. This is self-evidently true in the cases where a costume designer or production designer is interviewed in, say, a DVD feature, solely for the purpose of making some pronouncement on her or his work. However, when a claim of authority over design is one of a number of authorising statements made by a showrunner, whose power is already constructed as wide-ranging, this claim may carry even more weight than a designer's.

I am not suggesting that what is at stake here is the 'final' meaning of the design; polysemy of visual imagery is not really curtailed by any implicit or explicit authorial direction on how to understand a given design's significance. Attempts to canalise design's meaning through authorial commentary are interesting more for what they reveal about the process of authorisation than what they reveal about the design. Precisely because design is mute, because it is broadly redolent rather than narrowly signifying a particular signified, its co-option into a discourse such as auteurism is intriguingly suggestive of the scope and limits of that discourse. In the pages that follow, I shall examine several designs or clusters of designs produced in the Moffat era, and authorial statements about these by Moffat and others. Not all the designs are like in kind, and nor, significantly enough, are the statements. Some commentary was clearly scripted as an a priori claim of agency, and indicates recognition of the symbolic power of certain cardinal, 'iconic' designs (the Daleks and the TARDIS, and to an extent the Silurians). Other comments were still carefully calculated but evidently responsive rather than proactive, retrospectively resolving supposed disharmony among the different potential authors of a design (Matt Smith's first costume as the Doctor). Others again offered explicitly defensive, implicitly palliative or tacitly ironic responses to unexpected or undesirable readings of design (Amy's costumes).

'Something Old, Something New': The Rebranding of New *Who* and the Issue of Authority

For the first kind of authorial statement on design noted above, namely the showrunner's a priori gloss, there is ample precedent both within and without *Doctor Who*. Perhaps stimulated by the rapid improvement in the quality of the television-screen image, and an ever-greater espousal of televisual spectacle and self-conscious stylishness in 'quality TV,' claims for showrunners' minute control of design and *mise en scène* have become

increasingly common in recent years. Matt Weiner, writer-producer of *Mad Men* (AMC, 2007–), provides the most marked
example. DVD features, interviews and webcasts repeatedly note
Weiner's intervention in choices regarding props, palette, film
stock and overall lighting values for the series.[7] Albeit not to the
same extent, Russell T Davies evinced broadly comparable concern with details of design and aesthetic tone in *Doctor Who*. On
key decisions – such as the reimagining of the Cybermen and other
icons reintroduced from the classic series – deferral to Davies's
final authority became a mantra among contributors such as the
production designer Edward Thomas and the prosthetic artist
and 'monster maker' Neil Gorton. In short, there is both a broad
and an immediate context for envisaging Steven Moffat's as the
ultimate authorising voice for design imagery in his 'era'.

Some of the design choices apparently made in Moffat's
name, or with his intervention, are discursively no different from
those made under Russell T Davies's tutelage. Since the Daleks'
renaissance in 2005, the decision to bring back a monster from
the classic series has invariably entailed the programme makers' acknowledging changed audience expectations about monsters' plausibility, and generally also entailed discussing the new
technologies which enable fabricators to meet these expectations. When 'The Hungry Earth' saw the return of the Silurians,
who had first featured in the classic series in the early 1970s, the
challenges of reimagining them were duly rehearsed in *Doctor
Who Confidential*, the BBC's documentary 'shadow' to *Doctor
Who*. Following the *Confidential* precedent established during
Davies's incumbency, sound bites from the showrunner and several collaborators furnished details of the revision. The only slight
departure from most of the Davies-era precedent stems from
the fact that the episode's writer, Chris Chibnall, is given the
greatest airtime, and it is his preferences – for example, that the
new Silurians should be beautiful – not the showrunner's, which
are presented as central to the renovation process. Beyond this
minor shift, most of the rhetorical positions and material claims
are familiar: the creatures had to be reinvented 'for 2010'; they
had to be plausible as characters; these changes were facilitated
by cutting-edge silicone prosthetics which allow great flexibility
of facial expression, and so on. In short, the new Silurians, like
all the classic monsters previously revived under Davies, were

framed within the conceit of responsible modernisation, which between 2005 and 2008 was thoroughly established as part of the branding strategy for new *Doctor Who*.

Most of the redesigns for series five were not, as with the Silurians, updates of images from the classic series but significant revisions to work done in the new, while Davies was showrunner. As noted at the beginning of the chapter, statements in interview and documentary establish Moffat as not only instigating but also specifying aspects of the redesign of the TARDIS and the Daleks. Both of these avowedly embody nostalgia for 1960s *Doctor Who*, and more specifically for the two non-BBC film releases starring Peter Cushing, which were adaptations of the earliest Dalek serials on television. The body of the TARDIS police box prop for the Moffat era is painted an unprecedentedly intense, vivid blue, akin to Cushing's in *Dr Who and the Daleks* (1965), while the white trim on the window surrounds and glazing bars, and the St John's Ambulance badge on the door also echo the Cushing design (and indeed the original colour scheme for the BBC's TARDIS prop, which was altered in 1966 to the uniform blue used consistently thereafter).[8] The 2010 interior of the new TARDIS also recalls Cushing's both in the general sense that it is emphatically haphazard in layout rather than being polygonal and radially planned, and in the narrower sense that the central control station has an unprecedentedly Heath Robinson character, the console crowded with odd excrescences, hefty levers and vivid coloured lights, with myriad cables strewn both above and below.

If the TARDIS was given a nostalgic, 'Technicolor–Techniscope' makeover, the adjustment was arguably less startling than the renovation of the Daleks, for which Mark Gatiss's 'Victory of the Daleks' was essentially the showcase. Their remodel was apparently the subject of much discussion among Moffat, Gatiss and the art department. Once again the intertextual relay expressly records the fact that the new design was influenced by Moffat's and Gatiss's love of the Cushing Dalek movies.[9] In *Dr Who and the Daleks*, the Dalek props not only had more heft and greater height than those originally designed by Raymond Cusick for the television series, but were also much more colourful, with blues, black and red used in co-ordination with gold and silver trim. In 'Victory of the Daleks', the new models closely recall the Cushing-movie precedent in their massiveness but actually exceed their cinematic forebears in the array of bold colours they parade, with orange and primary yellow as well as blue, red and white.

Moving beyond details of the redesigns, there is overarching interest in the way that authorising statements about these changes interact with brand logic, which provides a coherence otherwise lacking in justifications for renewal within the intertextual relay. In fact, discrepancies are rife in authorising statements. For example, in a short behind-the-scenes video on the official *Doctor Who* site, released to coincide with the beginning of series five, Edward Thomas claimed to have been surprised by Moffat's decision to alter the TARDIS interior, having assumed that the existing set would continue in use.[10] Later, however, in the *Brilliant Book of Doctor Who*, he asserted that the art department 'always knew' that Moffat and his colleagues 'wanted to put their own stamp on the look of the TARDIS'.[11] There are even more marked discrepancies among Steven Moffat's statements about the new Daleks. In the *Brilliant Book,* he claims that the addition of five new props 'was prompted by me walking into the prop room, and realising that we only had three Daleks'.[12] Yet earlier, in the *Doctor Who Confidential* accompanying 'Victory', Moffat had implied that the change was, in a sense, gratuitous: 'It's all-new *Doctor Who*: what's the other thing we haven't changed? Let's change the Daleks too.'[13]

Moffat's tongue-in-cheek tone notwithstanding, there is actually greater resonance in the claim that the redesigned Daleks were expressive of 'all-new' *Doctor Who* than in the supposed practical justification for their manufacture. Swelling the ranks of the Dalek props need not have entailed any substantive change to their appearance. Indeed, if this was the primary concern, simply producing more units from the existing moulds – as eventually happened for the production of 'Asylum of the Daleks' – would surely have made better economic sense. At the time of the 'Victory' makeover, *Private Eye* claimed that there had been direct financial investment by BBC Worldwide in the new-look Daleks because of the potential they generated for increased merchandising. *Private Eye*'s allegation should not be wholly discounted: interestingly, the BBC 'spokesman' who responded to the accusation sidestepped the issue of BBC Worldwide's putative involvement, saying only that 'the scripts always come first and the coloured Daleks were in the script'.[14] Yet the matter of tie-in sales is ultimately subsumed into a larger issue, which is the role of design and redesign in the maintenance of brand equity. Change as a function of branding logic provides ample justification for the fact, if not the details, of the Dalek redesign.

Moffat's description of series five as 'all-new *Doctor Who*' clearly suggests that part of the stimulus for major redesigns was the arrival of the Eleventh Doctor and his new companion, Amy Pond – and, by implication, the simultaneous installation of Moffat and his fellow executive producers, Beth Willis and Piers Wenger. It is worth stressing that the total switch of principal cast is unprecedented in either new or classic *Doctor Who*. The continuing presence of the immensely popular Billie Piper as Rose Tyler had eased the only prior change of lead actor since the show's revival in 2005; this echoed a consistent pattern in the classic series, in which at least one ongoing character always offset the unfamiliarity of a new Doctor. In the context of wholesale replacement of the primary players and production personnel for the BBC's flagship program, deliberate and total rebranding, as opposed to piecemeal brand refreshment, was in a very real sense not just desirable but essential.

As Matt Hills has argued, the process of updating the *Doctor Who* brand was continuous throughout Russell T Davies's incumbency as showrunner, finding its clearest expression in the handling of the series' signature monsters, the Daleks and Cybermen. Each time either monster reappeared, a new variant was introduced: in the case of the Daleks, the Emperor and Imperial Guard in 'The Parting of the Ways' (2005); the Black Dalek in 'Doomsday' (2006); the red Supreme Dalek in 'The Stolen Earth' (2008) and so on. As Hills notes, these variants were 'always visually recognisable as revisions' in much the same way as each new generation of iPhone, and it is clear that every Dalek redesign was intended to translate smoothly into 'must-have' merchandise.[15] In a commercial context where brand renewal is routine and expected, it would in many ways have been odd if the simultaneous change of Doctor and companion had *not* been accompanied by comprehensive rebranding.

The fact that branding imperatives may underwrite redesign in *Doctor Who* does not necessarily belie Moffat's and Gatiss's claims for the influence of their own tastes over the revamping of the Daleks. Yet brand logic does complicate the way in which these claims can be understood as reflecting ultimate authorial power. While it would be excessive to imagine *Doctor Who*'s brand manager as an *eminence grise*, it is important to recognise that the activities and influence of 'creative' personnel are not in any absolute sense anterior to brand rollout. Given the contemporary television industry's 'will-to-brand',[16] design choices for a high-profile show such as *Doctor Who* are in some measure always already directed beyond the design's indicial role within the drama. The BBC spokesman's insistence, *vis-à-vis* the Daleks, that 'the scripts always come first', may technically be true, but far more telling is Steven Moffat's bald acknowledgement of his reluctance to make apparently money-saving episodes 'without a proper monster', because '*Doctor Who* with no monsters is *Doctor Who* with no toys'.[17]

'Who's wearing the trousers?' or How Design Authority is Skirted

Moffat's proclivity for such disarmingly blunt observations and pawky one-liners might be taken to imply a critical distance from the 'packaging' of *Doctor Who*, but his seemingly detached, even contrarian, commentary can itself also be understood as a function of branding. Hills has aptly commented that Moffat is 'the Tom Baker to Russell T Davies's Jon Pertwee', the new man's wilful perversity and transgressiveness in each case replacing his predecessor's suave air of establishment-oriented authority.[18] Yet within the intertextual relay of *Doctor Who*, Moffat's self-portrayal as waspish and oppositional is just as effectively canalised in service to the brand as Davies's avuncular paternalism. Take, for example, Moffat's origin story for the first costume of the Eleventh Doctor. At one level, his account of the costume's genesis represents a deliberate, not to say gleeful, debunking of his own authorial vision and control, in sharp contrast to Russell T Davies's emphatically documented role in defining Christopher Eccleston's look. Both Eccleston himself and the costume designer for the 2005 series, Lucinda Wright, recalled in interview that the choice of the Ninth Doctor's leather jacket was 'scripted' by Davies.[19] Moffat, on the other hand, told *Doctor Who Magazine* that Matt Smith had to argue for his first costume, especially the bow tie, in face of objections from Moffat himself, who claims to have called Smith's projected outfit a 'pantomime idea' of *Doctor Who*.[20] This evocation of an untidy and combative design process diverges strongly from reports of Russell T Davies's clear-sighted, harmonising influence over creative decisions. Yet in the last analysis, Moffat's account of his 'mistake' in relation to the choice of Smith's costume is in itself a kind of retrospective authorisation. In dramatising the dispute, Moffat exhibited his flair for storytelling, which is identified as his central area of responsibility. In this little tale, a minor skirmish has a satisfying denouement, with Smith/the Doctor victorious over Moffat/the monster.

Moffat has subsequently done something broadly similar within the series narrative itself, in a specially made 2011 *Comic Relief* miniature in two parts, respectively titled 'Space' and 'Time'. Here Moffat seemed to be slyly responding to a contested design choice, and one whose incendiary potential apparently caught some of *Doctor Who*'s creative personnel by surprise, namely Karen Gillan's 'look' for the role of Amy Pond. In certain respects, this displacement from explicit to implied comment, and from paratext to series narrative, is problematic.

From her debut, Amy's forthright sexuality was immediately the target of criticism in the popular press (see Chapter 4 of this book). These attacks focused partly on suggestive or risqué scripted representation of the character.[21] Yet negative criticism was also directed towards Amy's predilection for micro-miniskirts.[22] In eight of the 13 episodes in series five, and again in the following Christmas special, Amy wore either very brief skirts or, in one case, equally brief shorts. While arguably no more distinctive to the character than the vintage leather flying jackets or motorcycle jackets which dominated her outfits in six episodes, the skirts became *the* defining aspect of Amy's look purely because they were so much discussed in the press.

Given a media context in which authorising statements by creative personnel tend to be mutually reinforcing, the *cause célèbre* over Amy's costumes show the ease with which indicial slippage can happen when a key design in a high-profile television series is *not* coherently authorised. While there was some proactive commentary on Amy's costumes, it was riven with contradiction. This is true even of *SFX*'s joint interview with Piers Wenger and Ray Holman, the costume designer on series five, issued immediately prior to the new season's launch. Wenger, interestingly enough, focused on Amy's flying jacket and cowboy boots, which supposedly confirm 'the key thing for Karen', namely that Amy is 'a born adventurer'. In comparison to this crisp gloss, Holman's remarks are generalising and nebulous, and mostly confined to observations about the relationship between clothing, individualism and consumption: as Amy is a 'feisty, independent girl', Holman felt that nothing in her wardrobe 'could be clearly from Top Shop'. Unlike Wenger, Holman did briefly touch on her sexualisation and more specifically her miniskirts, noting on the one hand that 'she's very sexy, but she's not overplayed sexy' and on the other that 'Karen sometimes has her short skirts on because she can, because that's okay with the script'.[23]

Holman's appeal to the authority of the script, and his suggestive use of the possessive in noting that '*Karen*...has *her* short skirts', may indicate a wish to distance himself from this aspect of Amy's look. Karen Gillan has in fact from the first claimed that the skirts reflect her personal input into the costuming process,[24] and it seems to me logical to understand them in the way that Gillan generally professes to do – as unremarkable. While Gillan initially defended the short skirts as 'part of the plot',[25] she has increasingly used a different legitimating tactic, appealing to an external, social benchmark: 'I just don't get it with the skirts. It's what any girl on the street is wearing. I mean, Amy's not a schoolgirl, she's 21, pretty much the same age as me, and we all wear stuff like this.'[26] While this may seem to smack of protesting too much, it is important to recall that the profession of ordinariness was only necessary because Amy's outfits had already been coded as transgressively *extra*ordinary. The pattern persisted well into Amy Pond's incumbency with reference to her skirts routinely serving as a framing device even in the more benign interviews with or articles about Gillan.

The force of the very public, reiterated critique of Amy's outfits also inevitably meant that any substantive costume change was likely to be read as a tacit response to negative criticism. In pre-publicity materials for series six (and in five out of the seven episodes which made up the 'spring season'), Amy is seen wearing plaid flannel shirts with jeans – which, coincidentally or not, closely echo Gillan's outfit in her inaugural photocall in 2009. *Metro* duly carried a story claiming in the headline that the miniskirts were being 'ditched'. Ironically, *Metro* provided clear contrary testimony from Gillan herself in the body of the article[27], and short skirts continued to alternate with trousers throughout the 'autumn season' in 2011 and Gillan's final set of five episodes a year later. A few weeks after the publication of the *Metro* piece, Gillan specifically explained to the *Independent* that she 'didn't want to get rid of the short skirts completely', again on the grounds that 'that's what young girls wear', adding: 'I know that because I am one of them.'[28] By this point, Gillan's persistent representation of the miniskirts as unexceptional and therefore unexceptionable had crystallised into a coherent, positive authorial stance.

Having commented relatively little on the skirt controversy (in comparison with, say, Matt Smith, who has consistently rallied behind the costume choices for Amy), Steven Moffat did make an ironic nod to it in his two-part 2011 Comic Relief special, which aired shortly before series six. In this 'minisode' one of Amy's skirts really is a cardinal function of the narrative. Rory's glancing up between his wife's legs through the glass floor of the TARDIS control station leads him to drop a 'servo coupling', which in turn results in a space/time paradox. In the final line of dialogue, the Doctor instructs Amy to 'put some trousers on', effectively making her responsible for managing Rory's sexuality. Importantly, the whole scenario resonates with Rory's claim, made just before he drops the servo coupling, that Amy is an incompetent driver who only passed her test first time because she 'cheated' – by wearing a short skirt.

Satire notwithstanding, the Comic Relief special de facto affirmed that the furore about Amy's skirt was *not* unwarranted. Worse – and again, satire notwithstanding – the minisode provided explicit support for the idea that Amy/Karen Gillan and her outfits are somehow to blame for any 'uncontrollable' sexual excitation straight male viewers might, like Rory, 'naturally' feel in looking at her. Once again, I am not claiming that Moffat's authorial position is ultimately explanative. However, given the power of Moffat's voice as head writer, his facetious emphasis on the sexual connotation of Amy's skirt has the potential to carry as much weight as Gillan's consistent and serious attempts to *de*-emphasise it.

A Relationship Based on Looks: 'A Moffat-Era Aesthetic'?

So far I have treated various design initiatives of the Moffat era individually, because my main purpose in this chapter has been to highlight the complex, overlapping and sometimes contradictory ways in which design can be authorised in the context of a strongly branded prestige television series. In drawing to a conclusion, I should like to move beyond this atomised approach, briefly examining the larger question of whether there was a discernible 'Moffat-era aesthetic', during the first two and a half years of his incumbency as showrunner, and if so how it relates to the issue of rebranding and to the construction of Moffat's authorial 'signature'.

Authorisation is ultimately a matter of words, of verbal statement, of naming and claiming. Yet design imagery self-evidently does not operate in the realm of speech; on the contrary, the evocative power of costumes, sets, and so on, derives precisely from their embodying more than can be said. To adopt a strong authorial position *vis-à-vis* design, as Davies and his collaborators did in the publicity and documentary narratives for series one to four, is not only to restrict but in a sense to distort design's signification – though the positive value of such 'distortion' is immediately discernible in the context of branding discourse.

In the case of the Moffat era there is arguably less inducement to believe that design imagery bears the showrunner's individual imprint: as I have shown throughout this chapter, Moffat's authorisation of design is weaker than that of his predecessor. This means that it is ultimately easier to disentangle the significance of writing from the putative auteur status of the head writer. Scripts for series five, six and seven have unquestionably reoriented *Doctor Who* toward a more Gothic-Romantic, fairytale sensibility, which inevitably affected the work of designers. The settings for adventures during Davies's incumbency were predominantly urban or technological, the most oft-used environments being either contemporary London or a future metropolitan dystopia. By contrast, the Moffat era has given us, among other things, a spooky old house with a hidden room; a subterranean 'maze of the dead'; a dungeon-crypt beneath Stonehenge; a storm-racked castle on an island; Area 51; and an underground asylum – all bucolic or isolated locales strongly rooted in the literature, art and cinema of the uncanny. The same applies to monsters such as the quintessentially Gothic Weeping Angels, the Dream Lord, the Headless Monks, the lightning-animated Gangers, and in a different way the Silence, whose appearance is meant to evoke not only the stereotypical 'grey alien' of ufological speculation but also the distorted physiognomy of the main figure in Munch's *Scream*.[29]

Yet for all this coherence in terms of genre and tone in the writing of series five, six and seven, there are objections to envisaging a Moffat-era design aesthetic based on the scripts alone. It should be self evident that no scripted impetus for a design will comprehensively account for the way in which the designer develops and realises a given image, or indeed for the way in which the director of photography and editor mediate realised designs to the audience. In other words, the design process is not a simple conduit for writers' ideas, but one of a number of *filters* for those ideas, which condition the ultimate 'style' of a programme. So if there is a cogent design aesthetic in *Doctor Who*, it depends on much more than the vision of Steven Moffat and his writing colleagues.

Conclusion

In closing, I should like to make two divergent, but not irreconcilable, observations about the issue of the series aesthetic. The first concerns the design process, in which the role of the aleatoric must not be underestimated. When the first photographs emerged in July 2009 of Matt Smith in costume with the sixties-style TARDIS prop, the Eleventh Doctor's new outfit seemed to be part of a systematically conceived retro aesthetic. Quite apart from the fact that Smith's tweed jacket was supposedly of sixties vintage, aspects of his dress and grooming clearly recalled Patrick Troughton's mop-haired, bow tie wearing, drainpipe-trousered Doctor. Yet as we have seen, Smith's look was apparently far from being part of a larger design concept, retro or otherwise. We therefore have to acknowledge a potential mismatch between the commonplace notion of achieving a strong aesthetic 'by design' and the more haphazard, or organic, realities of design for television.

My second observation pertains to design not as a process but as an attribute of a final product. As I have already suggested in this chapter, design imagery in the new *Doctor Who* is ultimately circumscribed, if not defined a priori, by brand logic. However much happenstance may be involved in the development of a given image, brand imperatives will tend to bring all design elements into alignment, or at the very least create structures in which there is a powerful impulse towards synthesis. The unveiling of the Moffat/Smith era *Doctor Who* logo in October 2009, and the subsequent release of a teaser trailer in February 2010, made it clear that Smith's 'retro' look, and that of his TARDIS, had indeed by this time become part of a cohesive rebrand – and in the TARDIS's case the very core of a new graphic identity system. To offer a thorough exegesis of the evocative use of colour and form in this identity system exceeds the scope and purpose of the present chapter. Suffice it to say that the image of the Eleventh Doctor juxtaposed with the blocky, Constructivist-style typeface of the new logo, and the deep aqueous blue (or 'TARDIS blue') used so extensively in the title sequence, teaser trailer, official website and much tie-in merchandise in 2010 and 2011, precisely paralleled and complemented the earlier juxtaposition of the Tenth Doctor's features with a glowing amber and ochre palette and coolly modern sans-serif typography, even as they eclipsed it. In short, design-as-brand carried such a powerful charge that one hardly needed to watch *Doctor Who* in 2010 to be aware, subliminally at least, of the arrival of the 'Moffat era'.

Notes

1. I am extremely grateful to Matt Hills for reading an earlier draft of this chapter and offering comments.
2. On the concept of 'intertextual relay' – a term originally coined by Gregory Lukow and Steven Ricci – see Steven Neale, *Genre and Hollywood* (London, 2000), pp. 2–3.
3. Roland Barthes, 'An Introduction to the Structural Analysis of Narrative', *New Literary History*, vi/2 (1975), p. 249.

4. Ibid., p. 247.

5. C.S. Tashiro, *Pretty Pictures: Production Design and the History Film* (Austin, 1998), pp. xv–xvi, 12, 16; Piers D. Britton and Simon Barker, *Reading Between Designs: Design and the Generation of Meaning in The Avengers, The Prisoner and Doctor Who* (Austin, 2003), pp. 16–17.

6. Britton and Barker, *Reading Between Designs*: pp. 35, 46–55, 199.

7. Rachel K. Bosley, 'Pitch Perfect', *American Cinematographer*, xc/10 (2009), pp. 38, 40.

8. Tom Spilsbury, 'Takin' Over the Asylum' (The DWM Interview: Steven Moffat), *Doctor Who Magazine* 417 (2010), p. 24.

9. Zoe Rushton and Gillane Seaborne (producers), 'War Games', *Doctor Who Confidential*, (BBC), 17 April 2010.

10. 'The TARDIS Tour!', online video. Available at www.bbc.co.uk/doctorwho/dw/episodes/b00rs6t7/videos/p00765jg (viewed 10 April 2010).

11. Jason Arnopp, 'Designing the TARDIS,' in Clayton Hickman (ed.), *Doctor Who: The Brilliant Book 2011* (London, 2003), p. 19.

12. Quoted in Benjamin Cook, 'Meet the Boss', in Hickman, *The Brilliant Book*, p. 105.

13. 'War Games'.

14. Christian Cawley, 'Cynicism of the Daleks?', Kasterborous On-Line Magazine, 30 April 2010. Available at www.kasterborous.com/2010/04/cynicism-of-the-daleks/ (accessed 2 May 2010).

15. Matt Hills, *Triumph of a Time Lord: Regenerating Doctor Who in the Twenty-First Century* (London, 2010), pp. 66–8.

16. Ibid., p. 66.

17. Cook, 'Meet the Boss', p. 105.

18. Matt Hills, 'Steven Moffat's *Doctor Who*: Challenging the Format Theorem?', 2 May 2011. Available at http://blog.commarts.wisc.edu/2011/05/02/steven-moffats-doctor-who-challenging-the-format-theorem/ (accessed 3 May 2011).

19. Gillane Seaborne (producer), 'Bringing Back the Doctor', *Doctor Who Confidential*, (BBC), 26 March 2005.

20. Tom Spilsbury, 'The Time is Now!' (The DWM Interview: Steven Moffat), *Doctor Who Magazine* 418 (2010), p. 21.

21. 'Viewers Think New Doctor Who is "Too Sexy"', *Telegraph Online*, 5 April 2010. Available at www.telegraph.co.uk/culture/tvandradio/doctor-who/7554825/Viewers-think-new-Doctor-Who-is-too-sexy.html (accessed 10 April 2010); Paul Revoir, *Mail Online*, 'Who's Steamed up the TARDIS? The Doctor Shares a Passionate Kiss with Companion Amy', 1 May 2010. Available at www.dailymail.co.uk/tvshowbiz/article-1270166/Whos-steamed-Tardis-The-Doctor-shares-passionate-kiss-companion-Amy.html (accessed 3 May 2010).

22. Simon Cable, 'Doctor Ooooh! How the Doctor's Saucy, Short-Skirted Companion Sent Viewers into Orbit', *Mail Online*, 6 April 2010. Available at www.dailymail.co.uk/tvshowbiz/article-1263583/Doctor-Whos-racy-new-companion-Karen-Gillan-sent-viewers-orbit.html (accessed 8 April 2010).

23. Nick Setchfield, 'Dressing Doctor Who', *SFX Online*, 28 March 2010. Available at www.sfx.co.uk/2010/03/28/doctor-who-the-new-costume/ (accessed 1 April 2011).

24. 'Doctor Who Actress Says She Sexed Up Sidekick Amy Pond', *Telegraph Online*, 13 May 2010. Available at www.telegraph.co.uk/culture/tvandradio/7718487/Doctor-Who-actress-says-she-sexed-up-sidekick-Amy-Pond.html (accessed 13 May 2010).
25. ' "It just shows she's confident": New Assistant Karen Gillan Defends Her Short Skirts in Sexed-Up Doctor Who', *Mail Online*, 7 April 2010. Available at http://www.dailymail.co.uk/tvshowbiz/article-1264231/Karen-Gillan-defends-Doctor-Who-criticism-fans-appeared-slutty-show.html (accessed 10 June 2011).
26. Quoted in E. Jane Dickson, 'Twelve Weeks that Changed My Life', *Radio Times*, 19–25 June 2010, p. 23.
27. Amy Duncan, 'Doctor Who's Sexy Assistant Amy Pond to Ditch Mini-Skirt for Series Six', 19 April 2011. Available at www.metro.co.uk/tv/861316-doctor-whos-sexy-assistant-amy-pond-to-ditch-mini-skirt-for-series-six (accessed 20 April 2011).
28. Gerard Gilbert, 'Karen Gillan: Obsessive Fans, Short Skirts and Life with Doctor Who', *Independent Online*, 7 May 2011. Available at www.independent.co.uk/arts-entertainment/tv/features/karen-gillan-obsessive-fans-short-skirts-and-life-with-doctor-who-2278843.html (accessed 10 June 2011).
29. Tom Oglethorpe, 'He's a Real Scream! Get Ready to Dive Behind the Sofa as Doctor Who's New Enemy Makes the Daleks Look Like Dusty Bin', *Mail Online*, 15 April 2011. Available at www.dailymail.co.uk/tvshowbiz/article-1377089/Doctor-Whos-new-enemy-The-Silence-makes-Daleks-look-like-Dusty-Bin.html (accessed 10 June 2011).

9

SILENCE WON'T FALL

Murray Gold's Music in the Steven Moffat Era

Vasco Hexel

Television music on both sides of the Atlantic has throughout its short history followed trends and generally evolved with prevailing fashions and modes of production. This includes shifting preference for musical styles, performance media, and the actual source of music (composed or licensed).[1] Yet it seems as though in recent years music in mainstream television is changing more drastically and is slowly disappearing altogether. Across genres, but particularly in thriller/drama, music is either omitted entirely or reduced to innocuous drones and percussive pulses that hardly breach through other soundtrack elements. Programme makers seem to be in pursuit of what they conceive of as realism. Perhaps they are afraid of patronising their audience – or simply unsure of their dramatic intentions. In any case, television music has grown increasingly sparse, low profile, quiet and less than expressive. To the contrary, music continues to play a prominent, even vital role in *Doctor Who* where it accompanies the majority of scenes from front to end. Each episode contains over 30 minutes of composed underscore. Composer Murray Gold is a longstanding collaborative partner of Russell T Davies and has continued scoring *Doctor Who* since Steven

Moffat took over as the programme's lead producer and writer. Gold's scores have gained considerable extra-textual popularity in their own right, as evidenced by recent soundtrack album releases and high-profile concert performances. By the time Matt Smith arrived as the freshly regenerated Eleventh Doctor, nearly all music was performed and recorded by the BBC National Orchestra of Wales. As a result, series five, six and seven feature scores of a musical ambition and sophistication rarely heard in television music. Underlying budget considerations suggest that music was deemed important as a storytelling tool: television producers cannot normally afford the luxury of an expensive score if it is not directly justified by the programme's narrative requirements. This chapter illustrates pertinent aspects of Gold's scores in the Steven Moffat era and pursues questions as to music's role and function in the context of television in general and *Doctor Who* specifically. How does a musical underscore tinged in Hollywood tradition and its musico-narrative conventions serve *Doctor Who*'s less than conventional narrative style? What scoring strategies succeed in supporting Steven Moffat's *Doctor Who*?

The Main Title Music

Gold's 2010 re-arrangement of Ron Grainer's original *Doctor Who* title music ensures musical continuity at the extra-diegetic franchise level. As a recognisable entity, the well-known theme tune constitutes the sole musical constant across series, facilitating brand identity. Janet Halfyard observes that it is not unusual for (cult) television shows that thematic material established in the main title never actually appears during an episode.[2] The *Doctor Who* main title theme is thus attached to the brand and not to an intra-diegetic character or action. Gold's arrangement is driven by an angular drum loop that has a somewhat dated flavour, with romping synths and raucous brass atop, lending the theme a more swashbuckling swagger than ever. The signature theremin sound whistling the melody is perhaps the last remaining signifier of 'sci-fi' in a score that otherwise tends to place the Eleventh Doctor in other genres (see below). It is remarkable that *Doctor Who* has held on to its main title sequence, short though it may be, considering the widespread disappearance of television main titles. Music here sounds markedly different from the almost exclusively orchestral underscore that accompanies series five, six and seven. As a result, its occurrence in the programme makes for an idiomatic and aesthetic break that suspends – or even interrupts – narrative flow and affective process. The main title thus serves the dual purpose of hailing the *Doctor Who* brand and acting as a punctuation mark. In each episode, it is positioned after a narrative exposition, usually around four minutes into each episode, except for those which have extended expositions like 'The Pandorica Opens', 'The Big Bang' and 'Asylum of the Daleks'.

Television Scoring, its Influences and Genre

While the main title music thus continues to pay homage to *Doctor Who*'s musical heritage, Gold's scores otherwise explore new territory. The non-diegetic underscore of series five, six and seven occasionally incorporates drum loops, electric guitars, piano, and voices but is otherwise wholly symphonic. Making effective use of the orchestral medium, Gold's idiom is lush and neo-Romantic at its most expansive. Elsewhere, he takes a more minimalist approach, influenced by popular idioms. It has become unusual for British television programmes to use music performed by live musicians, let alone a full symphony orchestra. American television largely abandoned live scoring decades ago – for fiscal as much as aesthetic reasons – except for an eclectic range of programmes such as *Star Trek: The Next Generation* (Paramount, 1987–94), *The Simpsons* (Fox, 1989–) and *Family Guy* (Fox, 1999–). Most of the time, television composers have to economise by combining sample-based, computer-generated sounds with a few live players, which is the approach Gold took during series one to four.[3] Even widely acclaimed (and commercially viable) drama series such as *Downton Abbey* (Carnival Films, 2010–) are scored with a smaller chamber orchestra. George Fenton's scores for the BBC's flagship natural history programmes *Planet Earth* (2006) and *Frozen Planet* (2011) are notable exceptions, performed by the BBC Symphony Orchestra. It is all the more remarkable that increases to the music budget meant that Gold could use the BBC National Orchestra of Wales to record the scores for series five, six and seven.

The resulting scores are by their mere scale raised to a higher affective plane. Matt Hills posits that 'the use of "big" music works to "mainstream" *Doctor Who* discursively, articulating its textual identity with "Hollywood" fantasy-epic and thoroughly exnominating – writing out – any assumed science fictionality'.[4] He adds that 'grabbing and holding the attention of a twenty-first century audience called for aural "sensory overload", a "big" full sound and a frenetic pace'.[5] While the choice of medium (orchestra) may be thus explained, the neo-Romantic 'Hollywood' *idiom* has wider implications. Kevin Donnelly notes that 'British TV has a social-realist tradition in which "serious" television largely avoids music as aesthetization.'[6] Robyn Stilwell agrees that compared to British content, American television music tends to be more cinematic and to contain more music, due to its 'aesthetic adjacency to Hollywood' and greater financial resources.[7] However, Gold's musical language in *Doctor Who* is firmly grounded in a Hollywood film-music paradigm, at times verging on being derivative. Gold himself acknowledges the influences of Ennio Morricone, Bernard Herrmann, Danny Elfman, Thomas Newman, Jerry Goldsmith and John Williams.[8] The extent to which such influences transpire varies between cues. 'Always on Horseback' (in 'The Pandorica Opens') with its use of dissonant chords and woodwind figurations in repeating intervals resembles James Newton Howard's score to *Signs* (2002); the rhythmic drive and loop-based composition of 'River's Path' (in 'The Time of Angels') is reminiscent of composer John Powell's *Bourne* trilogy scores (2002, 2004, 2007); and 'Signora Rosanna Calvierri' (in 'The Vampires of Venice') features an extended melody in a minor mode similar to moments in Hans Zimmer's *Gladiator* (2000) score. Ron Rodman describes how 'textual knowledge [on the part of the viewer] contributes to facilitating meaning in television'.[9] Hollywood references infuse the music in *Doctor Who* with textual connotations seemingly at odds with the programme's production values, premise, form and style as a thoroughly British television institution. Beneath this potential incongruence at an aesthetic and cultural surface level lies the more fundamental question of *Doctor Who*'s generic position.

Piers Britton observes that by 2003 'Doctor Who was no longer a single text, unfolding along a trajectory defined by the production and consumption rhythms of real-time broadcasting', but rather an array of texts (television episodes, websites, books, magazines) 'bleeding between forms... in the age of cross-media communication'.[10] John Fiske notes that interpreting and decoding televisual texts generally requires interpreters' 'knowledge of the world (social knowledge); knowledge of the medium and the genre (textual knowledge); and the relationship between the two (modality judgments)'.[11] Film and television have also mutually influenced their respective developments in terms of narrative tactics and modes of storytelling. Mainstream film and television stories have traditionally dealt in established formats that are readily understood by audiences. The managing of expectations, creation of story arcs, tension and release (boy meets girl/hero slays dragon), and embedding culturally encoded meanings and subtexts makes for engaging film and television. Generic conventions help root programmes in discrete categories, which support viewer identification and fandom.[12] By employing idiomatic codes, film music can help provide genre identifiers. Rodman refers to these as 'style topics', which in 'television may also convey discursive narrative traits, such as "comedy," "the heroic," and "action." '[13] Hills claims that Murray Gold's contribution is crucial in 'mainstreaming' the once cultish Doctor Who, by steering away from the previously upheld sci-fi genre (depicting the conflict between humans and science and/or humans and aliens) and less widely accessible 'cult TV' vibe. Timothy Scheurer has drafted a taxonomy of sci-fi scoring in the Hollywood canon,[14] concluding that sci-fi music tends to draw on electronic and synthesised sounds and an atonal and dissonant musical language. It is safe to agree that Gold's music resides outside the realm of conventional sci-fi scoring, the re-arranged main title track being the sole sci-fi remnant. With music helping to transcend Doctor Who's sci-fi baggage, questions arise as to generic allegiance. If new Who is not sci-fi, what is it? When Hills asserts that Doctor Who's increased accessibility is facilitated by a 'newfound textual consistency' at score level,[15] it is worth asking whether and how this perceived 'textual consistency' is met at the programme's genre level. Arguably, recent Doctor Who and its accompanying music move freely between (period) drama, melodrama, comedy, thriller – and indeed sci-fi. As a generic label, the term 'telefantasy' is perhaps best suited to describe *Doctor Who*.

Narrative Television Music

The principles and functions of narrative film and television music in furthering filmic and televisual storytelling have been extensively discussed and are well understood.[16] Film music functions in the context of the visual and acoustic elements it accompanies (or co-exists with) and contributes to a film's aesthetic and affective properties. Due to prevalent production processes, music has traditionally been created in the final phase of production and would therefore be determined by timing considerations (i.e. the edit) and narrative requirements of the programme at hand. Both in terms of technology and musical language, the seemingly discrete spheres of film and television scoring are widely accepted to have mutually influenced and cross-fertilised each other,[17] enabling audiences to decode meanings embedded in the audio-visual experience. Addressing narratological perspectives on music, Claudia Gorbman posits that the film/television spectator 'receives much more than [a story], situated by the connotative systems of camera placement, editing, lighting, acting ... and music' and that 'ultimately, it is the narrative context, the interrelations between music and the rest of the film's system, that determines the effectiveness of film music' and vice versa.[18] Rodman agrees that music resides in the intra-diegetic space of technical codes including camera positions, sound quality, lighting, and so on, that help fill in certain details, tone and mood within the story: 'components of televisual discourse and usually not part of the story itself.' Paraphrasing Levinson, he continues that 'although they are not really part of the story of the television episode, discursive components such as music are part of the world or space of the television narrative'.[19] The written word and its delivery by the actors complement the semiotic system. Music in television is thus part of what Rodman has termed 'an interpretative network model of correlation',[20] whose components coalesce into the participatory experience of the programme at hand. In *Doctor Who*, the balance between

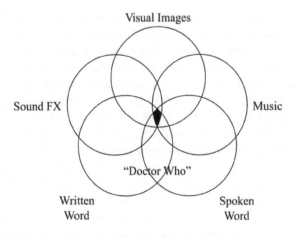

9.1 Network Model of Signification after Rodman

components is ever in flux (Figure 9.1). Prominently featured sound effects, busy musical cues, shaky camera frames, energetic (sometimes hysterical) acted performances, dazzling set-pieces and other-worldly encounters make for a dazzling, at times confusing, and occasionally overwhelming viewing experience. The programme's abundance of audio-visual stimuli ensures that many of its viewers cannot help but be entertained. An occasional lack of the dialogue's intelligibility results from loud sound effects but presumably does not detract from many viewers' enjoyment so long as other filmic elements keep the audience's mind occupied. Some viewers, however, may find *Doctor Who's* audio-visual style off-putting or find the music intrusive.

Narrative and Scoring Strategies in Moffat's *Doctor Who*

Series five, six and seven of *Doctor Who* extend the programme's established mythology, confronting the Eleventh Doctor with many familiar, and some new, villains, monsters and challenges. Despite all 'mainstreaming', *Doctor Who* expects a good deal of prior knowledge from its audience. For example, the fact that the Doctor and his companions Rory and Amy understand (and are in turn understood by) all persons and creatures they encounter is not explained.[21] In series five, the fact that they are heard to speak in foreign/alien tongues is not even hinted at until 'Vincent and the Doctor', when van Gogh comments on the Doctor's particular Dutch dialect. Such ellipses and understatement might confuse some viewers who are less familiar with the programme. On the other hand, omitting potentially redundant explanatory plot points makes for more strident, refreshing storytelling. Allusionism extends to *Doctor Who*'s narrative style as a whole: in virtually every episode, the Doctor encounters a series of unexpected and more or less mysterious (or plain bewildering) obstacles and challenges. More often than not, the Doctor seems to be well ahead of his companions (and the viewers) in trying to solve a problem. He always seems to know more than is made explicit to the audience. Pressured to explain himself, he exclaims, unnerved, 'Excuse me, I'm making perfect sense. You're just not keeping up' (in 'The Hungry Earth'). Amy and Rory are frequently baffled and overwhelmed whilst the Doctor races through an ever more complicated series of riddles and what appear to be series-spanning story arcs. Britton offers a most insightful analysis of narrative tactics in *Doctor Who*, calling it a 'vast narrative' that incorporates structuring motifs and patterns, cumulative thematic concerns, and also internal breaches or shifts in the text. He offers the fitting concept of the 'endlessly deferred narrative ... whose scale and complexity is hinted at but never fully explored. ... *Who* was not conceived with an eye to internal coherence; there was no need for it to be.'[22] This, however, has serious implications for *Doctor Who*'s music: effective narrative film music traditionally functions within teleological narratives with clear causal links and coherent emotive aims. Dan Martin, in his weekly *Guardian* blog during series six, pondered whether new *Who* had 'gotten too complicated?'[23] Editor of *Word* magazine Andrew Harrison feels that responses may differ by individual, stating 'one person's plot hole is another's unfathomable mystery – and I'm glad that Moffat is pushing the Doctor back into the realms of inscrutability'. Harrison continues, 'It's more fun that way, and it's best not to focus on plot holes in a show that's based on the flatly impossible.'[24] In recent *Doctor Who* anything goes: any plotline can ultimately be explained. Gold's music never questions or contradicts this narrative strategy. Consistently, no matter how opaque or mysterious the Doctor's monologues get, music affirms his authority, is quick to respond to unexpected twists and turns and heightens the dizzying pace at which he proceeds. When the Doctor proclaims 'I'm always okay' ('The Impossible Astronaut'), returning alive having apparently just been shot dead, the score's response is conclusive and reassuring. The audience is led to obligingly accept that anything is possible. The bundle of loosely related plot strands *Doctor Who* endlessly intertwines is at odds with the kind of teleological storytelling mainstream television audiences are generally accustomed to. This is of course part of *Doctor Who*'s appeal: the audience is never let to settle complacently for predictable plotlines. Britton concedes that even an *ideological* analysis of *Doctor Who* will reveal dissonances, inconsistencies and flaws but warns that such analysis would make for a depressing and redundant critique.[25] A closer look at scoring strategies employed to accompany this complex narrative should prove more constructive.

In tackling this less than connected narrative, Gold employs a two-pronged scoring strategy, assigning recurring themes to selected characters whilst taking a supple, reactive approach to effective incidental scoring. Stilwell has discussed the use of leitmotifs in series one, remarking that Gold's cinematic uses 'simple, occasionally simplistic ... recurring themes of most television but ... also demonstrates a more nuanced and rich use of leitmotifs, including multiple interpenetrating meanings'.[26] To some degree, Stilwell engages in the kind of 'theme counting' Royal S. Brown advises against,[27] warning that the mere cataloguing of themes and leitmotifs contributes little to one's understanding of the narrative and affective functions of film and television music. At the same time, Stilwell's observations on the importance and meaning-making capabilities of leitmotifs in series one veer on overstatement, reaching beyond those leitmotifs obvious function as signposts. According to Rodman, 'the ability of leitmotifs to ... connote extramusical traits, such as emotion, is one of the great semiotic powers of music in film or television.'[28] But such connotative abilities have equally been ascribed to non-motivic film music that can be evocative and referential outside the strictures of repeating motifs. The need for and function of leitmotifs in television scoring are generally debatable. Serial television as a repetitive format deals largely with familiar characters and plot configurations. Recurring leitmotifs (or themes) constitute an added layer of repetitiveness. When heard repeatedly in the on-screen presence of the character they accompany, leitmotifs are a redundant narrative device. Traditionally, television scoring has thus tended to be non-thematic and instead primarily situational and plot-driven.

In series five, six, and seven, Gold establishes a number of clearly recognisable, recurring themes. These serve indexically to identify, delineate and amplify characters but do not function as fully developed leitmotifs in the way Stilwell describes. Once introduced, themes remain largely unaltered and frequently identical recordings of the same theme are simply repeated across different episodes. This emphasis on character helps navigate the viewer through a seemingly incoherent (or at least highly complex) narrative. Amy technically has two themes: one that accompanies her childhood incarnation and one to go with her adult counterpart. Arguably, the audience becomes familiar sooner with 'Little Amy' (young Amy's theme) by the mere fact that it is repeated several times with little variation in the series five pilot episode, 'The Eleventh Hour'. It also generally recurs more frequently than adult Amy's theme (Figure 9.2). This theme is not introduced until 'The Beast Below'. A female voice with a soulful and gentle timbre renders this theme warm and caring, with a fairy-tale touch. Amy's themes' musical structure is markedly more linear than that of the Doctor's themes (see below), and only the beginning is shown here. The theme's linear, developmental nature, together with its fragile tone, perhaps expresses an awareness for Amy's humanness – and mortality – as opposed

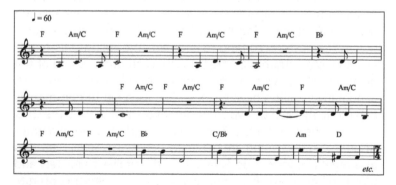

9.2 Amy's theme

to the alien, ever-regenerating Doctor whose themes are more cyclical. Both 'Amy' themes are used emotively and empathetically in her sombre or trying moments. Elsewhere, in 'The Girl Who Waited', they serve predictably to help characterise Amy's two incarnations as equally compassionate and loving, a companion, heroine, saviour, lover, and so on.

Matt Smith's energetic interpretation of the Eleventh Doctor elicits a range of emotions and character traits. These are presented (or imposed on the viewer) in a carefully constructed manner. The Doctor's serious side as the sole survivor of his race is captured in one of two recurring themes, 'The Mad Man with a Box' (Figure 9.3). Like Amy's theme, this is sung by a female voice, in a soft, mellow timbre. The tone of the voice paired with the theme's minor mode evokes a certain level of melancholy and nostalgia. The melody is confined in range, putting little strain on the singer's voice. Intervallic movements are mostly limited to stepwise motion except for a leap between the third to last and penultimate note in each phrase. The tune has a certain Romantic flavour and is reminiscent of Danny Elfman's neo-Gothic themes. The harmonic progression appears circular, departing from D-minor, to which it clearly aims to return upon the completion of the fourth melodic phrase (the leading tone in the melody over the dominant chord). The theme is heard in the Doctor's moments of uncertainty, hardship and self-doubt. A variation, 'The Sad Man with a Box,' accompanies a rare occasion of seemingly genuine emotion, in this case sadness (for example, in 'The Big Bang').

Repeated most frequently is the Doctor's second theme, 'I Am the Doctor' (Figure 9.4) introduced in 'The Eleventh Hour'.

9.3 'The Mad Man with a Box'

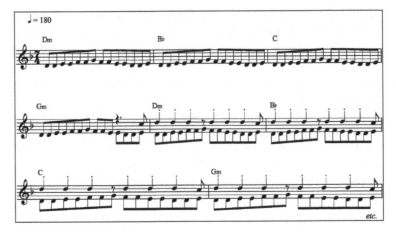

9.4 'I Am the Doctor'

The theme is notably non-melodic: a low-profile strings ostinato comprising a stepwise ascend and descend. In the current context of largely ostinato-based (Hollywood) film scoring, Gold's score here is perhaps at its most contemporary. Remarkably, the theme is set 7/4, commonly perceived as an irregular time signature, as compared to the more familiar triple and 4/4 metres that have for centuries prevailed in folk and concert music. Due to its asymmetry, a regular subdivision of the musical phrase is not possible. This results in a rhythmically unsettling, unstable feel. Non-musicians need only try to clap along or tap their feet in a regular 'beat' to consciously feel this rhythmic unsteadiness. The inherent rhythmic irregularity mirrors the Doctor's key character traits of a somewhat hyperactive, easily distracted time traveller. The theme's rhythmic complexity is further compounded by high accents on strings and woodwinds that set in soon after the theme starts. Although these are played with flair in a concise and snappy manner, they appear to be of ever-shifting emphasis, seemingly syncopated. This creates a suitable air of anticipation but also calculated precision. The recurring strings ostinato takes itself seriously in its assured, rhythmically flawless, mechanical delivery. Its self-confident manner supports the Doctor whenever he has an insight that will solve the mystery at hand, or when he asserts his power and authority as Time Lord over an opponent. The theme sometimes appears with an electric guitar and even drums accompaniment, which add depth and weight. Occasionally, dignified and grand brass chords colour the theme accordingly. Despite inherent complexities, 'I Am the Doctor' remains highly accessible through its repetitiveness and use of a looping four-chord harmonic accompaniment. The chosen progression is common in contemporary popular music and thus lends this theme wider appeal.

Discussing leitmotifs, Rodman outlines how 'as musical statements, leitmotifs function in much the same way as Morris's ascriptors'.[29] He then distinguishes between denotative and connotative signifiers, outlining that there are 'two kinds of leitmotifs: motifs that are arbitrarily assigned to a character or situation and that accrue meaning through repetition ... and motifs that are assigned to characters or situations that have intertextual reference ... the prior being denotative only, the latter being denotative and connotative'.[30] 'I Am the Doctor' is predominantly denotative to start, its musical characteristics being both suitable for and having some semblance to the character of the Eleventh Doctor. The theme later also takes on connotative capacities, most obviously in 'The Impossible Astronaut': the Doctor, sitting on the hood of a Cadillac and wearing a cowboy hat, welcomes Amy, Rory and River in Utah with a tongue-in-cheek 'howdy'. The cue 'I am the Doctor in Utah' with its cowboy-esque electric guitar strums transplants the Doctor's theme into a mythical Wild West setting whose nostalgic set-pieces of vintage cars and diners deal in filmic clichés. In this opening episode to series six, to the experienced viewer, the theme's familiarity in combination with a geographic and culturally coded variation creates an opportunity for added engagement.

Under Moffat, *Doctor Who*'s puzzling story arcs see its key characters relate in complex intertwined ways. River Song is a lead character throughout series five and six, yet her identity and background remain a mystery for some time. To further complicate matters, Amy's daughter, Melody Pond, is later revealed to be young River Song. Gold's music gives clues. A new River theme is first introduced when she kisses the Doctor near the end of 'Day of the Moon' (Figure 9.5). A female voice is double at pitch by an oboe, lending the theme a warm, caring quality. The first eight bars commence just as River kisses the Doctor goodbye. The second half of the theme comprises a D-minor

9.5 River's Theme A

9.6 River's Theme B (Regenerating in New York)

pedal and a recurring mordent in the vocal line. The tone is at once insistent and longing, underpinning River's obvious disappointment at the fact the Doctor does not remember ever kissing her before. Their unfolding relationship and River's reverse time travel play a major role in story developments.

In the same episode's ensuing final scene, moments after River's theme has been introduced, a little girl (Melody Pond) regenerates in a New York alley. As the regeneration process engulfs the girl in blinding light, a short musical cue rises. The melody is again sung by a female voice, now doubled in the high strings (Figure 9.6). Gold ingeniously suggests a link between River Song and the girl: not only is the latter half of this cue near identical to the head of River's theme in melodic contour and rhythmic values. In the first two bars, the slower strings also provide the same mordent that concluded River's theme.

Both parts of River's theme return near the end of 'A Good Man Goes to War' when she reveals her identity, first to the Doctor and then to Amy and Rory. Very effectively, the mordent figuration first starts when River mentions Amy's child. A prolonged emotive musical build-up follows that paralleling Amy's realisation that River Song is her daughter, ending on part B, the same music that accompanied the girl's regeneration. River's theme helps channel strands of the narrative that have taken many episodes to connect. It is also, however, used, for example, in the concluding scene to 'Closing Time', long after River's identity has been revealed.

Aside from recurring themes, Gold's scores are highly incidental and reactive, focusing on individual scenes and their dramatic and emotive requirements. Music incessantly accompanies most scenes from start to finish. Rarely ever is there a moment of un-scored, unmitigated action. Obviously, decisions as to whether and where to place music – as well as that music's tone and intended narrative aim – are made collaboratively by the storytelling team. Throughout series five, six and seven, Gold's scores have markedly conservative attributes, compared to the contemporary television canon that explores new devices and means of expression that include extended passages without music. Gold's cues are at times nostalgic, sentimental, generally unambiguous, perhaps manipulative, often over-the-top, even bombastic – in short, they have all the attributes of Hollywood's Golden Age film scoring.[31] Gold relies on a tried-and-tested, safe approach to scoring in localised affective vignettes. These are self-contained and internally logical and coherent. In decidedly unambiguous terms, the audience is pointed at, for example, comedic moments (see 'Fish Custard' in 'The Eleventh Hour', 'When a River Forms' in 'Let's Kill Hitler', 'Doctor Gastronomy' and 'You Must Like It Here' in 'The Lodger', 'Stormageddon, Dark Lord of All' and 'Ladieswear' in 'Closing Time', and various tracks in 'Dinosaurs on a Spaceship') or one that showcases a surprisingly sportive, youthful Doctor ('A Useful Striker' in 'The Lodger'). There is nothing subtle about Gold's scores. Britton identifies the 'epic vignette', as well as the 'touching' and the 'sobering' vignettes. Within these, music helps create, anchor, and affirm meaning. Each cue through over-coding encourages the viewer to a singular interpretative reading of each discrete scene at hand. The extent to which *Doctor Who* relies heavily on music for atmosphere reveals something about narrative tactics but also modes of production: despite evident advances in

DOCTOR WHO, *THE ELEVENTH HOUR*

computer-generated imagery, *Who* remains confined to a limited amount of sets and protagonists per episode – a circumstance *Doctor Who* has traditionally tackled with wordy and static delivery rather than action-filled, cast- and prop-reliant settings. In moments of peril and contest, music steps in to heighten the dramatic charge and helps compensate for what might otherwise be an obvious lack in production resource. Daleks thus become frightfully villainous creatures ('Victory of the Daleks'), and when the Doctor is shouting at obviously computer-generated visuals of space ships above ('Words Win Wars' in 'The Pandorica Opens'), the opulent and distinctly *filmic* accompanying score lends gravitas to his word and performance. This helps transpose his individual struggle to protect the Pandorica's content from one Doctor's plight to an audience-bonded collective plight against alien forces. Marcia Landy acknowledges that 'orchestration... contributes to the illusion of transcendence, or surpassing both individual and collective struggles'.[32] It would make for a telling experiment in audience reception if one were to ask a group of volunteers to sit through that same scene with its music omitted from the soundtrack. One can reasonably predict that the moment's effect would be greatly diminished without Gold's music's considerable meaning-making and affective influence.

Hills has addressed the use of diegetic rock/pop songs during the Russell T Davies era and their effect on the socio-cultural and historic positioning of these series. He acknowledges that '*Doctor Who*'s time-travelling scenarios greatly reduce possibilities for using pop music diegetically'.[33] He also notes the use of non-diegetic pop music, which is ubiquitous elsewhere in contemporary television. Not only are pop songs incongruous with the historic settings the Doctor traverses. The use of pop songs also carries cultural connotations of potentially short-lived currency, immediately dating the programme or film they accompany. It is therefore not surprising that recent *Doctor Who* eschews the use of contemporary popular music. In a rare exception, the song 'Chances' by the band Athlete commences as the Doctor and Amy lead a baffled van Gogh into the Musée d'Orsay near the end of 'Vincent and the Doctor'. The song dominates the soundtrack for much of its duration and rather blatantly imposes a contemporary feel to the segment. Although it could be read as a refreshing change of pace and tone, the stylistic break is nevertheless disruptive. Most intrusively, the song's sudden dynamic surge upon the drums' entry momentarily overpowers the on-screen narrative. As the creative decision-making process is never conclusively observable on the final result, one can only speculate as to why 'Chances' was chosen for this segment. The choice may, admittedly, provide pleasure for fans of the band Athlete, or add emotion to the scene. Otherwise, this one-off use of a non-diegetic pop song may be perceived as stylistically inconsistent or crudely sentimental.

Conclusion

Doctor Who's lack of teleological coherence and genre adherence as well as its stylistic (in-)congruency are concerns that during each episode are eloquently brushed over or circumnavigated but never settled. Music is a key component in helping propel the narrative forward at all times. If *Doctor Who*'s narrative and affective aim is 'make-believe' in the literal sense, then Murray Gold's music helps guide the audience to singular readings of moments in this complex, multi-faceted text. Music in recent *Doctor Who* helps carry the audience through the proverbial choppy waters of seemingly disjointed narrative *vignettes*. The music provides a certain level of coherence through a consistent instrumental medium, tone, and colour. Recurring themes act as signposts and anchors for key characters. Overall, the large-scale orchestral score raises the programme's aesthetic and affective impact. In times when shrinking budgets impose considerable restrictions on the instrumental forces employed, Murray Gold has the privilege of commanding a full symphony orchestra. If *Doctor Who* aims simply to entertain, then Gold's music in the guise of traditional narrative film music, tinged in Hollywood tone and style, contributes to making *Doctor Who* palatable and accessible to a wide mainstream audience. The orchestral instrumental forces and largely nostalgic, conservative musical language help position the score (and in turn the programme) in a realm culturally and historically removed from current trends and tastes that might otherwise quickly date the programme. This sits well with *Doctor Who*'s premise by which the Doctor traverses time and space rather than staying put in a fleeting present. In their scale, scope, and ambition Gold's scores constitute a refreshing change from prevailing trends in contemporary television music whereby sentimental and generally prominent scoring is being shunned. Music is largely absent or toned down to mere pulses and drones; (musical) silence has fallen in many television sound-tracks, but silence won't fall in *Doctor Who*.[34]

Notes

1. See also Jon Burlingame, *TV's Biggest Hits: The Story of Television Themes from 'Dragnet' to 'Friends'* (New York, 1996), p. 12.
2. Janet K. Halfyard, 'Boldly Going: Music and Cult TV', in Stacey Abbott (ed.) *The Cult TV Book* (London, 2010), p. 126.
3. Gold interviewed in Matt Bell, 'Murray Gold: Composing for *Doctor Who*', *Sound On Sound* 2007. Available at www.soundonsound.com/sos/jun07/articles/drwho.htm (accessed 17 June 2012).
4. Matt Hills, *Triumph of a Time Lord: Regenerating Doctor Who in the Twenty-First Century* (London, 2010), p. 179.
5. Hills, *Triumph of a Time Lord*, p. 183.
6. Kevin J. Donnelly, *The Spectre of Sound: Music in Film and Television* (London, 2005), p. 115.
7. Robyn J. Stilwell, 'Bad Wolf' – Leitmotif in *Doctor Who*', in James Deaville (ed.) *Music in Television*, (London, 2011), pp. 119–41.
8. Murray Gold, 'Murray Gold (*Doctor Who* composer) Interview'.
9. Ron W. Rodman, *Tuning In: American Narrative Television Music* (Oxford, 2010), p. 43.
10. Piers D. Britton, *TARDISbound: Navigating the Universes of Doctor Who* (London, 2011), pp. 3–4.
11. John Fiske, *Introduction to Communication Studies* (London, 1990), pp. 64–84; cited in Rodman: *Tuning In*, p. 39.
12. On film scores' contribution to generic categorisation see Timothy E. Scheurer, *Music and Mythmaking in Film: Genre and the Role of the Composer* (Jefferson, 2008); Robert S. Hatten, *Interpreting Musical Gestures, Topics, and Tropes: Mozart, Beethoven, Schubert* (Bloomington, IN, 2004), pp. 1–2.
13. Ron W. Rodman, ' "Coperattas", "Detecterns" and Space Operas – Music and Genre Hybridization in American Television', in James Deaville (ed.) *Music in Television* (London, 2011), p. 43.
14. Scheurer, *Music and Mythmaking in Film*, p. 50.
15. Hills, *Triumph of a Time Lord*, p. 181.
16. See, for example, Claudia Gorbman, *Unheard Melodies* (London, 1987); Royal S. Brown, *Overtones and Undertones: Reading Film Music* (Berkeley, 1994); Irwin Bazelon, *Knowing the Score: Notes on Film Music* (New York, 1975); Kathryn M. Kalinak, *Settling the Score: Music and the Classical Hollywood Film* (Wisconsin, 1992).
17. See Burlingame, *TV's Biggest Hits*; Deaville: *Music in Television* (London, 2011); Rodman: *Tuning In*.

18. Gorbman, *Unheard Melodies*, pp. 11–12.
19. Rodman, *Tuning In*, p. 49 referring to Jerrold Levinson, David Bordwell and Noel Carroll (eds) 'Film Music and Narrative Agency', in *Post-theory: Reconstructing Film Studies* (Madison, 1996), pp. 283–306.
20. Rodman, *Tuning In*, p. 43.
21. The fact that the audience (along with characters) hear alien tongues in English was first acknowledged in the classic series story 'The Masque of Mandragora' (1976) and more recently in the 'The End of the World' (2005).
22. Britton, *TARDISbound*, p. 25.
23. Dan Martin, 'Has *Doctor Who* Got Too Complicated?', *Guardian*, 20 September 2011. Available at www.guardian.co.uk/tv-and-radio/tvandradioblog/2011/sep/20/doctor-who-too-complicated (accessed 17 June 2012).
24. Helen Lewis-Hasteley, 'Is Time Up for *Doctor Who*?', *Observer*, 9 October 2011.
25. Britton, *TARDISbound*, p. 192.
26. Stilwell, 'Bad Wolf', p. 120. 'Leitmotifs' are musical gestures that once established in conjunction with a character, object, or situation can then allude to or represent these in their absence. The use of the very term 'leitmotif' is somewhat tenuous in the context of *Doctor Who*, given the way recurring motifs are repeatedly deployed but hardly developed. The term 'theme' seems more appropriate and is less laden with connotations of the concert music/opera sphere. For the purpose of this chapter, the terms 'leitmotif' and 'theme' can safely be used interchangeably.
27. Royal S. Brown, 'How Not to Think Film Music', *Music and the Moving Image* 1 (2008), pp. 2–18.
28. Rodman, *Tuning In*, p. 117.
29. Rodman, *Tuning In*, p. 115, citing C.W. Morris, *Signs, Language and Behavior* (New York, 1946), p. 351.
30. Rodman, *Tuning In*, p. 113.
31. Hollywood's 'Golden Age' lasted from the late 1920s until the early 1960s.
32. Marcia Landy, *Cinematic Uses of the Past* (Minneapolis, 1996), p. 111.
33. Hills, *Triumph of a Time Lord*, p. 194.
34. The editor wishes to acknowledge Professor Stanley C. Pelkey for raising the idea of Murray Gold providing a 'musical key' to River Song's identity. However, this chapter has expanded on his point and has used the idea to further a quite different argument.

PART FOUR

BEYOND THE EPISODES

10

HYPING *WHO* AND MARKETING THE STEVEN MOFFAT ERA

The Role of 'Prior Paratexts'

Matt Hills

Up to this point, this book has looked at what distinguishes the episodes of the Steven Moffat/Matt Smith era of *Doctor Who*. The Moffat era is distinguishable in other ways, however, for example through its density and range of paratexts. The casting of Matt Smith in the role of the Eleventh Doctor set the tone for what was to come, since news of this was broken via a special edition of *Doctor Who Confidential*, broadcast on 3 January 2009 at 5.35 p.m. (almost a year ahead of Smith's first diegetic appearance in 'The End of Time', Part Two). Rather than enacting its usual role – as a behind-the-scenes, making-of show transmitted on BBC3 immediately after each new BBC1 episode of *Doctor Who* – in this case the TV 'extra' became the main event; a stand-alone text aimed at maximising publicity for the announcement of a brand new Doctor.

More keenly than ever before, *Doctor Who* under Moffat's tenure has become a focal point for activities of official marketing, publicity and online brand extension. The first post-Tennant series in 2010 was even accompanied by a promotional bus tour of various schools across the UK, and as Frank Collins notes, the marketing activities surrounding Moffat's *Who* have been many and varied:

> Moffat and his producers oversaw: the distribution of 3D cinema trailers; a BBC Outreach tour to launch the new series and screen the first episode 'The Eleventh Hour' to local schoolchildren in Belfast, Inverness, Sunderland, Salford and Northampton; a major promotion for the series in America; three newly developed, downloadable computer game episodes … two BBC Proms featuring the music of composer Murray Gold; and a touring arena show *Doctor Who Live*.[1]

To this list we might add *The Doctor Who Experience*, an interactive exhibition again involving 3D cinema, as well as various BFI Southbank events to promote the show. Some of these, such as the downloadable games, *Doctor Who Live* and *The Doctor Who Experience*, will be returned to in Neil Perryman's chapter. But this helps us realise that although some of these types of promotional activities surrounded the Russell T Davies era, there has been an intensification of the show's marketing linked to its 2010 re-branding. In what follows, I will consider a range of *Doctor Who* 'paratexts'.

Paratexts: Definitions

The concept of paratextuality was introduced and explored in a literary context by Gerard Genette in his book *Paratexts: Thresholds of Interpretation*, translated into English in 1997. Genette argues that any literary work

> is rarely presented in an unadorned state, unreinforced and unaccompanied by a certain number of … other productions, such as an author's name, a title, a preface, illustrations. And although we do not always know whether these productions are to be regarded as belonging to the text, in any case they surround it and extend it, precisely in order to present it, in the usual sense of this verb but also in the strongest sense: to make present, to ensure the text's presence in the world, its 'reception' and consumption.[2]

Genette calls this the 'paratext', viewing it not as a boundary but rather as a threshold, 'a zone between text and off-text, a zone not only of transition but also of transaction: a privileged place of ... strategy, of an influence on the public'.[3] He goes on to define different modes of paratext, analytically separating the peritext and epitext. The peritext covers all paratextual elements within the same volume – title, preface, notes, and so on – whereas the epitext means 'distanced elements ... located outside the book'.[4] Genette observes that 'our "media" age has seen the proliferation of a type of discourse around texts'.[5] My focus is therefore more accurately on *Doctor Who*'s epitexts, although applying ideas taken from literary theory to contemporary television raises a number of questions.

Other writers have already begun this process of application, most notably Jonathan Gray in his *Show Sold Separately* (2010) which considers, amongst other things, trailers and spoilers as forms of paratext. With regards to Steven Moffat's *Doctor Who*, the subject of spoilers really requires its own dedicated study.[6] My focus in this case will instead be on official, industry-created or licensed paratexts rather than 'viewer-created' ones.[7] And even within this massive terrain, I will be tackling a subset of official paratexts, excluding merchandise such as Character Options toys (and myriad other products), and instead focusing on *promotional, marketing activity which precedes the broadcasting of Moffat's Doctor Who* rather than following in its wake (this also places *Doctor Who Confidential* outside my remit as well as, for example, the P.S. after the first five episodes of series seven updating the viewer about what happened to Rory's dad, Brian Williams). Appropriately enough for a series about time travel and 'timey wimey' scenarios, it remains important to consider the '*temporal* situation of the paratext',[8] and I am restricting myself to '*prior* paratexts'[9] in this instance. Even this distinction becomes somewhat blurred, though, since *Doctor Who*'s contemporary promotion involves publicising clips from each episode at the BBC *Doctor Who* website[10] before broadcast, meaning that excerpts from 'the text' arguably become prior paratexts in their own right. Clips from *Doctor Who Confidential* have also been officially made available before its broadcast, converting extracts from a post-broadcast paratext into online prior paratexts. There is thus a kind of paratextual time travel at work here, with texts and '*later* paratexts'[11] retooled as 'prior paratexts', in Genette's terms.

Given the massive volume of textual analysis accumulating around *Doctor Who*, including textual studies focused on the Moffat era,[12] it is perhaps surprising that less attention has been given to the show's paratexts. This relative absence might suggest that scholars have viewed paratextual material as secondary, and as subordinated to the TV programme. But given the industrial importance of marketing *Who* – especially after the loss of a highly successful Doctor and production team – as well as the intense scrutiny to which prior paratexts are subjected by fan audiences, I would argue that it is necessary to push paratexts up the academic agenda. Paratexts represent a way for producers and marketing professionals to frame texts, setting up audience expectations and putting interpretive frameworks in play:

> We can regard paratexts as game-pieces in a game of interpretation. Many industry-created paratexts try to set limits for interpretation around a program, inviting audiences to look at a program in a certain way. And even within industry-created paratexts, we may see several players jockeying for power – a…marketing team may choose to highlight certain aspects of a show and…sell it as one entity, while the showrunner or stars may subsequently…insist on other interpretations.[13]

Paratexts are centrally concerned with delimiting parameters of audience interpretation, but they are also highly ludic – necessarily playing a game with audiences where certain narrative information is revealed, teased and withheld. As Jonathan Gray and Amanda Lotz have also noted, 'through paratextuality, the study of ' "television" often requires the study of many other media',[14] and with that in mind I shall begin by considering a cinema trailer and a magazine cover. Studying prior paratexts means considering 'the text's first initial outposts, in particular trailers…and hype'.[15] Hype surrounding Matt Smith as the Eleventh Doctor entered a new phase.

'Cool' *Doctor Who*: 3D, British and American Trailers

A change of lead actors synchronised with a change in production team was clearly going to be a moment of some anxiety for the BBC, keen for *Doctor Who*'s popularity to be maintained. As well as the 'Outreach' activity, series five was also promoted via a cinema trailer shown in 3D along with the UK release of Tim Burton's *Alice in Wonderland*, and made available in 2D online and on TV.[16] No production credits were given with this trailer, but Andrew Pixley's study of production documentation identifies it as '2010 Series Trailer: The Journey', made by Red Bee Media, directed by Michael Geoghegan, and overseen by Tony Pipes.[17] Elizabeth Evans has considered the fact that transmedia content – often prior paratexts, as in this case – will tend to go uncredited:

> the non-televisual transmedia elements of *Doctor Who* display no visible evidence of any individual author, no person is credited with writing, directing or producing the content despite someone clearly having done so. This lack only further positions the BBC as the author; they are the visible source of *Doctor Who* content and that source remains constant across the platforms of the transmedia narrative.[18]

Unlike TV episodes, then, this trailer does not carry markers of Steven Moffat's author-ity. It is corporately branded, sustaining a sense of *Doctor Who*'s ongoing consistency and identity as well as placing the BBC as a 'constant source' of production. By exnominating production credits, 'The Journey' obscures changes in production team and showrunner. The only visible changes are, instead, linked to a new Doctor–companion pairing. And even here, the BBC's strategic intent was one of smoothing over transition:

> The brief from the BBC for the launch was fundamentally to introduce Matt Smith as the Doctor. "The aim was to reassure and excite the fans so that, although the Doctor had changed, he was still the amazing character…we all know and love", explained creative Tony Pipes who helmed the project, "We wanted to invite the viewer on a journey with him – as you would be invited every week – and experience the familiar and the new with the new Doctor in total heroic control".[19]

Reassurance and familiarity are crucial watchwords in the BBC's brief. The new Doctor is thus viewed as an opportunity (to refresh the brand) and a threat (if change is too marked, then viewers may be frightened off). Familiarity is represented in the trailer via the brief appearance of a Dalek, although *not* the new redesign that would appear in 'Victory of the Daleks'. Ironically, then, *Doctor Who*'s monsters become the key element of non-scary, comforting familiarity in this prior paratext, as the Doctor also does battle with a Weeping Angel. This sequence is more extended than the Dalek's fleeting presence, however, and offers a way of implicitly recuperating Moffat's author-ity as showrunner, given that it was he who created the Angels in 'Blink'. The trailer also fuses the Eleventh Doctor's heroic omnipotence with quirky humour, repeating a long-standing joke:

> Amy (looking up at the stars in the sky): That one's flickering.
>
> The Doctor: Yeah, sorry, thought I'd fixed that.
>
> Amy: Who are you?
>
> The Doctor: I'm the Doctor.
>
> Amy: Doctor who?

Creating a sense of mystery and intrigue around the character, while reiterating the show's core identity – *Doctor Who*? – this also represents the Doctor comically, with a flickering star becoming akin to a faulty gizmo. The brief exchange of dialogue is again readable as Moffat-esque, shifting audience expectations via comedic incongruity, and drawing on heightened, snappy, dialogue almost as a special effect in its own right.

'The Journey' then depicts Amy and the Doctor being drawn into a vortex seemingly located under the ground on which they've been lying. As such, the geography depicted in the trailer is repeatedly impossible. Along with this fracturing of the earth, a Silurian warrior mask bursts out of the ground at the very end of the trailer. Such effects evidently aim to show off the presence of 3D, 'enhanced through the layering of objects and ... unexpected intrusion ... into the frontal plane'.[20] Although the Silurian's appearance from underground nominally fits into diegetic continuity, 'The Journey' is more interested in generating 3D's sense of 'moving through space' rather than representing a plausible environment.[21]

Appropriately enough, given that the trailer was shown in cinemas with *Alice in Wonderland*,

> [the] idea for the trailer was to take a page from the classic 1865 children's fantasy *Alice's Adventures in Wonderland* and have the Doctor take both the viewers and his new companion Amy 'down the rabbit hole'. ... [Using] one of the most iconic images from *Doctor Who*, the time vortex ... "We aimed to make something breathtaking and visually stunning but also something that looked 100% *Doctor Who*", commented Tony [Pipes].[22]

Realist space is thus fragmented both in line with a fairy-tale sensibility, and in line with deploying 3D as 'visually stunning'. While downplaying the newness of the Eleventh Doctor via familiar monsters, and seeking to reassure audiences that the show will continue to be '100 per cent' BBC *Doctor Who*, the trailer also promotes a sense of *Doctor Who*'s now-ness. 3D is an effect very much of the moment, having risen to prominence since James Cameron's *Avatar* (2009), thus connoting 'state-of-the-art', up-to-date visuality. And while the time vortex may signify *Doctor Who* as a brand, it also offers the possibility of 'intensifying motion [and] depth cues'[23] thereby enabling the 3D illusion to operate more effectively.

Before any 3D effect kicks in, however, the image of the Doctor and Amy lying side-by-side in a field draws on another intertext altogether. It is reminiscent of the first *Twilight* film (2008) and its well-known scene where Bella lies down beside Edward in an idyllic rural setting. Arguably, this intertext is stronger in the trailer than *Alice*, and like the use of 3D, it aims to integrate *Doctor Who* into 'cool' popular culture that is 'of the moment' for younger audiences. Although 'The Journey' is perhaps more *Twilight* than *Alice*, it is unsurprisingly the latter which is nominated in production discourse, carrying a sense of 'classic' English cultural value. This trailer isn't really about an 1865 intertext, though: it reassures audiences in an overdetermined manner, defusing change by combining 'iconic images' (Dalek/Weeping Angel/vortex) with intertexts and connotations of popular-cultural now-ness (*Twilight*/3D technology). Drawing on *Twilight* implies romantic possibilities between Amy and the Doctor, and though the series does not ultimately make good on this, Amy's sexuality and desire for the Doctor do become a key aspect of the Moffat era.

3D was also linked with a series of non-TV paratexts surrounding series five and six; the standard edition series five DVD box set had a lenticular 3D-effect cover, while the limited edition release of series six also included four lenticular 3D cards. *SFX* magazine 194 (May 2010) promoted the beginning of the Moffat era with an 'Exclusive 3D cover', and *Doctor Who Adventures* followed suit with a 3D cover on issue 173: an 'awesome collector's edition ... [t]o celebrate the explosive end of Series 5'.[24] Three-D has evidently provided one strategy for positioning the TV series as more than 'ordinary' television – as visually impressive as well as of-the-moment. Akin to *Doctor Who Adventures*, *SFX*'s editor Dave Bradley linked its 3D cover with paratextual discourses of celebration, but also stressed 3D's 'exclusivity':

> the internet is not the natural predator of the printed page. ... [M]agazines excel at the delivery of physical commemorative material, like this month's amazing 3D *Doctor Who* cover. We're celebrating the Eleventh Doctor's arrival on our screens with this unique lenticular photograph. ... That's a picture we took ourselves ... and it's a treatment that you won't find anywhere else.[25]

Just as 3D movies aim to make cinema attendance essential – combating piracy and illegal filesharing/downloading – so too does Bradley use 3D to valorise the consumption of 'physical' media. But quite unlike 'The Journey' cinema trailer, which aims to connote now-ness while defusing threatening novelty, as an unofficial prior paratext *SFX* links its 3D cover to novelty: '"It's the first 3D *Doctor Who* cover"', Jon [Coates, Art Editor] tells us. '"It's new technology, and the new Doctor seemed like the perfect opportunity to try it out"'.[26] New Doctor; new 3D.

Tapping into a commercial, media zeitgeist emphasising 3D's distinction and cultural value, Moffat's *Who* aims for a specific profile as immersive quality TV rather than merely being 'new'; novelty is a problem to be overcome in the rebrand, meaning that change has to be carefully managed. The type of 'now-ness' and 'cool' that association with 3D cinema can bring is also significant, given that the Moffat era refuses to align itself with participatory, social media (it was a desire to promote

Sherlock which brought Moffat to Twitter, and not the marketing of *Doctor Who*). Likewise, *Doctor Who* during Moffat's tenure has not yet opened with a Twitter hashtag publicised on-screen, as did BBC3's (2011) paranormal drama *The Fades*. *Doctor Who* could have been re-positioned in 2010 as social-media-friendly in order to demarcate it as 'of-the-moment', but such a strategy was evidently rejected as out of line with the showrunner's target aesthetics – storytelling that the viewer has to concentrate on, be absorbed in and pay close attention to. Moffat has emphasised this in prior paratexts accompanying series six, for example in a *Radio Times'* interview preceding 'A Good Man Goes to War':

> "you have to pay attention", says Moffat severely. He sounds like a teacher, and then I remember he was an English teacher in his 20s. "You can't watch it when you are doing the ironing. And you certainly can't watch it when you are tweeting. You have to sit down and focus, and a child audience certainly does that."[27]

Such paratexts don't so much enter into a 'game' of interpretation as attempt to spell out its rules, and the Moffat era has perhaps appropriated 3D as a result of *Doctor Who's* perceived non-alignment with social media, leaving cinematic/lenticular 3D as one possible strategy for connoting 'now-ness'.

The showrunner's paratextual emphasis on close reading is also reinforced by specially shot teasers promoting series six. Rather than deploying 3D, these promotional paratexts – again overseen by Tony Pipes – instead incited audience immersion by acting like a televisual game of spot the difference: 'Two versions ... [were] made, one with and one without a Silent, to make people question what they had seen and create a buzz around the forthcoming episodes.'[28] This time directed by Jason Thomson,[29] the present/absent teasers paratextually guided audiences by rewarding 'forensic fandom',[30] or careful scrutiny of the images for clues. Rather than merely building buzz, this marketing reinforces Moffat's author-ity, and the show's post-2010 aesthetics, even where the flesh-and-blood showrunner himself has little or no involvement in constructing such campaigns (the production credits include BBC One's Marketing manager, Anna Skelton, and Brand Executive Daniel Buchuk, but there is no writing/concept/exec-producer credit given to Moffat).[31] Though Gray and

Lotz remind us that a 'marketing team may choose to highlight certain aspects of a show...while the showrunner...may...insist on other interpretations',[32] it is equally possible that marketing can successfully reinforce the showrunner's preferred interpretive game, as occurs here.

However, the marketing of the Moffat era is not restricted to BBC One or Red Bee Media strategies. *Who* has been hyped differently in overseas markets such as America. While Simone Knox earlier argued that Moffat's *Who* is broadcast in the Anglophiliac environment of BBC America and that it reclaims heritage as cool, promotion in the US lends Matt Smith's Doctor an air of conventional masculine heroism that is somewhat at odds with his portrayal of the role, so as to draw in as wide an audience as possible. The American version of 'The Journey' trailer for series five features the Doctor telling Amy, 'FOLLOW ME', in a commanding, authoritative tone. Series six was also marketed in the US via a variant promotional poster not used in the UK. Deploying the strap-line 'TRUST YOUR DOCTOR', this marketing implied US ownership of the lead character, positioning Matt Smith's Doctor – wielding his sonic screwdriver as if it were some kind of weapon – as a cool, enigmatic action hero. Facing an open road, picked out by low-key lighting, and set against ominous dark clouds, the Eleventh Doctor is given a noir-ish tinge, recontextualising him within a history of American pop-cultural heroes. Significantly, the Doctor here is not sporting his stetson, which might have appeared touristic or inauthentic to US audiences. *Doctor Who*'s popularity in the US has indeed been attested to by its being featured on the cover of *Entertainment Weekly* in 2012.

In the next section, I want to consider a range of other 'prior paratexts' that, like the use of specially shot trailers, have been routinised across the Moffat era (online prequels/*Radio Times* covers and episode guides/'Production Notes' in *Doctor Who Magazine*). These iterate promotional practices established under the previous showrunner and production team, but like the specially shot trailers I've already examined, they also reinforce specific interpretations of Steven Moffat's *Doctor Who*. Along with routinised paratexts, I will also address exceptional cases where cracks have opened up between production/fan discourses, and where normative limits to the show's paratextual positioning are highlighted.

Routinised and Exceptional 'Prior Paratexts': The Prequels, Series 'Fnarg' and *Gay Times*

The 2006 series of *Doctor Who* used 'TARDISodes' as teasers for each episode, these being designed for audiences to watch on mobile phones (also being available on the web). Each TARDISode diegetically extended the following TV episode, offering an extra scene akin to a pre-credits sequence. The experiment was deemed unsuccessful, however, and discontinued until series six when diegetic 'prior paratexts' were finally returned to, this time purely as a form of online promotion. Rather than having to consider 'parameters of [a mobile phone's] miniature screen ... [and] the nature of the phonisode as an emerging genre',[33] each 'online teaser'[34] could instead function as an additional, conventionally televisual sequence. These were labelled 'prequels', making explicit their status as a lead-in to the primary TV text, being prior to its narrative events and its time of broadcast.

In common with other online, transmedia content, the prequels lacked production credits,[35] although Andrew Pixley confirms that the first prequel was written by Steven Moffat, whilst naming no writer for the prequel to 'The Curse of the Black Spot' (2010: 37 and 50). Prequels for 'The Impossible Astronaut',[36] 'The Curse of the Black Spot',[37] 'A Good Man Goes to War',[38] 'Let's Kill Hitler'[39] and 'The Wedding of River Song'[40] were made available online. Four of these were the split series' opening/closing episodes written by Steven Moffat and presumably deserving of 'special' promotion in order to build audience anticipation. The online prequels can therefore be read as paratextually contextualising select stories as 'event' episodes given their place in the series' story arc. The presence of a prequel for 'Curse of the Black Spot' is puzzling, however, since it doesn't fit this predominant (para)textual logic. Unlike other prequels, though, the second amounts to little more than a voice-over, representing a playful intertextual reference to *Star Trek* since it involves pirate Captain Avery (Hugh Bonneville) recounting his 'Captain's Journal' or Captain's Log. Avery's account is effectively a mood piece, building a sense of impending doom and dread, but empty shots of the episode's setting offer relatively little to hold the viewer's attention.

Otherwise, the prequels tend to function by posing key narrative questions. 'The Impossible Astronaut' reveals one of the Silents, but out of focus in the background. As well as this lure, the prequel sets up the mystery of how a young girl could have gained access to the President of the United States, Richard Nixon. This model of economy, condensing together diegetic puzzles, is matched by the prequel to 'A Good Man Goes to War' which focuses on the character of Dorium, and hints that Amy's baby may, in fact, be the Doctor's. Though the possibility is ultimately textually discounted, this paratext knowingly provokes fan speculation over Melody Pond's paternity, helping to intensify the audience's anticipation of major plot developments. By contrast, the prequel to 'Let's Kill Hitler' is far less focused on story-arc progression, instead offering a minimalist emotional scene set entirely in the TARDIS. Like the first prequel – and like practices of fanfic – this fills a gap in the associated episode, this time by showing one of Amy's phone calls referred to in 'Let's Kill Hitler'. It also presents a twist in its final shot, revealing that the Doctor has heard Amy's plea for help. The final prequel of series six also offers a reveal of sorts in its closing shot, since it shows River Song wearing an eye patch, posing the question as to what her Kovarian-esque appearance means. It also shows the Silence under surveillance in 'Area 52', implying some sort of parallel-world version of the Area 51 we see in the series' opening episode.

Although these prequels are typically structured around the series' hermeneutic code – setting up mysteries – they are rarely televisually compelling; 'Black Spot' and 'Hitler' consist almost entirely of cutaways (to parts of the 'good ship Fancy', and to the TARDIS console). Of the sequence of five prequels, only 'The Impossible Astronaut' and 'A Good Man Goes to War' include significant teasers: the glimpse of a new monster, and the implication that Melody is the Doctor's unearthly child. And the final shot of the 'Wedding' prequel – made available on Saturday 24 September 2011– markedly fails to offer dedicated (fan) followers of *Doctor Who* paratextuality anything new, since an image of River Song sporting an eye patch had already been included in the series six part two trailer, available prior to 27 August.[41] Thus, although the prequels reinforce a notion that key show-runner-written episodes are TV 'events', they do so with limited paratextual success. Not always sparking significant diegetic puzzles, they are sometimes teasers without much of a tease.

Series seven adopted a rather different approach to the online provision of prequels. Here, it was the series launch that was framed by a sequence of five daily *Pond Life* episodes released Monday – Friday at bbc.co.uk/doctorwho before 'Asylum of the Daleks' was broadcast on BBC1, Saturday 1 September 2012.[42] Showing the home life of Amy and Rory Pond intersecting with the Doctor's adventures, these vignettes were credited to a producer (Denise Paul), director (Saul Metzstein) and writer (Chris Chibnall), placing them closer to 'textual', canonical TV *Who* rather than the uncredited transmedia content discussed by Elizabeth Evans. *Pond Life's* third part references one of classic *Doctor Who's* most infamous paratexts – Jon Pertwee's comment about encountering 'a Yeti sitting on your loo'[43] – by comedically depicting an 'Ood on the loo'. Writer Chris Chibnall thus draws on fan knowledge to blend very different paratextual eras in *Doctor Who's* history.

As well as *Pond Life*, series seven also used prequels to 'Asylum of the Daleks' and 'A Town Called Mercy', which were made available commercially, at first via the US iTunes site, and then via UK iTunes. Although fans have become accustomed to DVD-only additional content, released many months after TV broadcast, the fact that these prequels were commercially available so close to transmission made them somewhat controversial in fan circles (as did their initial availability only to US audiences). Significantly, also, although labelled 'prequels', these were released *after* the episodes had been screened and so fall outside my main concern in this chapter to examine 'prior paratexts'. Steven Moffat authored the 'Asylum of the Daleks' prequel, but did not significantly add to the episode's diegesis, instead showing an incident the televised episode told viewers about (the Doctor's summons to Skaro). Likewise, the 'Town Called Mercy' prequel added little to the narrative universe of the TV episode. Perhaps reflecting BBC anxiety about directly commercialised story content, then, these pay-to-view paratexts displayed a high degree of narrative redundancy.

Along with specially shot trailers and prequels – aimed at framing *Doctor Who's* launch and key episodes as 'event' television – promotion of the Moffat era has followed a number of other established patterns. Like Russell T Davies before him, Moffat has written a regular 'Production Notes' column for *Doctor Who Magazine*, and the *Radio Times* has also been given exclusive content, with Moffat contributing an 'ultimate episode guide' to each new run of stories.[44] The *Radio Times* has also frequently put new *Who* on its cover, with some of these paratexts becoming textually celebrated in their own right. For example, the 30 April–6 May 2005 'Vote Dalek' cover from the Russell T Davies era, made available as a poster, was voted the best British magazine front cover of all time[45] and was itself intertextually cited by the 17–23 April 2010 collectable cover which featured three variants: red, yellow and blue redesigned Daleks from 'Victory of the Daleks'.[46] While promoting the Daleks' return in the 2010 series, this paratext primarily referenced the earlier, highly successful *Radio Times* paratext (which in turn referred back to a 1964 episode of *Doctor Who*). *Who*'s promotional paratexts have thus occasionally taken on a life of their own as award-winning, merchandised texts. Akin to *Pond Life*'s 'Ood on the loo', 'Vote Dalek' is a paratext-referencing-paratext, indicating how paratextuality can possess a sedimented and specific history rather than merely being an ephemeral prop to TV drama.

However, the first part of series seven went a step further than offering the *Radio Times* cover as a poster. Instead, specially created poster art was made available online for each of the five episodes.[47] Reinforcing a logic of 'event TV', where each week's story was paratextually represented as if it were a film with its own poster, *Doctor Who Magazine* #451 and #452 also published variant cover designs, each promoting a specific episode, complete with movie-style 'BBC WALES PRESENTS' credits. Like the series five cinema trailer ushering in 'the Moffat era', this strategy again paratextually placed *Doctor Who* in a cinematic rather than televisual paradigm. Whilst 'film poster' promotion makes sense in relation to spectacle-heavy, high-concept *Who* ('Asylum of the Daleks'; 'Dinosaurs on a Spaceship') and episodes intertextually citing film genre (the Western-themed 'Town Called Mercy'; noir-ish 'Angels Take Manhattan'), it arguably clashed with the character based 'Power of Three'. Here, the TV text and its movie poster paratexts seemed poorly aligned, with the concept of a 'slow invasion' challenging *Doctor Who*'s archetypal, action-adventure temporality being difficult to reduce to promotional poster art. For instance, the notion of a gradual countdown is wholly absent from the cubes depicted in the episode's online poster, which instead all show the number three (reiterating the episode's title). Monolithically rendering series seven as 'blockbuster' storytelling, these paratexts fail to engage with key aspects of *Doctor Who*'s broadcast textuality, glossing over the series' multiple tones, varied narrative structures and differing relationships to filmic intertextuality.

While the *Radio Times* is a regular supporter of the show, major news stories such as the casting for the 2011 Christmas Special are typically entrusted to UK tabloids, reinforced by the BBC's own *Doctor Who* website.[48] At the same time, special access has been granted to broadsheet journalists in order to secure in-depth feature coverage, e.g. Neil Midgeley's account of shadowing the programme's production, published in the *Saturday Telegraph* on 13 March 2010.[49] Press releases tend to be synchronised with location filming so that official images and copy are used in the media rather than 'paparazzi'-style photos captured by fans. These different strands of PR strategy therefore routinely aim to achieve the following: targeting the dedicated fan audience; recognising the heritage and history of *Who* (and how it has been promoted in the past, e.g. giving the *Radio Times* a privileged role in marketing); targeting the 'mass' audience as well as differentiated readerships for broadsheets/tabloids; controlling and securing the advance information that appears in print media/online.

As I have noted elsewhere, a form of 'info-war' circulates around the programme's promotion, since spoiler-phile fans will seek information on *Doctor Who* stories far ahead of official press releases and announcements.[50] For example, the website *Doctor Who Spoilers* revealed River Song's true identity on 27 April 2011, just a few days after series six had premiered on the 23rd (see 'The Companion's Daughter').[51] Although Steven Moffat was duty bound not to draw further attention to this breach of *Doctor Who*'s production security – and significant loss of PR control over 'prior paratexts' – it seems likely that it nevertheless informed his decision to go on the offensive, and attack fansourced spoilers in a BBC interview: 'You can imagine how much I hate them. ... It's only fans who do this, or they call themselves fans. ... I wish they could go and be fans of something else.'[52]

By contrast, the launch of series seven proceeded without key spoilers circulating among online fandom. Despite a BFI preview screening on 14 August 2012, Jenna-Louise Coleman's radically unusual role in 'Asylum of the Daleks' remained wholly absent from series seven's prior paratexts. The media maintained the illusion that Coleman's first appearance would be in the 2012 Christmas special. However, in a media context when *Who* is so intently promoted and hyped, its paratexts need strong, clear and immediate hooks for fans and general viewers alike. Arguably, 'Asylum of the Daleks' only succeeded in obscuring Coleman's debut because it used an alternative paratextual strategy, focusing on the involvement of every type of Dalek ever. Steven Moffat has conceded that this narrative ploy was 'mostly about publicity'.[53] It promises enough scale, spectacle (and story potential) to appear readable as convincing, appropriate hype. Keeping huge spoilers – and silencing industry-standard paratexts such as those surrounding the introduction of a new lead actress – means making other huge paratextual promises instead, given the institutional need for series' marketing.

Given the routinised, co-ordinated nature of much of *Doctor Who*'s contemporary marketing, leaks such as April 2011's 'Rivergate' and Moffat's denigration of certain audience-generated prior paratexts are notable exceptions to business-as-usual. However, other prior paratexts also become exceptional, either by virtue of fracturing a coherent, overall marketing strategy, or by focusing on types of information not otherwise circulating in media promotion. As an example of the former case I'll consider Moffat's jokes about series nomenclature in *Doctor Who Magazine*, and then address a promotional interview in *Gay Times* as an instance of the latter.

Writing in *Doctor Who Magazine* 417, Moffat introduced 'the Writers of Series Five!', but then began to question whether this was the correct term:

> Or [Series] One! Or 11! Or 31! Or 32, if you count the Specials as a series, and why not! Or 33, if you count the Paul McGann era – or movie – as a series! Look, I'll start again. ... [T]he writers of Series Fnarg (it's a whole new number – I haven't decided yet, but I think it's even).[54]

This humorous debate nevertheless gestures to an 'issue which remained inconsistent during production'[55] – series numbering. According to archivist Andrew Pixley's account, BBC branding and licensing were concerned that '"Series Five" …made *Doctor Who* look like an ageing brand, so it was decided that this term would not be used for production purposes or in press releases'.[56] Instead, Series 31 was used to demonstrate the show's 'longevity' and to emphasise that the current production was part of the same programme which began in 1963, whilst series one demonstrated 'a fresh era for a new Doctor'.[57] Indeed, shooting scripts for the 2010 series were headed '*Doctor Who* 1' and then the episode number,[58] with the next series' scripts being identified as '*Doctor Who* 11–2'[59] followed by episode numbers from 1 to 13. (No differentiation was made between parts one and two of the 2011 series.)

By referring to the nonsensical, parodic series 'Fnarg', Moffat seemingly satirises disputes over numbering, but at the same time he also draws attention to and highlights these disagreements. His 'Production Notes' discussion of series six likewise mocks the notion of deciding a series number once-and-for-all, drawing on a managerial/marketing discourse of 'meetings':

> [T]ime to meet the writers of Series…um. Six and a bit? Six part two? Seven? Thirty-Two? Or is it Thirty-Three? Do the Specials count as a series, and if not, why not? What did we decide at the last meeting? Actually, never mind, I think I got it right the first time…here come the writers of Series Um.[60]

In fact, inconsistent, fractured 'prior paratexts' disputing the identification of series five/one/thirty-one/fnarg were eventually overwritten by the BBC DVD of 'THE COMPLETE FIFTH SERIES'. The 'Fnarg' *DWM* column shows that cracks had started to appear between BBC marketing and fandom's commonsensical view that the Moffat era was series five. As Gray and Lotz note, in relation to paratexts 'we may see several players jockeying for power – a…marketing team…and…the showrunner. …Audiences are then able to play this game themselves'.[61] Where series five was concerned, apparent disagreements between marketing, the showrunner and (some) fans in 'prior paratexts' were repaired via 'later paratexts'. Moffat's Fnarg/

Um 'Production Notes' remain unusual prior paratexts because they comedically highlight and subvert debate between different industry and audience 'players' rather than reinforcing an official, branding/marketing line.

Gay Times stands as another example of an exceptional prior paratext. In a series of interviews promoting the 2010 series, the magazine discussed Steven Moffat's sexuality, as well as that of executive producer Piers Wenger, and the programme's appeal to gay fans. None of these subjects have formed part of the show's routinised paratextual meanings, and the discursive introduction of sexuali*ties* is thus striking. For instance, Moffat is asked about the fact that he is the first 'straight producer since 1979':

> I know all the *Doctor Who* fan facts. I was thinking 'first straight man here'. What I loved best about that was when there was quite a lot of press about Amy's short skirts and they're all saying 'that's Steven Moffat ...'. It's not. It's the bloody gays! It's got nothing to do with me! Like I spend a lot of time in the costume truck...I think I came up with...gayer jokes [than Russell T Davies]...But I think the sexuality I share in common with Russell is that we're *Doctor Who* fans! I think that's 90% of our brains.[62]

In the very moment that this prior paratext acknowledges sexuality, it seeks to contest any straightforward reading of it, with textual outcomes supposedly attributable to heterosexual desire being an outcome of 'gay' competencies in costume design, and with Moffat's writing outdoing Davies's for 'beard' jokes. Moffat instead curiously subsumes debates over sexuality into a catch-all category of 'fandom', proposing *Doctor Who* fandom as a 'sexuality' of its own. He thus repeatedly destabilises the concept, and the cultural politics, of homosexual difference by queering any homo/hetero binary. By contrast, the magazine's interview with Piers Wenger directly nominates the Doctor as not a 'stereotypical heterosexual male', seeking to explain the show's appeal to the gay audience:

> I just love the Doctor's kind of rebellious streak, completely on his own terms. ... [H]e's not a conventional action hero and he doesn't approach the fight with a traditional stereotypical heterosexual male gung-ho macho approach. He does it all with

brains and style and brilliance and that is probably what a lot of gay men respond to, it's certainly what I respond to.[63]

Moffat and Wenger thus tackle the explicit nomination of sexuality in very different ways. The former deconstructs or queers homo/hetero binaries while seeking to unify *Doctor Who* fandom (and drawing on specific stereotypes of gay culture); the latter posits homo/hetero binaries, reading the Doctor as non-heteronormative. What the two executive producers share in these prior paratexts, however, is an emphasis on *Doctor Who* as a queering force. As Piers Britton has argued, the 'Eleventh Doctor queers the *new series* precisely because of the potency of the "straight" precedent established under Russell T Davies's tutelage ... marking the Ninth and Tenth Doctor as clearly if chastely heterosexual'.[64] Yet this repositioning of Matt Smith's Doctor as eccentrically, blithely unaware of sexuality, and its 'destabilization of straight masculinity ... is hardly surprising: ambiguous sexuality and gender powerfully signify the "alien" ... because our society is so rigidly heteronormative'.[65] The Moffat era may have reintroduced 'strangeness' to the Doctor's depiction, yet this queering seems to paradoxically and problematically uphold heteronormativity.

Britton's analysis of the Moffat/Smith era introduces such topics within a critical, academic paratext; discussion of sexualities is extremely rare in *Doctor Who*'s prior paratexts and marketing. *Gay Times* represents a predictable but still important exception to the show's paratextual exnomination of sexualities. Steven Moffat says to interviewer Darren Scott, 'tell your gays they're in safe hands with me',[66] but such discourses are very much restricted to a target-marketed publication rather than being allowed any wider industrial and public circulation. *Doctor Who*'s prior paratexts carefully play a 'game of interpretation'[67] within the norms and parameters of hegemonic culture. Britton expresses surprise at the 'mainstream success for Smith's more theatricalized and queer version of the character',[68] but this challenge to the show's 'relentless branding'[69] is, I would argue, exnominated and contained by 'mainstream' marketing paratexts. There is thus a powerfully hegemonic, normative dimension to much of *Doctor Who*'s ('child-friendly') hype which exceptional paratexts such as the (2010) *Gay Times* promotion can serve to highlight.

Conclusion

In this chapter I've considered a range of 'prior paratexts' from the Moffat era, focusing on official marketing and hype that occurs in advance of the TV show's broadcast. By definition this is a vast field, and so I have focused on specific, key paratexts, for example specially shot trailers for series five and six, both in Britain and the US, and routinised promotion via the *Radio Times* and *Doctor Who Magazine*. I have also considered online teasers or story 'prequels' as well as exceptional paratexts where conflicts between different 'players' in the game of *Doctor Who*'s branding have surfaced, or where normative paratextual delimitations of the series' meanings have been challenged.

In the corpus of paratexts I've addressed here, however, Steven Moffat's status as showrunner and his authorial 'signature' are generally reinforced. This is very much true of the British series five and six trailers, even though these are typically uncredited and Moffat's direct involvement in their production is hard to gauge. By contrast, the numbering of series one/thirty-one/five/ Fnarg indicates how cracks had opened up between production/ fan/branding discourses, with these finally being closed via the shift from 'series one' or 'thirty-one' in prior paratexts to 'series five' for the DVD release. As such, paratexts can alter how the TV series is viewed, engaging with fan discourses in some cases, or seeking to silence certain forms of interpretation while typically reinforcing how Moffat's *Who* should be read – as 'cool', of-the-moment, and as a sequence of 'event' episodes (premieres/ finales) deserving audience attentiveness. While there's no single role played by prior paratexts – given their multiplicity – nevertheless paratextual patterns have been drawn around, and in relation to, the Moffat era. And while the 'later paratext' *Doctor Who Confidential* was ultimately axed as part of BBC cost-cutting after series six, *Doctor Who*'s prior paratexts show no sign of abating in range, scope or significance.

Notes

1. Frank Collins, *Doctor Who: The Pandorica Opens Exploring the Worlds of the Eleventh Doctor* (Cambridge, 2010), p. 1.

2. Gerard Genette, *Paratexts: Thresholds of Interpretation* (Cambridge, 1997), p. 1.
3. Ibid., p. 2.
4. Ibid., p. 5.
5. Ibid., p. 3.
6. Matt Hills, *Triumph of a Time Lord: Regenerating Doctor Who in the Twenty-First Century* (London, 2010); Matt Hills, 'A Showrunner Goes to War: *Doctor Who* and the Almost Fans?', 6 June 2011. Available at http://blog.commarts. wisc.edu/2011/06/06/a-showrunner-goes-to-war-doctor-who-and-the-almost-fans/ (accessed 24 September 2011).
7. Jonathan Gray, *Show Sold Separately: Promos, Spoilers and Other Media Paratexts* (New York, 2010), p. 143.
8. Genette, *Paratexts*, p. 5.
9. Ibid.
10. BBC *Doctor Who* site. Available at www.bbc.co.uk/doctorwho.
11. Genette, *Paratexts*, p. 6.
12. Collins, *Doctor Who*; Alec Charles, 'The Crack of Doom: The Uncanny Echoes of Steven Moffat's *Doctor Who*', *Science Fiction Film and Television* 4/1 (2011), p. 1–23; Matt Hills, 'New New *Doctor Who*: Brand Regeneration', 19 April 2010. Available at http://blog.commarts.wisc.edu/2010/04/19/new-new-doctor-who-brand-regeneration/ (accessed 24 September 2011); Matt Hills, 'Steven Moffat's *Doctor Who*: Challenging the Format Theorem?', 2 May 2011. Available at http://blog.commarts.wisc.edu/2011/05/02/steven-moffats-doctor-who-challenging-the-format-theorem/ (accessed 24 September 2011).
13. Jonathan Gray and Amanda Lotz, *Television Studies* (Cambridge, 2012), p. 134.
14. Gray and Lotz, *Television Studies*, p. 135.
15. Gray, *Show Sold Separately*, p. 47.
16. BBC *Doctor Who* site. Available at www.bbc.co.uk/doctorwho/newyear/ (accessed 1 April 2010).
17. Andrew Pixley, *The Doctor Who Companion: The Eleventh Doctor Volume 1* (2010), p. 39.
18. Elizabeth Evans, *Transmedia Television: Audiences, New Media and Daily Life* (London, 2011), p. 33.
19. Pixley, *The Doctor Who Companion Volume 1*, p. 39.
20. Alison Griffiths, *Shivers Down Your Spine: Cinema, Museums, and the Immersive View* (New York, 2008), p. 103.
21. Ibid., p. 104.
22. Pixley, *The Doctor Who Companion Volume 1*, p. 39.
23. Griffiths, *Shivers Down Your Spine*, p. 103.
24. Moray Laing, 'What's Inside', *Doctor Who Adventures* 173 (2010), p. 3.
25. Dave Bradley, 'Brave New World', *SFX* 194 (2010), p. 3.
26. Nick Setchfield, 'The First Eleven', *SFX* 194 (2010), p. 59.
27. Moffat in Rosie Millard, 'Best Job in the Universe', *Radio Times*, 4–10 June 2011, p. 19.
28. Andrew Pixley, *The Doctor Who Companion: The Eleventh Doctor Volume 3* (2011), p. 36.
29. Ibid.

30. Jason Mittell, 'Lost in a Great Story: Evaluation in Narrative Television (and Television Studies)', in Roberta Pearson (ed.), *Reading Lost* (London, 2009), p. 128.
31. Pixley, *The Doctor Who Companion Volume 3*, p. 36.
32. Gray and Lotz, *Television Studies*, p. 134.
33. Charles Tryon, 'TV Time Lords: Fan Cultures, Narrative Complexity, and the Future of Science Fiction Television', in J Telotte (ed.) *The Essential Science Fiction Reader* (Lexington, 2008), p. 304.
34. Pixley, *The Doctor Who Companion Volume 3*, p. 37.
35. Evans, *Transmedia Television*, p. 33.
36. 'The Impossible Astronaut' prequel. Available at www.bbc.co.uk/doctor-who/dw/videos/p00fxf06 (accessed 22 April 2011).
37. 'The Curse of the Black Spot' prequel. Available at www.bbc.co.uk/doctor-who/dw/videos/p00gmybn (accessed 6 May 2011).
38. 'A Good Man Goes to War' prequel. Available at www.bbc.co.uk/doctor-who/dw/videos/p00h74x2 (accessed 3 June 2011).
39. 'Let's Kill Hitler' prequel. Available at www.bbc.co.uk/doctorwho/dw/videos/p00jthfd (accessed 26 August 2011).
40. 'The Wedding of River Song' prequel. Available at www.bbc.co.uk/doctor-who/dw/videos/p00kn2y6 (accessed 30 September 2011).
41. '*Doctor Who* Series Six: Part Two Trailer', 4 August 2011. Available at www.doctorwhonews.net/2011/08/dwn040811173008-doctor-who-series-six.html (accessed 4 August 2011).
42. www.bbc.co.uk/programmes/p00wqr12/features/pond-life (accessed 1 September 2012).
43. Tat Wood and Lawrence Miles, *About Time: The Unauthorised Guide to Doctor Who 1966–1969. Seasons 4 to 6* (IL, 2006), p. 163.
44. Steven Moffat, 'The Ultimate Episode Guide', *Radio Times*, 3–9 April 2010, pp. 20–1; Steven Moffat, 'The Ultimate Episode Guide', *Radio Times*, 16–22 April 2011, pp. 12–13; Steven Moffat, 'The Ultimate Episode Guide', *Radio Times*, 27 August–2 September 2011, pp. 12–13.
45. Nicole Martin, 'Vote Dalek Image Voted Best Magazine Cover of All Time', 29 September 2008. Available at www.telegraph.co.uk/news/3102812/Vote-Dalek-image-voted-best-magazine-cover-of-all-time.html (accessed 1 September 2011).
46. Mark Gatiss, 'Let battle begin again ...', *Radio Times*, 17–23 April 2010, p. 14.
47. www.denof geek.com/tv/doctor-who/22496/doctor-who-series-7-episode-posters.
48. 'Claire Skinner on Doctor Who at Christmas', 21 September 2011. Available at www.thesun.co.uk/sol/homepage/showbiz/tv/3825919/Claire-Skinner-on-Doctor-Who-at-Christmas.html (accessed 21 September 2011); BBC *Doctor Who* site Available at www.bbc.co.uk/doctorwho/dw/news/bulletin_110920_01/Christmas_Special_The_Stars (accessed 30 September 2011).
49. Neil Midgeley, 'Crunch Time', *Telegraph Magazine*, 13 March 2010, pp. 40–5.
50. Hills, *Triumph of a Time Lord*, p. 72.
51. Available at http://doctorwhospoilers.com/2011/the-2011-series/set-reports-and-photos (accessed 30 September 2011).

52. 'Doctor Who boss 'hates' fans who spoil show's secrets', 11 May 2011. Available at www.bbc.co.uk/news/entertainment-arts-13353367 (accessed 1 September 2011).
53. Moffat in Nick Setchfield, 'Doctor Who', *SFX* 226 (2012), p. 52.
54. Steven Moffat, 'Production Notes', *Doctor Who Magazine* 417 (2010), p. 4.
55. Pixley, *The Doctor Who Companion Volume 1*, p. 17.
56. Ibid.
57. Ibid.
58. Ibid., p. 23.
59. Pixley, *The Doctor Who Companion Volume 3*, p. 41.
60. Steven Moffat, 'Production Notes', *Doctor Who Magazine* 437 (2011), p. 6.
61. Gray and Lotz, *Television Studies*, p. 134.
62. Moffat quoted in Darren Scott, 'Look Who's Back', *Gay Times*, April 2010, p. 39.
63. Wenger quoted in Scott, 'Look Who's Back', p. 43.
64. Piers D. Britton, *TARDISbound: Navigating the Universes of Doctor Who* (London, 2011), p. 103.
65. Britton, *TARDISbound*, p. 108.
66. Moffat quoted in Scott, 'Look Who's Back', p. 39.
67. Gray and Lotz, *Television Studies*, p. 134.
68. Britton, *TARDISbound*, p. 108.
69. Ibid.

11

'OH, NO, THAT WON'T DO AT ALL.... IT'S RIDICULOUS!'

Observations on the *Doctor Who* Audience

Brigid Cherry

Viewers of a sensitive disposition might want to hide behind the sofa – *Doctor Who*'s back, complete with a new body as usual.[1]

Now get ready to duck behind the sofa.... The famous time lord returns to our screens for a Christmas day special and guess what, the Doctor looks a tad different.[2]

These almost identical introductions to news reports on the casting of Christopher Eccleston in the role of the Doctor prior to the return of *Doctor Who* to British television in 2005 and of David Tennant taking over the role illustrate two points about the perception of the programme within British popular culture. First, it is a newsworthy event when an actor is cast in the role. Second, it is impossible to avoid the linking of the series with its audience. One of the most iconic images that the series brings to mind, alongside the TARDIS, a Dalek, a sonic screwdriver and perhaps a very long scarf, is a delight-fully scared child watching from behind the sofa – a myth that both Channel 4 and the BBC reproduce in their introductions to the news segment. But this image gives us only a hint of the complexities of the audience, their reasons for viewing and their responses to both the narrative and to the extra-textual production contexts of the series.

We might, for example, expect viewers to grow accustomed to the current version of *Doctor Who*, or perhaps to have a favourite Doctor, companion or type of story that they are reluctant to let go of. Further, fan audiences are notorious in their attachments to cultural texts, but may be attached to specific elements whilst not caring for others. In this instance, some fans might not like a particular Doctor or 'era' of the programme and be waiting in anticipation of the next cycle of change. How, then, do audiences, fans and more casual viewers respond to change in a text they love but which is in a constant state of flux? This chapter explores such responses in both the wider mainstream (and perhaps more casual) audience and in the specifically intense fan audience.

Researching the Audience

The reboot of the series in 2005 formed an opportunity to explore questions about the *Doctor Who* audience, and specifically the fan audience in the context of online audience practices, communication of emotional responses in computer-mediated discussion and fan discourses that grow up around the pleasures – or, since fans are not always satisfied with the way 'their' series is produced, displeasures – of viewing.[3] *Doctor Who* had maintained a core fan following during the gap between the end of the classic series in 1989 and the announcement of the new series, generating its own text creation and professional fan writers via the Virgin New Adventure novels and the Big Finish audio plays. The online fan community was therefore strong, if small, and made an ideal case study to track discourses around the series. The primary data was drawn from participant observation in online fan forums and discussion groups, including Gallifrey Base,[4] Roobarb's Doctor Who Forum, and the Doctor Forum on Digital Spy, together with supplemental observations of Facebook communities. The fan demographic being studied was initially focused on the responses of classic *Who* fandom, but as the new series generated an influx of new fans, the methodology design expanded.

In terms of gauging responses of a wider audience segment than the fan forums, particularly since a manageable alternative to undertaking mass audience research was required, the comments posted on the *Guardian* reader feedback pages, the Reading Festival forum and the CBBC *Newsround* pages were analysed. These data sources were selected in order to give an indication of responses from the BBC audience in general, a middle to highbrow audience with an interest in culture generally, young adult viewers and the children in the audience. Whilst these data sources cannot guarantee a representative profile of the entire audience responses (there may well be overlap with the fan audience since there is nothing to prevent fans posting on these sites), they do provide a snapshot of the wider audience and form a control group against which fan responses can be measured.

A Family Audience

BBC audience research confirms that the core audience for *Doctor Who* is children, and adults in the 35–44 age range; in other words, a broad-based 'family audience'. Since the series' reboot, *Doctor Who* has regularly topped the viewing charts and attracted audiences of between 6 and 10 million. During series five to the first part of series seven with Smith in the lead and Moffat as showrunner, audiences have continued to hold above 6.5 million (see Figure 11.1) and have averaged 7.9 million. More significantly, the share in terms of its proportion of the total audience during the timeslot has been consistently high (Figure 11.2). This means that *Doctor Who* is amongst the most watched dramas in the BBC's top ten charts and regularly wins in its time slot.[5] This represents the continuing popularity of the series and its economic and cultural importance for the BBC and British television in general.

Quantitative measures of audience reach cannot provide the qualitative responses and judgements that observations of family and friends opinions can provide. The fans themselves are interested in what the wider audience thinks of each episode, Outpost

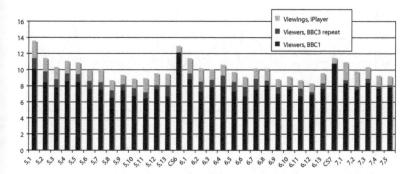

11.1 Audience reach (millions of viewers) for series five to seven (CS = Christmas Special)

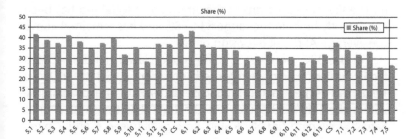

11.2 Audience share for series five to seven (CS = Christmas Special)

Gallifrey/Gallifrey Base having a 'What did the kids and the "Not We" think' thread for each episode. Similarly the BBC is interested in specific demographic responses to each episode. Focus shifts, therefore, to the Appreciation Index (AI), giving a measure of how much the audience enjoyed the programme. The AI for 'The Eleventh Hour' was 86, compared with 76 for 'Rose' and 84 for 'The Christmas Invasion'. In general, this suggests that viewers enjoyed Smith and Moffat's first episode as much as, if not slightly more than, the first episode of the returning series with Eccleston and the previous change of Doctor to Tennant. The breakdown of the AI figures for this episode indicate that female viewers and viewers in the 35–54 age group enjoyed the programme the most, though in all groups some viewers indicated that they missed David Tennant.[6] As Figure 11.3 indicates, the AI

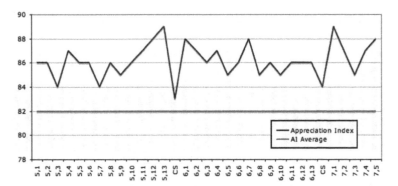

11.3 Audience appreciation index for series five to seven (CS = Christmas Special)

for the first three seasons of the Smith and Moffat era has been consistently high, in the range 83 to 89, and has remained above the average AI for all television of 82.

For the BBC, however, it is the young viewers (and associated family audience) who are regarded as the core audience for *Doctor Who*. This relates to the broadcast patterns of the programme within the BBC's schedule, first the time it is transmitted on a Saturday evening (usually a start time of between 6 and 7 p.m., sometimes later) and second the season in which it is broadcast. From the re-launch and up until series six (which was split mid-season, with the second half being broadcast at the end of August/ early autumn), *Doctor Who* was scheduled around Easter/late spring and early summer. This meant that it was still daylight at the time of broadcast and there was a higher likelihood that the weather was mild or fine. In fact, the *Daily Mail* blamed the sunny weather on low audiences for 'The Impossible Astronaut': 'It was billed as one of the scariest Doctor Who episodes ever. But when the series returned on Saturday, the Time Lord found himself facing an unexpected enemy – the sunshine.'[7] It is difficult to correlate the audience reach with the weather since this can be variable across the country, though the lighter evenings in the late spring and early summer may mean fewer families are at home and indoors. To a greater extent, it is the latter that is perceived to be a potential problem and is one factor in the move of the series to the autumn, certainly for Moffat, although series seven was again split into two parts, with the second part screened in Spring 2013:

> Doctor Who in the summer? All that running down tunnels, with torches, and the sunlight streaming through your windows and bleaching out your screen? All those barbecues, and children playing outside, while on the telly there are green monsters seething in their CGI-enhanced lairs? It's just not right, is it?[8]

Here Moffat extrapolates not just the problem of children being outdoors at the time of broadcast but the incompatibility of the *Doctor Who* aesthetic with broad daylight. It is the scariness of the programme that is one reason it is enjoyed so much by children (as the hiding behind the sofa myth demonstrates). The point that Moffat makes about the darker and scarier nature of *Doctor Who* is significant in this respect. *Doctor Who* has long been labelled as too frightening for children – as Mary Whitehouse did in the mid-1970s – and parental concerns have been raised about Moffat's *Who* (as for example the *Guardian* blog debates on the series being both too scary and too complicated[9]).

Alongside the aspects of romance and relationships introduced by Russell T Davies, this reflects a sophisticated family audience in the twenty-first century, and indeed the *Doctor Who* reboot has led to the recognition that it is still possible to attract a family audience in the fragmented multi-channel and internet age. The BBC's audience research reports that over 90 per cent of the viewers polled said that *Doctor Who* was 'good family viewing', though around 19 per cent were concerned about their children being scared by the series. This is not a deterrent to the younger audiences though; rather that it is older viewers who are in decline. The 4–15 age group has risen to 19 per cent and the 16–25 group to 9 per cent of the audience in the Smith/Moffat era (from 15.6 per cent and 7 per cent respectively in 2005), whereas the over-65 share has fallen from 15 per cent to 11 per cent across the same period.[10]

Whilst this audience research undoubtedly includes fans as well as parents (indeed many fans are also parents), the focus on the family audience obscures specific fan responses to the series. The female audience is particular important; classic *Who* fandom was predominantly male, but this has changed significantly with the reboot and especially with the casting of David Tennant. Classic *Who* fandom also contained a significant proportion of gay fans, and this has been reflected in the series itself to some extent;

Davies is respected for his portrayal of sexuality in his TV work, and this continued into *Doctor Who* (though it was primarily on *Torchwood* where he explored the sexuality of characters such as Jack Harkness). Audience data also fails to account for changes in the nature of fan culture itself (and indeed what it might mean to talk of fans within the context of online cultures and Web 2.0).

We're All Fans Now

With the overlaps between audience segments, it is problematical to explore any one segment at the exclusion of others. Children are fans too, and (adult-)fans-in-the-making. Viewers might be fans of the classic series, the reboot or both. They might be fans of David Tennant or Russell T Davies, solely or in addition to being fans of the series as whole. We might expect that some fans in these groups would stop watching the series when Tennant and Davies left. Or they might become more casual viewers or even remain intense fans. Fans might also be active in that they participate in producerly fan activities, but equally casual viewers might join, read and participate in online communities discussing *Doctor Who* (though not necessarily dedicated fan communities). They might also be fans of other aspects of the transmedia narrative – the Big Finish audioplays or the various novel series. Any discussion of the audience, fan or otherwise, is thus complex and contradictory. As Henry Jenkins and other fan scholars have pondered, how can we discuss the fan audience in an era when fan communities are accessible and open to anyone who can go online and participate, when everyone is (potentially) a fan now? As Jenkins points out, Web 2.0 has 'made visible a set of cultural practices and logics...expanding their cultural influence by broadening and diversifying participation'.[11] Since this can be considered 'fandom without the stigma', the question of differentiating between the fan audience and the mainstream audience for *Doctor Who* is not clear cut. If any viewer, and this includes the children amongst the family audience, is able to go online and read or post his or her own responses to the series without having to join an overtly fan community (and avoiding the stigma that this may still carry) then distinctions between fan and other audience segments are moot.

Such fannish activities broaden and diversify participation within online communities that are similar in some respects (though not all of course) to fandom. As Kristina Busse argues when discussing this mainstreaming of fan culture, the fannish behaviours encouraged when casual viewers engage with trans-media texts in the context of Web 2.0 should not be wholly con-flated with fandom per se. However, as she proposes, the notion of 'a continuum that acknowledges the more intense emotional and actual engagements of many TV viewers today without eras-ing the strong community structures which have developed through media fandom' is significant. The *Doctor Who* audience includes 'different trajectories that combine into levels of fannish-ness'.[12] These different trajectories might incorporate being a sin-gular fan, participating in a fan community or enacting fannish behaviour (perhaps without even self-identifying as a fan), as well as whether people consider themselves to be a fan of a particu-lar text, a member of a fandom or a fan per se. In the context of this research, such trajectories or levels of fannishness might include viewers with intense emotional attachments to *Doctor Who* who have no or little experience of organised or participa-tory fandom, as well as active members of participatory *Doctor Who* fan communities. Given the role of *Doctor Who* as an iconic element of British popular culture, we might expect the former to be as significant a component of the audience as the latter. Their attachments might be in terms of nostalgia for the programme they watched in childhood or because the Doctor, the TARDIS or the Daleks represent an important image for them (the idea here being that all these elements are recognisable independ-ently from the text, as something that scared or fascinated them when they were children) or because they found a particular actor – Doctor or companion – appealing. While these 'casual' fans may not participate to the same extent in the same com-munities, online or face-to-face, as the 'intense' fans, they might nonetheless contribute to or lurk in online spaces frequented by both fans and others with fannish interests. They might also buy the DVDs for repeated viewings, or watch on iPlayer, check out the BBC website and watch the prequel webisodes or talk about the show 'around the water-cooler'. Furthermore, fans are not separate from the family audience or other audience segments. The Outpost Gallifrey/Gallifrey Base forum has regular threads for

DOCTOR WHO, *THE ELEVENTH HOUR*

each episode on what the 'Not We' (their term for *Doctor Who* viewers other than themselves) think. In these threads they report and discuss the reactions and responses of their wives, girlfriends, partners, children, younger siblings, nieces and nephews and parents. This illustrates levels of contact and overlap between different audience segments and interest in what the wider audience thinks. At the very least, these different trajectories of fannishness mean it is not necessarily appropriate to differentiate between a fan and a mainstream audience. Exploring the responses to the announcement of a 'new Doctor' reveals that there is indeed continuity and overlap across these different trajectories of fandom.

Regeneration: Negotiating Change

Given that the concept of 'regeneration' is embedded in the programme, the Doctor's appearance, personality and mannerisms are highly mutable, though his memories and core character traits such as his problem-solving and inherent eccentricity remain stable.[13] This does mean, however, that viewers who have developed attachments with the character have to negotiate the changes, potentially affecting not only their investment in the series but their viewing pleasures. Amber Davisson and Paul Booth suggest that complicated identity play occurs in online fan cultures: 'three identities ... are present in the activities [of fans] – the fan, the character, the community'.[14] The change of actor is thus highly significant to understanding audience responses to the series as a whole, but particularly in terms of fan responses within the context of fan communities. These eras also, to some extent, mark divisions in the production of the series, with lead production personnel often changing at or around the same time as the change in actor, though they can also change *within* actor era. Whilst viewers might *prefer* certain versions of the Doctor or the stories and stylistics of particular production teams, the appeal of *Doctor Who* usually transcends such changes. However, this is not necessarily an unproblematic negotiation.

As a case in point, reactions to the announcement of Smith as David Tennant's replacement were ambivalent at best and hostile at worst. In part this could be attributed to the viewers' lengthy discussions of who (or at least what kind of actor) they would like

212

to see cast in the role. Such discussion is not restricted to fans, since the media frequently participates in speculation which is picked up on by viewers generally; for example, the *Daily Mail* included an article entitled 'Billie Piper Leads the Space Race to Become the New Doctor Who' on 4 November, two months before a casting announcement.[15] Whilst suggestions of possible actors are always varied, on this occasion there was a great deal of speculation amongst fans – and also in the media, as with the *Daily Mail* article '*Casualty* Star Patterson Joseph could become first black Doctor Who' of 2 January[16] – as to whether a black actor would be cast. The possibilities that this offered for contemporary representations were foremost in a lot of fan discussion taking place, but primarily this involved speculating on whether Paterson Joseph, Adrian Lester or Chiwetel Ejiofor would make the best Doctor. The majority of fans felt it was acceptable and even appropriate in the twenty-first century for the Doctor to be played by a black actor, though this did initiate some contention and accusations of racism whenever fans said a black Doctor would not work for them.

In the *Doctor Who* and *Torchwood* forum on DigitalSpy,[17] for example, ED (male, 20s) replied to the discussion of Adrian Lester wanting to play the part, 'Not being a racist here, but as I have said before, The Doctor is a white british male and always will be.' AB (no stats) points out the fallacy in this by reminding ED that 'You surely mean the Doctor has been PLAYED by white british males, as he is clearly anything but!' H (male, 30s) writes 'The Doctor will always be a British (accented) male, but the colour of his skin has never seemed "set in stone" in that way, to me.' N (no stats) also points out that one of the faces shown to the second Doctor upon his enforced regeneration was black. ED follows this up by saying:

> I really dont like the idea ... nowdays, the casting of black actors in a previously white role is done for impact ... or at least seen that way. I think he would be great as the Doctor but it would all be over shadowed. I want to see headlines about the new doctor ... not the 'FIRST BLACK DOCTOR!'

Again, posters point out that this is not necessarily true. H says:

> Piffle. What about Jeffrey Wright as Felix Leiter in Casino Royale? Or Michael Clarke Duncan as Kingpin in Daredevil. Or Halle

Berry as frigging Catwoman? If those buttons aren't pushed, nobody seems to care but a bigoted fanboy minority, or a hack on a slow news day.

SS (no stats) points out that it actually works narratively for the Doctor to be played by a black actor: 'Becoming black works for the Doctor more than any character. He's a guy which changes his looks and character!' They also largely come to a consensus that the Doctor does not actually have any essential character traits that can be defined as 'white'.

Overall, the majority of posters in this thread specified that they would be happy to see a black actor in the role provided he (and it must be a he) was a good actor (Chiwetal Ejiofor being widely regarded as the best choice). The possibilities of a female Doctor had often been discussed in the past (and was frequently a favourite speculative topic in the *Daily Mail*, as with their Billie Piper speculation), but most fans felt that the Doctor should always be male. SS, for example, states, 'I'd be happy for a black Doctor. I can't see why not. A female doctor? No way', and B12 (female) replies, 'I second this. Totally happy with a black MALE doctor. But never a female. (and Im a female so Im not being sexist!)' SS also reasons that, 'As I see it, colour just changes the way you look, sex changes what you are. Which is why a black Doctor, yes, a woman Doctor, No.' The majority of fans, then, would not, as M (male, 40s) says, 'bat an eye if the Doctor was black' though most would have 'a tough time' in adjusting to a change of sex. It is generally accepted that the best actor for the role should be chosen regardless of appearance.

Nevertheless, the discussion did open up when contributors discussed where they might draw the line on what physical or character type could play the Doctor. Physical characteristics are not deemed to be important, there having been 'a fat Doctor', 'a senile old dithering cantankerous Doctor' and 'a goofy ugly scary one', while ED points out that the Doctor as played by Jon Pertwee even had a tattoo. Interestingly with respect to the direction Moffat and Smith have taken the character (as asexual in some ways), H says:

I'd have a problem with an overtly gay Doctor in the same way I currently have a problem with an overtly straight Doctor. I do not want a sexualised Doctor at all. He is an alien, and all the romance crap [with humans] they've introduced since the McGann Doc can sod off.

This response indicates a problematic negotiation of a dominant theme of the Davies era and for these fans Moffat offers a hope for return to 'their' Doctor of old. However, given that these fans felt that skin colour and other aspects of appearance did not matter, their immediate response to the announcement of Smith (made on an episode of *Doctor Who Confidential* on 3 January 2009) reveals contradictory emotions. The choice of Smith was completely unexpected for most members of the fan forums being studied and this seemed to have the effect of a 'bombshell', eliciting heated and excessive reactions from a large number of fans. That their expectations were not only not met, but not even remotely touched upon, can be interpreted as highly significant. These kind of fans (active participants in online forum discussion) are often heavily invested in demonstrating their knowledge and cultural competencies about the series and how it will develop. Whilst some of the reactions were straightforward disappointment that a black actor was not cast (for many fans, although this was something they would have been happy to see, they were not heavily invested in the possibility), the majority of responses were extremely emotional.

One aspect of this particular fan trajectory is timeliness and responsiveness (thus establishing a presence in the forum) in posting about a new episode or, as here, an important announcement.[18] There is a great deal of emotional investment in being part of the online group, as well as in the series itself at this moment of transition. Waiting online, in the group, is part of such fannishness, as RG's (no stats) post on Roobarb's demonstrates:

> Am I alone in being a nervous wreck about this? I barely slept last night; when I drifted off I dreamt about the announcement; I'm one step away from hyperventilating and I can feel every heartbeat in my chest. I've loved this show since I was four and feel that, up until now, I've been living through one of its golden eras. One bit of miscasting could bring the whole thing crashing down. God, I need a Tardis to take me to 5.35

SB replies, 'This will be announced at the end of the show, right? It'll be an effort to concentrate on the first 30 minutes of the show – might have to watch it again later', and cmc says, 'I have to say, that I'm getting rather excited! I shall need a cup of camomile tea in a minute to calm me down.' RG says he is 'tipsy on port and borderline cardiac arrest'.

Even before the casting is announced, this discourse of excitement, impatience and anxiety primes the fans for outpourings of passionate feelings. This sharing of emotional responses via computer-mediated discourses then exacerbates reactions to the announcement itself. EP (female 30s) says:

> I have a really bad sinking feeling about it all. So afraid it will all go tits up with a terrible choice. Still the proof is in the performance I guess, so will try to resist from judgement until I have seen whoever it is in the role. It will take someone pretty bloody spesh to make me feel any better about Tennant going, to be honest.

Here, the fan accepts she will have to wait and see what the actor will be like in the role, but knows that her feelings for Tennant will get in the way. Participation in forum discussion can therefore exacerbate a build-up of both positive and negative emotion.

Certainly, some fans became over-emotional and over-reacted when the casting was announced. LF writes 'Worst. Doctor. Ever.' in 36pt boldface font. BR (male, 40s) feels ill, BH (no stats) '*sobs quietly*' and CG is lost for words, simply posting 'OMFG!!!!!!!!!!!!!!!!!!!!!!!!!!!!!!!!!!!!!' He follows this up one minute later, now being able to express himself more coherently but still emotionally, by posting, 'the show is dead to me'. Similarly, CC writes 'Well, that's the end of Doctor Who for me. Smith? Absolute bullshit. I never thought I'd be sorry to see RTD and David Tennant go, but that's it, I give up. Total fucking crap.' DMG (male) says 'Well, that's pretty much the final nail in the coffin for the fan in me.' These instantaneous responses (posted during or immediately after the announcement on the episode of *Confidential*) are purely emotional reactions; they involve no or very little reasoned arguments and simply express an outpouring of their 'crashing disappointment'. They therefore represent the moment of shock when the object of the fans' focus changes dramatically. In the active fans' demonstration of their timeliness and presence, the immediate response is extremely important. Like any such moment of shock, however, these feelings develop into a more measured response. This takes place within a few minutes, and is either a change of mind in the instance of the early posters or a calmer first post by fans who have waited a short while to 'let it sink in' before posting. Most of these posts express reservations but the fans say they will wait until they have seen Smith's performance as the Doctor before making up their minds.

Notably, most of the early posters do reflect and later express a wait and see approach, hedging their bets because they do actually still want to keep watching the show. (Only one of these fans continued to maintain that he will no longer watch the series.) Some fans act as the 'voice of reason' and remind their fellow forum members that such reactions are nothing new. AH, for example, says that, 'When Pertwee regenerated back in 1974, I took an instant dislike to Tom Baker & said out loud to my Sister & dear departed Brother that I would not watch the show anymore. How I came to eat those words!'

It is interesting that some fans go into denial for a short time. (One point of discussion that developed on DigitalSpy argued that the announcement was a smokescreen and it would be revealed closer to the regeneration episode that it really was Ejiofor after all.) Other fans rationalise away the casting choice, putting the blame on the segment of the audience they tend to despise. In this case, it is the female segment of the audience that is often referred to as the 'squee brigade' (these are mostly female fans, but some male fans too, whose online presence is characterised by squeals of pleasure over their desired fan object typified by posts that consist largely of the onomatopoeic word 'squee', expressing an emotional response and little more). The classic *Who* fans on Roobarb's (the large majority of whom are male) are very protective of their community and make active attempts to keep out squee, which they see as having taken over Outpost Gallifrey/Gallifrey Base during the Tennant era. SC (male) reflects this discourse, blaming Moffat for pandering to this audience segment in casting Smith. He writes: 'Steven Moffat. The first DW Producer whose honeymoon period expired 15 months before the transmission of his episode. Still gotta keep that all important teenage girl audience on board, eh?' To which LF says, '[Smith]'s probably great if you're a 12-year-old girl who loves "Twilight" and owns a few emo albums.' These problematically gendered responses reflect the differences that might exist between classic series (male) fans and the more active female fandoms around the new series (and of David Tennant fangirls in particular). This illustrates clearly that different trajectories of fandom are at work in segmenting *Doctor Who* fan culture.

Age, Appearance and Bearing

Age was a factor in considering an actor suitable for the role even before Smith was announced, although it was not as great an objection as sex and mentioned far less frequently. In the immediate aftermath of the announcement by the BBC that the actor would be revealed on 3 January 2009, speculations began on Roobarb's (this again indicates how the rhythms of fandom are determined by the production contexts of the series). On this occasion, Ben Whishaw was discussed, having been linked to the role earlier in the media and on fan forums. CC (male) writes 'Hmm, you know, I'm starting to get a sinking feeling about this. ... At 28 he seems too young, and he doesn't look particularly interesting ...' LF (no stats) replies, 'That was my first thought as well. Too young and – more importantly – looks *way* too young. I doubt he'd have any gravitas in the role at all, but would probably be great news for the squee brigade.'

There is a sense for these fans that the Doctor is an authority figure and this relates to the character's history as someone who is hundreds of years old and has a great experience and wealth of knowledge. The traits of 'gravitas' and 'bearing' are ones that these fans deem most important, as when BF (male 30s) speculates on Julian Rhind-Tutt, saying he has 'the bearing to keep the fanboys happy'. For these fanboys, these signifiers of authority are linked to 'being the right age', which is '40-ish', but there also needs to be charisma and an 'alien-esque' quality. (The fans also need to be confident the actors can evoke the zany eccentricities of the Doctor.) However, there is also a feeling of discomfort for these older fans surrounding the fact that the actor would be younger than they are. In terms of projected interactivity or how they see the character, the Doctor is someone to look up to and admire, perhaps as a grandfatherly or fatherly figure or as someone who is always knowledgeable and experienced whilst also being friendly and eccentric. This is part of their enjoyment of the character and a reason they became a fan, though they are aware, of course, that it is they who are getting older whilst the series is still designed for the age group they were in when the series first appealed to them. (This is true of fans in their early thirties as well as of older fans.) TW (no stats) says, 'As for the Ben Wilshaw chappie – NOOOOOOOO! I'm too young to have a Doctor younger than me. He was born in 1980? 1980? He's not long out of short trousers for Troughton's sake.' Others deflect the issue by making jokes about the Doctor still using Clearasil. Accordingly, the typical response on the announce-ment of Smith was simply that he was too young. 'Isn't Matt Smith, like, 24 years old?' asks DF, for example, and CC says 'Oh dear, don't like the look of Matt Smith. Zero gravitas, far too young.' Interestingly, though, the 'too young' response is not limited to the older, male fans. While, rightly or wrongly, the fans discussed above assume that the casting of someone young is to keep the younger fans happy, a significant proportion of the young viewers posting to the *Newsround* website give the same reaction. Just over 15 per cent of the posts from 7 to 15-year-olds say that Smith is too young to play the Doctor.

Whilst the 'too young' response seems to be a response to the match between actor and character, more complex negative reactions were expressed around Smith's looks. On Roobarb's, SB (male, 30s) writes, 'Cor, he's an ugly looking bas-tard'. Responses were even more extreme on other forums and groups. Postings on Facebook were especially vitriolic (reflecting the way in which the more open nature of the social networking site permits unrestrained comment). Across the forums, Smith is compared to Herman Munster, an Auton, Rocky Dennis – the character with the facial deformity from *Mask* (1985) – and Joseph Merrick, the 'elephant man'. In one sense, this seems like an anomalous response; the actors playing the Doctor have never been cast for their glamour or 'movie-star' good looks. However, this was certainly a significant factor in David Tennant's appeal to female fans of the series (and 81 per cent of the posts on the *Newsround* thread were from girls aged 8 to 15, 39 per cent claiming Tennant as their favourite Doctor or that they loved Tennant, indicating the appeal to women cut across age groups). Pages were set up on Facebook, with titles such as 'Official Page to get Matt Smith to regenerate back into David Tennant' (with 4,955 fans), 'People, who already think that Matt Smith Is gonna suck as the 11th Dr' (263) and 'No, no no no no no ... I'm sorry but no' (22), appearing within minutes of the announcement. As an example of vitriol, the 'get Matt Smith to regenerate back' page posts a picture of John Hurt playing Merrick in *The Elephant Man* (1980) next to Smith under the heading 'Spot the Difference – There Isn't One!!!' Comments on the page include 'lookes like a gay dog', 'he is so uglllllllyyyyyyyyyyyyyyyy', 'i hate him,hes a drip and but ugly!', 'a gimp', 'doofus' and 'the new kid shud just go die :L'. The poor spelling, grammar and punctuation, as well as the non-PC language, are perhaps more indicative of this kind of online discourse, but these examples illustrate the extreme emotions that can be generated at the loss of a favoured actor from a series.

Fans dissenting from this viewpoint were in a minority, but the level of discussion was not conducive to reasoned argument in the Facebook groups cited above (though there is a lot of irony and sarcasm). Even on forums such as Roobarb's, contributors who express opinions that looking 'frikkin' odd' is a bonus for playing the Doctor are often put-down in a jokey way. When DG suggests that Smith has '*something* interesting there in a Who-ish wayy', N (male 40s) asks 'what drugs are you on' (DG specifies PG Tips). More tellingly of different trajectories of fandom, one Facebook fan page, 'The 11th Doctor' (set up after the casting announcement), was bombarded with negative comments after the regeneration scene in 'The End of Time'. The page gave a status update illustrating the discourses constructed around different kinds of fans:

> This page is being spammed of late by childish haters, who fancy David Tennant so much they can't bear the thought of the show featuring anyone else. Tennant himself has expressed his desire to see the show continue for years to come – slagging Matt so soon shows how little you actually care for Doctor Who itself. This fanpage is for the FANS of the show, not its former lead actor. Let's play nice, eh?

Comments at this point included acknowledgement that changes have to be got used to ('everyone hates new stuff'), that this is part of what being a *Doctor Who* fan is about ('Accepting the changing faces of the Doctor is part and parcel of being a fan. If you can't handle that, leave those of us who can alone.') and that it is only a minority who are excessively negative ('I'm getting sick to death of that small minority out there who thinks Matt will ruin the show'), while 'fangirls' are othered ('get over it fangirls', 'Oh it does my head in when the David Tennant fan-girls leap on Matt' and 'i hate how fangirls are like that id love to get a gun and shoot them'). This example highlights the fact that different trajectories of fandom co-exist, but sometimes contentiously and problematically. It must be noted that these references do not include all female fans, a significant number of whom belong to the older, classic fans (and some of the comments quoted in the example cited above are from female fans). Clearly, the negative comments on Facebook are an expression of the tension that some fans experienced around the loss of 'their Doctor' and can be attributed to the intense love that they had for David Tennant specifically. This kind of female fandom involves erotic and sexually explicit fan fantasies[19] and these female fans of Tennant are heavily invested in the sex appeal of and desire for the star. Although they are clearly invested in Tennant's specific role as the Doctor, this kind of star fandom is a very different trajectory than that of the *Doctor Who* fans specifically.

By comparison, discourses organised around the casting of the new companion are rather less emotional. On previous changes of lead actor, the companion has often remained to provide a bridge to the new 'era' (as Rose did when Tennant took over from Eccleston). However, the series of specials from Christmas 2008 to New Year 2010 (forming Tennant's finale) saw the Doctor without a regular companion and the series under Moffat thus saw a new companion cast alongside Smith. The announcement of Karen Gillan as the new companion was some-what subsumed under the concerns expressed around Smith; nevertheless, early fan responses reveal notably gendered fan discourses. Whereas those female fans expressing sexual interest in Tennant as the Doctor, especially the so-called squee brigade, were often looked down on in male fan circles, male interest in companions is seen as 'normal'. Thus, interest in Gillan centred around her physical appearance and in particular model shots of her in lingerie and sexually provocative poses. Fans did mention that she was a relative unknown, that she had previously appeared in *Doctor Who* playing a small role in 'The Fires of Pompeii' (2008) and that she was, like Smith, very young, but in the main discussion focused around her appearance and sexiness. The tone of this discussion is frequently suggestive, the reposting of the modelling shots making the threads 'not safe for work' (NSFW). On Roobarb's, BR points out that the notes on the photo of Gillan and Smith on the BBC press release on 29 May 2009 state 'not in costume', to which LF replies, 'I'm hoping she's "not in costume" quite a lot'. V says that he is off work ill and 'taking a break from my Deadwood marathon to look up sexy photos of Karen Gillan', TP replying, 'So, not so much "dead" wood as...oh please yourselves'. On Gallifrey Base, TT (male) posts a poll asking for members to vote for the 'sexiest female television companion'. Although she had not yet appeared in any episodes, Amy (Gillan) came top with 337 votes (51 per cent). Such masculine objectification of women is clearly still commonplace amongst the heterosexual male fan audience and reinforces the traditional view that the *Doctor Who* companion is there to appeal to the dads. It may well be then that a change of companion for these fans is not a major concern as long as she is attractive (and it is worth noting that there was a largely negative response to the announcement of Catherine Tate as companion). Whilst such positions are not representative of all groupings of fans (female and gay fans may feel marginalised or even take up oppositional views) they do create a particularly gendered discourse within the fan community as a whole.

Certainly female fans invested in the relationship between Tennant's Doctor and Rose are less accepting of subsequent companions. Another interesting response observed in the female fan communities was the way the attitude towards the character River Song changed from the Davies/Tennant era to the Moffat/Smith one. Many female fans, especially those who were intensely emotionally invested in Tennant's Doctor, disliked River when she first appeared in 'Silence in the Library'. The female *Who* fans observed in the feminine handicraft community Ravelry mention not liking her proprietorial interest in the Doctor with its suggestion of a close relationship (possibly her being his wife) and refer to her as a Mary Sue figure (a disliked original female character in fan fiction who is a perfect woman and thinly veiled version of the writer). However, they changed their minds and like her a lot in episodes with Smith. They agree that this is because they have less sexual interest in Smith and therefore she no longer 'gets in the way' of their feelings for Tennant.

Other Changes

The issue raised by the posts in the moment of Smith's casting, namely that fans express their emotional reactions without forethought or reflection, means that they do say things they might not have said with hindsight. Also, complaints are more frequently expressed than positive responses. Smith's performance was largely accepted because the fans realised when they saw his performance that he perfectly captured the immutable traits of the Doctor. This response was reflected in the wider audience suggested by the comments on the *Guardian* TV and Radio Blog.[20] The BBC also picked up on this in the wider audience, including a report on *Points of View*: 'Well, before Matt Smith had uttered his first line as the Eleventh Doctor viewers were queuing up to predict how much they'd hate his portrayal but in a huge collective U-turn you loved him.'[21] It was an aspect of stylistics, however, that viewers complained about, namely the 2010 theme tune. The *Points of View* report continues:

> [You] refocused your sights on a completely different aspect of the show. Noel Wallace emailed 'New Doctor – excellent. New TARDIS – excellent. New assistant – excellent (and sexy). New theme tune – an abomination.' Ouch, Noel.

These responses to the rearrangement of the theme tune were echoed on fan forums. Such a reaction is interesting; it harks back to the immediate discomfort around change and suggests a need for some stable elements when so much else has changed. Fans shifted their concerns about change onto the production decisions, with Moffat being the main focus of their disquiet.

The response to Smith's casting is not representative; when Eccleston left, many fans welcomed the change to Tennant, since the latter was seen as a self-confessed fan in whose hands the character would be safe. Similarly, many fans rated Moffat's episodes as writer amongst the best examples of the Davies era and initially welcomed the change of showrunner together with the promise that his creative input into the series – the Weeping Angels in particular, and also River Song – would be developed further. Whilst responses to 'The Eleventh Hour' were generally positive, as the series progressed, however, some fans became very vocal about the things they were not happy about. Many were unhappy with the redesign of the Daleks, referring to them as Fatleks, Daftleks, Dulux and Power Ranger Daleks on Gallifrey Base. It was storylines, plot-holes and over-complexity, though, that some fans were vocally negative about. This resulted in many forum threads with titles such as 'RTD leaves and the show sinks faster than titanic' and 'Doctor Who becoming too complicated' (DigitalSpy) and 'Has it officially become cringe-worthy?' (Gallifrey Base). Such threads are countered by others (demonstrating different allegiances) such as 'Hey, Russell, watch it and weep' (Gallifrey Base) and 'Surprised at negative reaction to this series' (DigitalSpy).

Haters and Naysayers

These reflect individual preferences and tastes of course, and the fans themselves frequently acknowledge this. Many are aware that this sends out the impression that they are never happy with the series they love. Custard's Doctor Who Forum describes itself as 'A Carnival of Moansters!', and fans with particular tastes are referred to by labels such as 'resident Moff haters'. Some fans have a reputation for contrariness or nitpicking in a particular community, as DF (male) says to LF: 'Well, I knew *you'd* disagree for a start. The universe would collapse in on itself otherwise.' Some fans, however, do become bored or sick of the negative discourses that emerge. It may be that this is a factor that stops less intense fans and members of the casual audience engaging with these intense trajectories of fandom. When one poster on the Reading Festival forum (young male fans) mentions 'the Doctor Who forum', another asks if he is 'on Gallifrey Base'. The reply – 'Kind of I dont really post just read some of the over the top reactions and when some of the big finish cd's come out. I would only get into an argument why tate is pony if i began posting over there' – does suggest the extremes of fan discourse can be off-putting to less intense fans.

As Nicholas Abercrombie and Brian Longhurst have set out, not all fans are the same; a spectrum of involvement exists even within the positive involvement typical of a fan.[22] According to Jonathan Grey, the category of anti-fan that exists alongside that of fan represents different viewing practices and proximities from the text.[23] The nitpickers and naysayers of *Doctor Who* fandom, however, do not fit neatly into this category, though they do resemble Grey's notion that 'fans can become anti-fans of a sort when an episode or part of a text is perceived as harming a text as a whole'.[24] They are not outright 'haters' of *Doctor Who* – to borrow a term from Lisa Lewis[25] – since they only take an exceptional dislike to parts of the text. One area of interest that emerges from this research is evidence of the fans' sense of cultural ownership of the text – what Matt Hills terms the 'dialectic of value'.[26]

Conclusion

As previous studies (from Henry Jenkins on) have suggested, fan audiences can be notoriously contradictory, vocal and even argumentative, and the *Doctor Who* fans' responses to the rebooted series as it continues to evolve are no different in this respect. In fact, the second Doctor's response to the Time Lords' choices for his new body (as quoted in the title of this chapter) is echoed by the negative or ambivalent responses of many fans to the announcement that Smith was David Tennant's replacement for the 2010 series, and then later – with the series under way – to their expressed concerns about the direction the production of *Doctor Who* was taking under Moffat. However, fans do not lose their strong attachments to the fan object. In fact, it is rather the opposite, with the 'naysayers' attachment to the series being as intense and passionate as the embracers of change. With change being integral to the text, LOT's (male, 20s) voice of reason on DigitalSpy (23 April 2010), however, stands out: 'Doctor Who embraces change and so should it's fans.'

Notes

1. Krishnan Gura-Murthy, *Channel 4 News*, 2 April 2004. Available at www.youtube.com/watch?v=jRoydwtNadE (accessed 26 May 2011).
2. Sian Williams and Dermot Murnaghan, *BBC Breakfast*. 10 June 2005. Available at www.youtube.com/watch?v=_CtuzKml7ng (accessed 26 May 2011).
3. Brigid Cherry, 'Squee, Retcon, Fanwank and the Not-We: Computer-Mediated Discourse and the Online Audience for NuWho', in Christopher J. Hansen (ed.) *Ruminations, Peregrinations, and Regenerations: A Critical Approach to Doctor Who* (Newcastle, 2010), pp. 192–208.
4. Previously run as Outpost Gallifrey.
5. See 'BARB Weekly Top 30 Programmes'. Available at www.barb.co.uk/report/weekly-top-programmes-overview.
6. Scottish viewers also enjoyed the programme slightly more than other groupings, reflecting perhaps the new Scottish companion and several jokey references to Scotland in the episode.
7. Simon Cable, 'New *Doctor Who* Episode Billed as Scariest yet Sees Ratings FALL by 1.5m', *Daily Mail*, 25 April 2011. Available at www.dailymail.co.uk/tvshowbiz/article-1380150/Doctor-Who-sees-ratings-FALL-1-5M-Britains-Got-Talent-slide.html (accessed 15 October 2011).
8. Steven Moffat, 'Production Notes', *Doctor Who Magazine* 442 (2011), p. 6.
9. See Dan Martin, 'Has Doctor Who Got Too Complicated?', 20 September 2011. Available at www.guardian.co.uk/tv-and-radio/tvandradioblog/2011/sep/20/doctor-who-too-complicated (accessed 21 September 2011) and Michael Hann and Pete May, 'Is Doctor Who Now Too Scary for Children?', 4 May 2011. Available at www.guardian.co.uk/tv-and-radio/tvandradioblog/2011/may/04/is-doctor-who-too-scary (accessed 30 September 2011).
10. Tim Glanfield and William Gallagher, 'Matt Smith is a Hit with Children and Middle Classes', *Radio Times*, 27 September 2011. Available at www.radiotimes.com/news/2011-09-27/doctor-who-exclusive-matt-smith-is-a-hit-with-children-and-middle-classes (accessed 15 October 2011).
11. Henry Jenkins, 'Fandom, Participatory Culture and Web 2.0'. Confessions of an Aca/Fan, 9 January 2010. Available at http://henryjenkins.org/2010/01/fandom_participatory_culture_a.html (accessed 24 March 2010).
12. Kristina Busse, 'Fandom-is-a-Way-of-Life versus Watercooler Discussion; or, The Geek Hierarchy as Fannish Identity Politics', *Flow TV* 5/13 (2006). Available at http://flowtv.org/2006/11/taste-and-fandom/ (accessed 24 March 2010).
13. Michelle Cordone and John Cordone, 'Who is the Doctor?: The Meta-narrative of Doctor Who', in Hansen (ed.) *Ruminations, Peregrinations, and Regenerations*, pp. 8–21.

14. Amber Davisson and Paul Booth, 'Reconceptualizing Communication and Agency in Fan Activity: A Proposal for a Projected Interactivity Model for Fan Studies', *Texas Speech Communication Journal* 23/1 (2007), p. 41.
15. Liz Thomas, 'Billie Piper Leads the Space Race to Become the New Doctor Who', *Daily Mail*, 4 November 2008. Available at www.dailymail.co.uk/tvshowbiz/article-1082602/Billie-Piper-leads-space-race-new-Doctor-Who.html (accessed 19 July 2011).
16. Simon Cable, '*Casualty* Star Patterson Joseph Could Become First Black Doctor Who', *Daily Mail*, 2 January 2009. Available at www.dailymail.co.uk/tvshow-biz/article-1104333/Casualty-star-Patterson-Joseph-black-Dr-Who-BBC-set-announce-David-Tennants-replacement.html (accessed 19 January 2011).
17. Note that in all quotes the original spelling, punctuation, grammar and use of vernacular terms has been retained.
18. Matt Hills, *Fan Cultures* (London, 2004), p. 141.
19. Cornel Sandvoss, *Fans* (Cambridge, 2005), p. 76.
20. See Dan Martin, 'Doctor Who: Matt Smith's debut in The Eleventh Hour – the Verdict', 3 April 2010. Available at www.guardian.co.uk/tv-and-radio/tvandradioblog/2010/apr/03/doctor-who-eleventh-hour (accessed 6 June 2010).
21. *Points of View*, 11 April 2010. Available at www.youtube.com/watch?v=Mb8N1wN2lhI (accessed 5 June 2010).
22. Nicholas Abercrombie and Brian Longhurst, *Audiences: A Sociological Theory of Performance and Imagination* (London, 1998), p. 141.
23. Jonathan Grey, 'New Audiences, New Textualities: Anti-Fans and Non-Fans', *International Journal of Cultural Studies* 6 (2003), pp. 64–81.
24. Grey, 'New Audiences, New Textualities', p. 73.
25. Lisa A. Lewis, 'Something More than Love: Fan Stories on Film', in Lisa A. Lewis (ed.) *The Adoring Audience: Fan Culture and Popular Media*, (London, 1992), pp. 135–9.
26. Hills, *Fan Cultures*, p. 63.

12

'I AM THE DOCTOR!'

Transmedia Adventures in Time and Space

Neil Perryman

There aren't 13 episodes of *Doctor Who* this year, there are 17 – four of which are interactive. Everything you see and experience within the game is part of the *Doctor Who* universe.[1]

W hen I originally surveyed *Doctor Who*'s transmedia output in 2006, the practice was still in an emergent state. While the series undoubtedly developed new and innovative ways to expand its fictional universe and extend audience engagement, the last seven years have seen a number of widespread changes; not only has the programme's lead actor and producer changed, but its transmedia output has shifted focus as well. As I write this chapter, the series no longer produces metatextual websites, podcasts or mobile-specific content to support the parent text, and this only serves to remind us that the BBC's transmedia experiments have been just that: *experiments*.[2] No definitive process or formula has emerged, and as technology and audience behaviour continues to evolve, so does transmedia storytelling.

On 8 April 2010, the BBC unveiled its latest, and arguably most ambitious, experiment in transmedia storytelling so far – 'The Adventure Games'. Commissioned for BBC Online by the corporation's Vision multiplatform division, and developed by Sumo Digital, a leading UK game design company, the BBC marketed the games as 'interactive episodes' that would 'complement the new series'.[3] The games would be available to download and play on either a Mac or a PC, with no additional cost to the UK licence-fee payer,[4] and they promised to take audiences to 'locations impossible to create on television'.[5] In this chapter I will examine how the 'The Adventure Games' function as transmedia texts, and their relationship (if any) to the series that spawned them.

Defining Transmedia Storytelling

As Jonathan Bignell has pointed out in his chapter for this collection, in the early years of the twenty-first century, television broadcasts have started to outgrow the television set. As media content began to flow across an expanding range of devices and platforms, from mobile phones and websites, to game consoles and computer laptops, a new series of terms was introduced to deal with what was rapidly becoming a completely new model of broadcasting. The broadcasters promoted buzzwords like 'multi-platform', 'cross-platform' (with and without the hyphen) and '360 degree commissioning',[6] while academics developed their own terminology, which included 'overflow',[7] 'media convergence'[8] and 'second shift aesthetics',[9] which they then employed to examine the ramifications of this emerging model on producers, broadcasters, scholars and audiences alike.

However, when it comes to discussing the relationships and interplay between medium-specific content, another term has emerged: 'transmedia storytelling'. Introduced by Henry Jenkins in an article for *Technology Review*,[10] and later refined for his book *Convergence Culture*, Jenkins' original definition described 'a new aesthetic that has emerged in response to media convergence', where audiences act as 'hunters and gatherers, chasing down bits of the story across media channels' – a participatory process that can potentially result in a 'richer entertainment experience',[11] which he later refined to

a process where integral elements of a fiction get dispersed systematically across multiple delivery channels for the purpose of creating a unified and coordinated entertainment experience. Ideally, each medium makes its own unique contribution to the unfolding of the story.[12]

As I write this chapter, a great deal of debate and controversy surrounds the definition of the term *transmedia*, and *transmedia storytelling* in particular,[13] and this has led Jenkins to clarify his original definition: In short, *transmedia* means 'across media' and *transmedia storytelling* is just 'one logic for thinking about the flow of content across media. We might also think about transmedia branding, transmedia performance, transmedia ritual, transmedia play, transmedia activism, and transmedia spectacle, as other logics.'[14] Furthermore, transmedia storytelling should not be confused with 'transmedia engagement',[15] which involves the *same* content being distributed across different media platforms; for example, watching an episode of *Doctor Who* on the BBC's iPlayer service, or downloading an episode to watch on an iPad via iTunes, and neither should it be confused with traditional franchising models.

The First Adventures

Transmedia texts have become less about promoting a central television programme or film and more about creating a coherent, deliberately cross-platform narrative experience.[16]

Traditional models of production based on licensing or merchandise – where a parent company sells the rights to a third party to create products based on that franchise – have invariably resulted in incoherent and contradictory end products. The results of this model can be seen in the earliest *Doctor Who* computer games, where the lead protagonist would only bear a passing resemblance to his counterpart on television.

Contrary to Steven Moffat's claim that 'there should have been [a *Doctor Who* game] ages ago',[17] the first computer game with a connection (albeit tenuous) to the television series arrived on users' monitors early in 1983. Unofficial, unlicensed and even untitled, the game was published within the text of the March edition of *Computer and Video Games Magazine* and readers were invited to input – by hand, no less – hundreds of lines of raw machine code into their Atari 400/800s if they wanted to play it; if they managed to complete this arduous task successfully, they could then interact with a very simple pyramid game that pitted the Doctor's pixellated wits against the Master's. To win the game, the Doctor has to *kill* his arch-nemesis – a fairly typical example of the lack of consistency that was a staple ingredient of some of the franchise's early ancillary spin-offs (licensed or not). In much the same way that Patrick Troughton's Doctor displayed a hitherto unimagined bloodlust in the *TV Comic* strips of the late 1960s,[18] the Doctor could be just as violent and trigger-happy in these early video-game appearances. This disturbing trend reached its nadir with 'Dalek Attack' (1992), a game that featured the Doctor leaping from tall buildings as he blasted swarms of Daleks with his very large – and very deadly – gun. Before the game was released, the actor Sylvester McCoy was moved to comment: 'When I got the job of the Doctor I didn't want him to be violent. I didn't want him to beat monsters to death. If my Doctor is doing anything violent [in the game] then I'm really against it',[19] a statement that was later echoed by contemporary reviewers: '[it's] a rejection of the programme's whole ethical stance ('Quick thinking, agile reflexes and a tactical use of weapons are needed' – so what happened to outwitting the villains?)'.[20]

This is not to say that links between the television series and these early transmedia experiments did not exist, if only superficially. The first official *Doctor Who* video game, appropriately entitled 'The First Adventure' (1983),[21] featured the Black Guardian (a classic series villain) as an integral part of the game's storyline (although this manifests itself more in the game's extensive manual than it does in its rudimentary game play) and the release of the game was tied into the revival of the same character in the serial 'Mawdryn Undead' that was broadcast on television earlier that year. Sadly, the Doctor's role in the game is once again reduced to blasting aliens to smithereens and performing heroic acts more suited to Buck Rogers than an eccentric Time Lord famous for favouring brain over brawn.[22]

However, while it is certainly possible to find antecedents for rudimentary transmedia storytelling (in the case of *Doctor Who*, this stretches back to the release of its first Annual in

1965), these are examples of what we would now recognise as franchising:

> There has been an attempt to move icons and brands across media channels, but not necessarily an attempt to extend the story in ways which expanded its scope and meaning. Most previous media franchises were based on reproduction and redundancy, but transmedia represents a structure based on the further development of the storyworld through each new medium.[23]

It has been argued that transmedia storytelling can result in a more coherent and unified entertainment experience but that it requires 'a stronger sense of integration' between its elements to succeed,[24] and 'true transmedia storytelling is apt to emerge through structures which encourage co-creation and collaboration'.[25] When it came to the release of 'The Adventure Games', the BBC took a number of steps to ensure that audiences regarded them as integrated and authentic extensions of *Doctor Who*. In promotional interviews, Piers Wenger and Steven Moffat both stressed that the games would be 'like *Doctor Who*. ... [It] will be like being in an episode, participating in an episode.'[26] This connection was made even more explicit when the games were advertised on BBC television; in the short 30-second promotional trailer, the Eleventh Doctor's live-action features suddenly dissolve into his pixellated counterpart – the same man in a different medium (or 'dimension', as the voiceover puts it) and this synergy between the game and the television series is cemented when Matt Smith's voice emerges from the lips of his avatar, adding a level of verisimilitude the *Guardian* was keen to emphasise when they reassured 'worried' viewers who still harboured memories of those early forays into *Doctor Who* video gaming:

> [The fans] should be impressed by the involvement of senior *Doctor Who* staff. Steven Moffat, the head writer and executive producer on the show will also be one of the executive producers on the games. ... Plus, Matt Smith and Karen Gillan have provided full voice-overs.[27]

In fact, publicity material for 'The Adventure Games' emphasised the collaborative nature of the project (further reinforced by the involvement of the television writers, James Moran and Phil Ford, and script-editor Gary Russell) and, above all, it consistently highlighted the games authored seal of approval: 'Steven Moffat wanted to do something big and innovative, and they're his vision: the games are part of the *Doctor Who* canon.'[28] Put simply: these games *count*.

As Elizabeth Evans says, 'New Media elements are no longer added on to support or promote a more recognisable form; the balance between the different elements of a transmedia text has become more equal'[29] and 'The Adventure Games' reflect this new paradigm. By affording the games canonical status, and by stressing their connection to the television series as part of a co-ordinated and collaborative vision, BBC producers have also demonstrated that they understand the value that an audience can place upon this model of production, a model that cannot be underestimated, as Geoffrey Long warns when he criticises George Lucas for failing to engage with his own Expanded Universe:

> If the primary auteur behind the franchise considers all of these spin-off works optional, how then are audiences supposed to treat them? ... [P]ity the poor casual fan who enjoyed *Return of the Jedi* enough to pick up an authorized *Star Wars* novel, then found himself completely bewildered when *The Phantom Menace* directly contradicted the events in the book. It doesn't take very many of these experiences for casual fans to develop a diminished opinion of these secondary media types – consequently, creating 'tiers' of canon leads directly to tiers of perceived narrative value.[30]

In the next section I will examine how 'The Adventure Games' function as a transmedia extension into the universe of *Doctor Who*, and in doing so I will examine Jenkins' claim that a true transmedia work 'needs to combine radical intertexuality and multimodality for the purposes of additive comprehension to be a transmedia story'.[31]

Transmedia Adventuring

Transmedia storytelling is not the same thing as 'radical intertexuality', where stories and characters move across texts in the *same* medium. This type of mono-medium movement already occurred freely between the three established television texts – *Doctor Who*, *Torchwood* and *The Sarah Jane Adventures* – the Saxon meme leaked into *Torchwood*, for example, while characters from both spin-offs have appeared in the parent programme. However, for storytelling to be truly transmedia, this movement has to take place across *different* media.

> Games are perhaps, on the surface, the most explicitly *different* from television drama episodes and involve a radical shift in viewer expectations and experience; they must go from watching a television episode to having to have direct input in a game. However, by being constructed as part of a transmedia drama they are also positioned as part of an integrated, coherent narrative experience.[32]

When 'The Adventure Games' were launched in June 2010, transmedia games were nothing particularly new or innovative. In addition to a series of emergent transmedia games already linked to *Doctor Who*,[33] games had also been developed for a number of other franchises, including *24*, *Spooks*,[34] *Battlestar Galactica* and *Lost*.[35] In Derek Johnson's analysis of 2006's 'The Lost Experience' he describes 'content [that] positioned the viewer not as an external spectator looking in on the story, but as a resident situated within the diegetic universe in which the story unfolded',[36] and this description could equally be applied to 'The Adventure Games'.

Every episode of 'The Adventure Games' is structured exactly like a modern episode of *Doctor Who*. The episodes begin with a short – and non-interactive – pre-titles teaser sequence that ends on a mini-cliff-hanger (the revelation that the Daleks have invaded London in 1963, for example) which in turn mirrors a convention that has been used by the series since it returned to television in 2005 to replace the loss (in most cases) of its traditional end-of-episode cliff-hangers.[37] This teaser is then followed by the series' title sequence that has been faithfully re-created in animated form to match that for series five and six and which includes the same arrangement of the theme tune by Murray Gold; the same font is even used to denote the title of the episode and its author. In fact, the narrative structure of these games closely mirrors the traditional three-act structure familiar to viewers of television drama – set-up, confrontation and resolution[38] – and in some ways the games are, strictly speaking, *adaptations* of an existing medium rather than a uniquely structured experience in their own right.

When Piers Wenger described the format of 'The Adventure Games' to journalists, he drew parallels between the show's central character and its game play: 'the Doctor ... doesn't fire a gun under normal circumstances, doesn't take alien life for the sake of it, will always try and find a clever way out of it because he's such a big show-off',[39] and this ethos was shared wholeheartedly by Charles Cecil, the executive producer of the games themselves:

> Right from the beginning we worked closely with the production people. ... Right from the very, very beginning. The key thing in our approach is that the Doctor doesn't use combat to overcome his enemies, so you'll see that a lot of the focus is on the stealth side.[40]

The resultant game play is, on the whole, non-violent; instead of engaging a Dalek in direct combat, the Doctor and Amy are expected to avoid confrontation at all costs. In fact, engagement with the enemy usually results in instant death for the player and in 'City of the Daleks' it takes a peripheral – and non-controllable – character named Sylvia to detonate any explosives. The end of the game sees the Daleks hoisted by their own petard, when the Doctor turns their technology against them, and in the game 'TARDIS' the antagonist is even shown forgiveness by the Time Lord at the end of the adventure, a far cry from the brutal antics of 'Dalek Attack' twenty years earlier. There is also significant emphasis placed on problem solving throughout these adventures, and this is achieved via a number of mini-puzzle-games that test the players' memory, logic and reflexes, instead of their trigger-fingers.

But if the games resolutely mirror the structure and the ethos of the television series, another important factor for any transmedia story is its 'multimodality', a term introduced by Gunther Kress to explore how each medium affords different types of representation.[41] In transmedia terms, 'each medium has different kinds of affordances – the game facilitates different ways of interacting with the content than a book or a feature film. A story that plays out across different media adopts different modalities.'[42]

However, while these games do afford the player the ability to explore and interact with the storyworld in a unique way (for example, piloting the TARDIS or exploring its interior), I would argue that these opportunities are still, at present, limited. For example, when players attempt to explore these game's 'worlds', they are continually forbidden to do so until an appropriate part of the game has been reached or unlocked, and instead of giving players total freedom of movement, they are instead steered through what is still essentially a very linear experience, a possible side-effect of adapting an existing medium (linear television) instead of embracing the type of open-ended modality that computer games can bring.

Another important element of any successful transmedia story is its ability to provide 'additive comprehension', a term borrowed from the game designer Neil Young and developed by Jenkins to describe the degree to which a text can enhance and contribute to the overall understanding of a fictional world. For Jenkins, additive comprehension can take many forms, from simple back story (for example, a webisode prequel; a technique used extensively in series six), to mapping a world (exploring the TARDIS interior and how it operates in the game of the same name), or by offering an alternative perspective on events; a technique used by the mobile game '24: Conspiracy' that was set during the show's fourth season but which featured a new set of characters reacting to its events.[43]

For Jenkins, 'Ideally, each individual episode must be accessible on its own terms even as it makes a unique contribution to the narrative system as a whole'.[44] This ideal is echoed by Evans, who claims that 'different components should contribute different facts to the narrative, ensuring that together they build to a whole that is greater than the sum of its parts'[45] and yet 'The Adventure Games' do *not* contribute to the primary narrative being pursued in the television series; namely, the recurring motif of the mysterious crack in time and the overarching role of the Silence. In fact, while every televised episode of series five features an appearance – however fleeting – by the crack, it is conspicuous by its absence in the games. As Piers Wenger explains, 'I think it's something we can consider in future',[46] but when Steven Moffat was asked if he planned to tie the games into the television series, his reply was unequivocal: 'No. You try to make any individual thing complete in itself.'[47] This is understandable, especially when you consider that 1.6 million people downloaded the first three adventures,[48] a mere fraction of the audience that watched the television episodes. It would be unreasonable if the games were designed as a delivery system for important plot points. A recent example of moving too far in the opposite direction can be found in the recent reboot of *Star Trek* (2009) where it is impossible to fully understand the role and motivations of the characters Spock and Nero if you haven't read the prequel comic books. Furthermore, even if this approach was deemed to be a favourable one, as a public-service broadcaster the BBC operates under a unique set of restrictions, as Russell T Davies made clear during the early transmedia experiments of 2005: 'If you had to buy a BBC novel in order to understand the plot as transmitted on BBC1, then we would be breaking the BBC's guidelines.'[49]

Christy Dena[50] describes two types of transmedia projects. The first disperses a single story across media and the audience is required to engage with *every* text on *every* platform to make complete sense of that story, while the second model is 'a collection of mono-medium stories' that '(continue) across media, (and) can involve the same writer teams, and undergo careful continuity controls. In a transmedia context, all of the stories in each medium are seen as equal contributors to the meaning of the overall storyworld.' 'The Adventure Games' are firmly situated within this second model. While Dena argues that 'the expansion of an existing mono-medium story has it pitfalls – the obvious reason being that the original story was designed to be self-contained and often conclusive' – I would argue that *Doctor Who* is a unique case in this regard. Its fictional universe was created 50 years ago, and while it was certainly never conceived as a transmedia text from the beginning, the story of the Doctor and his TARDIS continues to unfold, with no definitive conclusion in sight, and it is this open-ended narrative that allows transmedia stories to be told within its storyworld without them necessarily impinging or contradicting other mono-medium extensions into that world.

However, while the games do not engage with the primary storyline that remains the focus of this particular era of *Doctor*

Who, they do provide additive comprehension in other ways. First, they introduce new facts to the expanding mythos of the fictional universe (we visit Kaalan, the Dalek's capital city on Skaro, for example) and users are encouraged to harvest discretely packaged chunks of additive comprehension as they travel through the game: hidden within the first four games are 50 cards for the user to collect and each card provides additional information about the television series, including facts about the Doctors, his companions and his enemies. The game even provided educational facts about the game world; for example, in 'City of the Daleks' you can learn about the origin of Nelson's Column, if you can get close enough to it without being spotted by a Dalek, while the final Adventure Game, 'The Gunpowder Plot', came with a Teacher's Resource Pack that was designed to help primary school children use the game to explore key historical facts through game play.[51]

> I used to hate it when I was a kid, where the *Doctor Who* annual wouldn't fit [into the continuity]. It wasn't right. I wouldn't think it was authentic. These [Adventures] are intimately part of the *Doctor Who* universe, and are consistent with it.[52]

While it is never explicitly stated where the first series of 'The Adventure Games' take place in series five, either in official publicity or within the texts themselves, it is possible to deduce their chronological location from the evidence that is provided. The fact that Amy and the Doctor have visited several alien planets and are travelling *sans* Rory in 'City of the Daleks' suggests that the games must take place between the television episodes 'Cold Blood' and 'The Pandorica Opens'. However, in 'Blood of the Cybermen', the second game in the series, Amy seems to be unfamiliar with the titular monsters, and while this would not be a problem per se, she is *still* unfamiliar with them when she is menaced by one in 'The Pandorica Opens'. In fact, it does not matter where one places these games in series five, the end result is always the same: Amy encounters the Cybermen for the first time – *twice*. This discrepancy is exacerbated by the relatively short interval that existed between the transmission of the television episode (19 June 2010) and the release of the game itself (26 June 2010).

Fans who accept the premise that the games are fully-fledged episodes have argued on forums that the fault lies not with the game but with the television episode:

> The games and the television programme are both equally *Doctor Who* (they are both part of the canon), so the small continuity error is in the television programme with that dialogue, there is no continuity error in the game as such, as it is set (seemingly) before the finale.

Others remain more sceptical: 'The TV show doesn't even make sense by itself, so why would you treat the games as anything other than standalone [episodes]? It's fiction, people, it doesn't all have to fit together and sit properly on your shelf.' Meanwhile, others are more pragmatic, suggesting that it isn't possible for a single individual to spin this many narrative plates at once: '[T]hey clearly don't fit! Moffat admits he sometimes just says yes to stuff [because] he's actually focused on the TV product'. As transmedia stories grow larger and encompass more and more media, it becomes increasingly difficult to maintain a consistent and co-ordinated vision and it appears that even the most collaborative and 'authored' transmedia story can result in errors such as these slipping through the cracks.

Conclusion: Transmedia Futures

> There is no transmedia formula. Transmedia refers to a set of choices made about the best approach to tell a particular story to a particular audience in a particular context depending on the particular resources available to particular producers. The more we expand the definition, the richer the range of options available to us can be.[53]

In February 2012, BBC Worldwide announced that a previously commissioned season of 'Adventure Games' had been cancelled. They were replaced with 'Doctor Who: Worlds in Time'[54] in March 2012 – another free-to-play browser-based game.[55] But in a marked departure from the previous games, 'Worlds in Time' would be MMO (Massively Multiplayer Online). This type of networked game play gives users the opportunity to solve puzzles collaboratively with their online friends, reflecting the BBC's desire to tap into the phenomena of social gaming pioneered by the social networking platform Facebook: 'We're targeting not just core gamers, but the "new gamers" out there. The vast majority of the public that don't realise they are gamers, but are engaged online.'[56]

Once again, the BBC was keen to stress that the game's collaborative pedigree would result in an authentic experience for the end user. According to *Doctor Who*'s executive producer Caroline Skinner:

> The production team have been working in a very hand-in-hand way with the gaming team and the BBC Worldwide developers to make sure every storyline, every detail, every monster and the tone and the essence of the game feel as if they're as *Doctor Who* as they possibly can be.[57]

The game's producer, Robert Nashak, was also quick to dismiss any accusations of ancillary redundancy: 'We didn't come here just to deploy the content across platforms – we want to interact with what's happening with the show'[58] – a bold claim that led *SFX Magazine* to ask Caroline Skinner if the game contained spoilers for the upcoming television series (a claim that she did not dismiss).[59]

'Worlds in Time' continues to be updated and expanded, and, assuming its online community continues to grow, the potential exists for the game to reflect the ongoing narrative of the television show much more closely than ever before. As Skinner says: 'The game's going to be going for a very long time and I think that it will evolve and change and absorb storylines.'[60] How integrated these two mediums will become remains to be seen.

In addition to 'Worlds in Time', the corporation has also released a series of games aimed at the handheld market ('The Mazes of Time' for the iPhone and iPad and 'Evacuation: Earth' for the Nintendo DS), and exclusive titles for both the Wii console ('Return to Earth') and the PS3 and PS Vita ('The Eternity Clock'). But it isn't just digital gaming platforms that can deliver transmedia experiences; a wide range of innovative and experimental storytelling techniques have been employed to expand and build upon the fictional world of *Doctor Who* that don't require keyboards – or sometimes even screens – to work.

This process began with 'Doctor Who Live!' – an arena stage show that toured the UK in the winter of 2010.[61] Building on the success of the 'Doctor Who Proms' in 2008 and 2010, the show was part-transmedia performance, part-transmedia spectacle and part-transmedia storytelling (proving that these texts can fit within multiple logics), and the production was the result of another creative collaboration between a mono-medium specialist and the cast and crew of the primary text; it featured a pre-recorded performance by Matt Smith; its linking scenes were co-written by new series writer Gareth Roberts; the music was written especially for the stage show by Murray Gold; it was even pitched by Steven Moffat as a direct sequel to the 1973 television serial 'Carnival of Monsters'.[62]

'The Doctor Who Experience', an exhibition of props and costumes from the television series followed, opening its doors at London's Olympia Two venue on 20 February 2011.[63] What set the 'Experience' apart from *Doctor Who* exhibitions staged previously was the addition of an exclusive feature that was described by the BBC as 'an unmissable adventure featuring an exhilarating and unique walk-through experience'[64] and by Steven Moffat as 'a fan's dream come true – a fully interactive adventure. ... [T]his is the day the Doctor teaches you how to fly the TARDIS through time and space'.[65] Scripted by Moffat, this 'interactive adventure' also featured a pre-recorded performance by Matt Smith, and one especially tactile sequence sees him inviting participants to pilot the TARDIS itself. Presented as a direct sequel to 'The Big Bang' (the Doctor draws attention to the fact that the Alliance just happen to have a spare Pandorica lying around in which to trap him), this immersive walk-through also arguably provides a clue to a possible future direction of the show – when the 'classic' Daleks are seen to begin a civil war against the 'new' Daleks – and only time will tell if this is a possible spoiler or not. Even more additive comprehension is provided to visitors by a 'closed loop' mobile Wi-Fi platform that provides 'an immersive browsing experience related to the aliens, monsters and storylines at the show'.[66] And finally, in July 2011 'Crash of the Elysium', an hour-long theatrical show, placed audiences aged 6 to 12 in the middle of the Eleventh Doctor's investigations into an incursion by the Weeping Angels. Based on a concept by Steven Moffat and scripted by new series writer Tom MacRae, this transmedia theatre experience also featured a pre-recorded video performance by Matt Smith as the Doctor.[67]

In summary, the Eleventh Doctor is a transmedia Doctor. But as he journeys across an expanding media landscape – through television, comics, books, audiobooks, games, webisodes, exhibits and even live performances (did the character of the Doctor *really* appear on stage with Orbital at Glastonbury on 27 June 2010?) – what makes these extensions markedly different from those produced by the traditional model of franchising – a model that was based on repetition and redundancy – is that this iteration of *Doctor Who* is guided and co-ordinated by a true transmedia producer. And if true transmedia storytelling emerges from 'new aesthetic understandings of how popular texts work' that have been shaped in part by 'the rise of geeks and fans to positions of power',[68] then Moffat's position as both producer and fan makes *Doctor Who* an ideal site for transmedia engagement and experimentation to flourish.[69]

Notes

1. BBC Press Release, 'BBC Unveils *Doctor Who* – The Adventure Games', 8 April 2010. Available at www.bbc.co.uk/pressoffice/pressreleases/stories/2010/04_april/08/doctor_who.shtml (accessed 5 August 2011).
2. One reason for this is shift in emphasis is that in 2012 *all* media content is mobile. Instead of producing video previews (or TARDISodes) exclusively for handheld devices, the series now produces video material that can be accessed on every platform.
3. BBC Press Release, 'BBC Unveils *Doctor Who*–The Adventure Games'. Available at www.bbc.co.uk/pressoffice/pressreleases/stories/2010/04_april/08/doctor_who.shtml.
4. The games required a UK IP address to download them. The first two games were eventually released to Windows users in America via the company www.direct2drive.co.uk/ for $4.95.
5. BBC Press Release, 'BBC Unveils *Doctor Who* – The Adventure Games' http://www.bbc.co.uk/pressoffice/pressreleases/stories/2010/04_april/08/doctor_who.shtml.
6. Mark Thompson, 'Delivering Creative Future – Address to BBC Staff', 19 July 2006. Available at www.bbc.co.uk/pressoffice/speeches/stories/thompson_future.shtml (accessed 11 August 2011).

7. Will Brooker, 'Teen Viewers, Cultural Convergence, and Television Overflow', *International Journal of Cultural Studies* 4/4456–72 (2001).

8. Henry Jenkins, 'Transmedia Storytelling', *Technology Review*, 15 January 2003. Available at www.technologyreview.com/Biotech/13052/ (accessed 6 August 2011).

9. John T. Caldwell, 'Second Shift Aesthetics: Programming, Interactivity and User Flows', in Anna Everett and John T. Caldwell (eds) *New Media: Theories and Practices of Digitextuality* (London, 2003), pp. 127–44.

10. Jenkins, 'Transmedia Storytelling'.

11. Henry Jenkins, *Convergence Culture: When Old and New Media Collide* (New York, 2006), pp. 20–1.

12. Henry Jenkins, 'Transmedia Storytelling 101', 22 March 2007. Available at www.henryjenkins.org/2007/03/transmedia_storytelling_101.html (accessed 9 August 2011).

13. 'Your Mom is Transmedia' Available at http://4dfiction.com/2011/03/your-mom-is-transmedia/ (accessed 11 August 2011).

14. Henry Jenkins, 'Transmedia 202 – Further Reflections', 1 August 2011. Available at http://henryjenkins.org/2011/08/defining_transmedia_further_re.html (accessed 12 August 2011).

15. Elizabeth Evans, *Transmedia Television: Audiences, New Media and Daily Life* (London, 2011).

16. Ibid., p. 20.

17. Michael French, 'Who TV Bosses Talk Games', 8 April 2010. Available at www.develop-online.net/features/845/Who-TV-bosses-talk-games (accessed 2 August 2011).

18. In one memorable panel of the 800th edition of *TV Comic* (dated 15 July 1967), the Second Doctor is seen to fire a ray gun at a foe as he shouts, 'Die, hideous creature! Die!'

19. *Your Sinclair Magazine* 88 (1992), p. 50.

20. Jonathan Nash, '*Doctor Who* Dalek Attack Review', *Your Sinclair Magazine* 91 (1992), pp. 8–9.

21. The game was made by BBC Software for the BBC Micro.

22. To be fair to these early games, the television programme is guilty of this inconsistency, too (e.g. 'Day of the Daleks' 1972).

23. Jenkins, 'Transmedia 202'.

24. Evans, *Transmedia Television*, p. 27.

25. Jenkins, 'Transmedia 202'.

26. French, 'Who TV Bosses Talk Games'.

27. Stuart Keith, '*Doctor Who* Adventures – And the Future of Cross-Platform Entertainment', *The Guardian*, 8 August 2010. Available at http://www.guardian.co.uk/technology/gamesblog/2010/apr/08/doctor-who-adventures-bbc (accessed 7 August 2011).

28. Charlie Burton, 'Transmedia *Doctor Who*', *Wired*. 9 July 2010 Available at http://www.wired.co.uk/magazine/archive/2010/08/features/transmedia-doctor-who (accessed 10 August 2011).

29. Evans, *Transmedia Television*, p. 33.

30. Geoffrey Long, *Transmedia Storytelling: Business, Aesthetics and Production at the Jim Henson Company*, Unpublished MA thesis, MIT. Available at http://cms.mit.edu/research/theses/GeoffreyLong2007.pdf (accessed 9 August 2011).

31. Jenkins, 'Transmedia 202', http://henryjenkins.org/2011/08/defining_transmedia_further_re.html.
32. Evans, *Transmedia Television*, p. 84.
33. Neil Perryman, '*Doctor Who* and the Convergence of Media', *Convergence* 14(1), pp. 21–39.
34. Evans, *Transmedia Television*.
35. Derek Johnson, 'The Fictional Institutions of *Lost*: World Building, Reality and the Economical Possibilities of Narrative Divergence, in Roberta Pearson (ed.) *Reading Lost* (London, 2009), pp. 27–51.
36. Johnson, 'The Fictional Institutions of *Lost*', p. 42.
37. However, there is a cliff-hanger at the end of 'TARDIS' that leads directly into 'Shadows of the Vashta Narada'.
38. This adherence to a three-act structure is made even more explicit in the game's loading screens; if you choose to revisit the adventure you have option to join the action during one of three acts.
39. French, 'Who TV Bosses Talk Games', http://www.develop-online.net/features/845/Who-TV-bosses-talk-games.
40. P C Garner, 'The Adventures Games Interviews'. *Computer and Video Games* 9 April 2010. Available at http://www.computerandvideogames.com/241485/blog/doctor-who-the-adventure-games-interviews-steven-moffat-and-charles-cecil/ (accessed 8 August 2011).
41. Gunther Kress, *Multimodality: Exploring Contemporary Methods of Communication* (London, 2009).
42. Jenkins, 'Transmedia 202', http://henryjenkins.org/2011/08/defining_transmedia_further_re.html.
43. Evans, *Transmedia Television*.
44. Jenkins, 'Transmedia Storytelling 101', http://www.henryjenkins.org/2007/03/transmedia_storytelling_101.html.
45. Evans, *Transmedia Television*, p. 29.
46. French, 'Who TV Bosses Talk Games', http://www.develop-online.net/features/845/Who-TV-bosses-talk-games.
47. Ibid.
48. Tom Senior, '*Doctor Who* Adventures Get Second Series' PC Gamer. 20 September 2010. Available at http://www.pcgamer.com/2010/09/20/doctor-who-adventure-games-get-second-series/ (accessed 15 August 2011).
49. Russell T Davies, 'Production Notes', *Doctor Who Magazine* 356 (2005), p. 67.
50. Christy Dena, 'Do You Have a Big Stick?', *If: Book Australia*. 7 February 2011. Online. Available at http://www.futureofthebook.org.au/featured-articles/do-you-have-a-big-stick/ (accessed 12 August 2011).
51. BBC Schools. Available at http://www.bbc.co.uk/schools/teachers/doctor-who_adventuregame/ (accessed 30 May 2012).
52. Garner, 'The Adventure Games interviews', http://www.computerand-videogames.com/241485/blog/doctor-who-the-adventure-games-interviews-steven-moffat-and-charles-cecil/.
53. Jenkins, 'Transmedia 202', http://henryjenkins.org/2011/08/defining_transmedia_further_re.html.
54. *Doctor Who* Worlds in Time Official Website. Available at http://www.doctorwhowit.com/ (accessed 30 May 2012).

55. 'Worlds in Time' is free to play, but it comes with an option to purchase additional game upgrades.

56. Michael French, Interview with Robert Nashak, BBC Worldwide. 23 February 2012. Available at http://www.mcvuk.com/news/read/interview-robert-nashak-bbc-worldwide/091677 (accessed 30 May 2012).

57. Philip Bates, 'Introducing Worlds in Time'. 25 February 2012. Available at http://www.kasterborous.com/2012/02/introducing-worlds-in-time/ (accessed 30 May 2012).

58. French, Interview with Robert Nashak http://www.mcvuk.com/news/read/interview-robert-nashak-bbc-worldwide/091677.

59. Jordan Farley, 'Doctor Who: Worlds in Time – Caroline Skinner Interview'. SFX 23 February 2012. Available at http://www.sfx.co.uk/2012/02/23/doctor-who-worlds-in-time-caroline-skinner-interview/ (accessed 30 May 2012).

60. Ibid.

61. Live transmedia performances are nothing new to Doctor Who, with stage plays appearing in 1965, 1974 and 1985; the latter featured Colin Baker and Jon Pertwee as the Doctor.

62. Dave Golder, 'Doctor Who Live is a sequel to Carnival of Monsters'. SFX 1 September 2010. Available at http://www.sfx.co.uk/2010/09/01/doctor-who-live-is-a-sequel-to-%E2%80%9Ccarnival-of-monsters%E2%80%9D/ (accessed 11 August 2011).

63. It moved to Cardiff in July 2012.

64. BBC Worldwide Press Release, 'Step into the TARDIS and Be Part of the Adventure'. 1 November 2010. Available at http://www.bbc.co.uk/pressoffice/bbcworldwide/worldwidestories/pressreleases/2010/11_november/doctor_who_experience.shtml (accessed 11 August 2011).

65. Ibid.

66. BBC Worldwide Press Release. 'BBC Worldwide Breaks New Ground with Retail and Mobile Plans for Doctor Who Experience'. 8 February 2011. Available at http://www.bbc.co.uk/pressoffice/bbcworldwide/worldwidestories/pressreleases/2011/02_february/dwexp_retail.shtml (accessed 11 August 2011).

67. Matt Smith did appear in person for one performance: 'Doctor Who Actor Matt Smith Steps out of his Tardis at Salford Quays for surprise MIF appearance', Manchester Evening News, 15 July 2011. Available at http://menmedia.co.uk/manchestereveningnews/entertainment/manchester_international_festival/s/1426922_doctor-who-actor-matt-smith-steps-out-of-his-tardis-at-salford-quays-for-surprise-mif-appearance (accessed 11 August 2011).

68. Jenkins, 'Transmedia 202', http://henryjenkins.org/2011/08/defining_transmedia_further_re.html (accessed 4 October 2013).

69. Legacy Games intends to make the fifth instalment of The Adventure Games 'The Gunpowder Plot' available through Valve's Stream gaming platform.

13

FRIENDS REUNITED?

Authorship Discourses and Brand Management for *The Sarah Jane Adventures* 'Death of the Doctor'

Ross P. Garner

On 30 September 2010, the BBC press pack for series four of *The Sarah Jane Adventures* (BBC, 2006–11) – *Doctor Who*'s primarily child-targeted spin-off that aired on both the institution's CBBC service and within BBC1's afternoon children's schedules – was released. This set of documents provided potential buyers and publicity outlets with a summarising overview of the six adventures within the series and singled out the story 'Death of the Doctor' (2010) for special attention. Part of the reason for this was that the episode was to feature guest appearances by both Matt Smith as the Eleventh Doctor and Katy Manning, who would reprise her role as 'classic' companion Jo Grant for the first time since 1973's 'The Green Death'. Consideration of existing production trends on *The Sarah Jane Adventures* undermines this promotional rhetoric, however: outgoing Tenth Doctor David Tennant had featured in the previous year's 'The Wedding of Sarah Jane Smith' (2009), setting a precedent for crossovers to occur between *The Sarah Jane Adventures* and its parent series.[1] At the same time, the inclusion of Manning can be read as having been the continuation of an established production strategy used on *The Sarah Jane Adventures*. This strategy involved extending the programme's appeal beyond children alone by providing nostalgic pleasures for adult and/ or fan audiences. This was attempted through including stars from either 'cult' children's television – such as *Play School*'s (BBC 1964–88) Floella Benjamin as Professor Rivers in 'The Lost Boy' (2007) and 'The Eternity Trap' (2009) – or 'classic' *Doctor Who* – such as the reappearance of Nicholas Courtney's Sir Alistair Gordon Lethbridge-Stewart in 'Enemy of the Bane' (2008) – as supporting characters in individual stories.[2] Thus, although useful for marketing *The Sarah Jane Adventures*' fourth series, contextualisation of these aspects within the programme's history challenges their uniqueness.

However, further attention was directed towards 'Death of the Doctor' within official press material since it was to be written by Russell T Davies, *Doctor Who*'s executive producer between 2005 and 2009, and marked his first return to the franchise he helped reinvigorate. The press release suggests that Davies remains a 'recognizable thematic and stylistic presence'[3] within television's promotional practices by including a quote from Nikki Wilson, one of *The Sarah Jane Adventures*' executive producers, stating that 'to have a script written by Russell T Davies [for 'Death of the Doctor'] is the icing on the cake'.[4] This statement echoes Kim Newman's observation that '*Doctor Who* (2005–) was from the first seen … as *authored*' due to Davies's involvement and that, despite now being detached from the *Doctor Who* franchise, his status as an established auteur was still useful for marketing purposes.[5] This chapter extends these initial observations by considering the strategies employed for managing Davies's status as televisual auteur in relation to promotional material for 'Death of the Doctor' and the *Doctor Who* franchise post-2009. The discussion takes a post-structuralist approach to authorship, examining how Davies's author-function was constructed and negotiated within the cultural site of publicity discourses and examines a range of press sources. In doing so, it argues for a contextual approach to studying the construction of televisual auteurs that addresses how issues such as target audience and ownership impact upon how, where and when authors become articulated within publicity discourses. The advantages of contextually based research have been demonstrated elsewhere in Television Studies recently, such as Matt Hills' discussion of how *Doctor Who*'s status as 'cult' TV comes about due to the series' appropriation within this discourse in different historical and/or national contexts.[6] It is the argument of this chapter that a similar approach should be applied when studying contemporary television authorship discourses from an industrial perspective since this allows the mobilisation of individual author-functions to be aligned with practices used throughout the television industry nowadays, such as branding.

Crossing the Boundaries? Branding, Authorship Hierarchies and Intra-Franchise Complications

Catherine Johnson observes that 'branding has emerged as the defining industrial practice' within the present TVIII era and this is a point that has received widespread recognition amongst television scholars.[7] The importance of distinctly branded products to the television industry nowadays can be accredited to the combination of social, technological and political changes (amongst others) that have impacted upon television over the last 30 years and resulted in the continuing fragmentation of audiences across myriad channels and platforms of delivery.[8] It is unsurprising, then, that debates surrounding television and branding have addressed issues of authorship such as in Roberta Pearson's recognition that

> in the post-classic network system era the names of important hyphenates [i.e. showrunners occupying a role as head writer and/or executive producer on a series], the hyphenate brand as it were, [have] proved more attractive to demographically desirable audiences than ... the network brand.[9]

Similar to how within cinema marketing practices 'auteurs have become increasingly situated along an extra-textual path in which their commercial status as auteurs is their chief function', the marketing of a television series through the name of its hyphenate accrues distinction to the programme by allowing it to be promoted as authored.[10] However, within this promotional context, it should be remembered that the value of an authored television series arises through the correlation between that series and the singular name of its hyphenate. Think, for instance, of Joss Whedon and *Buffy the Vampire Slayer* (Fox/Mutant Enemy 1997–2003) or Aaron Sorkin and *The West Wing* (Warner Bros./John Wells Productions 1999–2006). This is because

> [t]he author's name serves to characterise a certain mode of being in discourse: the fact that the discourse has an author's name…shows that this discourse…is a speech that must be received in a certain mode and that, in a given culture, must receive a certain status.[11]

In terms of television promotion, because a specific programme can be credited to the agency of a specific individual, a series becomes culturally valued 'through the recuperation of the trusted Creator' within publicity material.[12]

One-to-one associations between hyphenate and series have been complicated with regard to *Doctor Who* since its post-2005 re-launch, however, in that 'the programme has been promoted as multi-authored, in line with egalitarian fan discourses'.[13] This observation appears, from one perspective, to have continued to be applicable to post-2009 *Who* since strategies of multi-authorship remained observable. Prior to its cancellation, *Doctor Who Confidential*, to take one example, provided opportunities for writers of individual episodes such as Neil Gaiman and Mark Gattis to reflect upon their work and their affiliation with the series. Despite this multi-authorship approach, it is nevertheless arguable that current head writer/executive producer Steven Moffat provided an overarching 'classificatory function…permit[ing] one to group together a certain number of texts, define them, differentiate them from and contrast them to others' on both this programme and beyond.[14] On *Doctor Who Confidential*, Moffat regularly provided further comments upon individual stories by either contextualising plots in relation to ongoing serialised arcs – see 'What Dreams May Come' (2011) – or appearing in footage which positioned him as the key creative influence upon the series. His presence presiding over a read-through session for the non-Moffat episode 'The God Complex' in the *Doctor Who Confidential* episode 'Heartbreak Hotel' (2011) provided just one example of this point. Similarly, Moffat's construction as auteur-hyphenate against a backdrop of multi-authorship is also readable from *Radio Times* articles credited to his name which either offer synopses of all of the stories in a series run[15] or provide explanations surrounding the themes/motivations behind each season.[16] This recurring construction of Moffat connotes a hierarchy of authorship to audiences in that, although individual writers are allowed to comment on their own work,[17] Moffat remains a consistent presence across publicity for post-2009 *Doctor Who* that invites audiences to classify these seasons through his name.

However, despite the authorial hierarchy constructed around post-2009 *Who*, consideration of the series' present approach to authorship can be complicated by expanding out to consider such issues in relation to BBC Wales' entire *Doctor Who* franchise. BBC Wales had developed 'three distinct continents' prior to its refranchising under Moffat's author-function that included two spin-off series – *Torchwood* and *The Sarah Jane Adventures*.[18] Taking *The Sarah Jane Adventures* as an example indicates how, since being commissioned in 2006, this series was continuously promoted by the BBC as '[c]reated by Russell T Davies's.[19] This should not be taken as evidence of Davies having being constructed as singular auteur for *The Sarah Jane Adventures*; however, since, in line with the strategies used elsewhere in the franchise post-2005, press releases for the programme also used a multi-authorship approach. For example, the official documentation for the launch of series five featured an interview with Phil Ford (identified as the series' head writer) whilst still attributing the programme as a whole to Davies's creative agency.[20] Once again, a hierarchy of authorship became connoted since, although writers of individual stories were constructed as authors for *The Sarah Jane Adventures*, these positions were ultimately secondary to Davies's overseeing of the programme. Davies's presence therefore provided 'a constant level of value' to *The Sarah Jane Adventures* by allowing the series to be promoted through the widespread recognition of his status as a contemporary televisual auteur for programmes including *Queer as Folk* (Channel 4/Red Productions, 1999), *Bob and Rose* (ITV/Red Productions, 2001) and *The Second Coming* (ITV/Red Productions, 2003).[21] Thus, whilst Moffat is presently constructed as hyphenate on *Doctor Who*, Davies retained an association with the wider franchise through occupying a similar role on *The Sarah Jane Adventures*.

'Death of the Doctor' therefore provides an opportunity for considering intra-franchise strategies for managing discourses of authorship within post-2009 *Doctor Who*. However, to fully understand the promotional discourses constructed for this story, an approach to studying authorship that addresses how contextual issues impact upon constructions of author-functions needs to be outlined. The next section introduces this method by examining one of the ways in which Davies's status as auteur was set up in press material for the story.

The Contexts of Authorship, or Why it is Important to Consider How, Where and When Authorship Discourses Become Constructed

John Ainsworth's coverage of 'Death of the Doctor' for the fan-orientated *Doctor Who Magazine* in many ways echoed the BBC press release for the story by highlighting Davies's script, and the presence of Smith and Manning as guest stars, as having been central to the story's appeal.[22] Within this article, quotes attributed to the episodes' guest stars provided one area where Davies's status as televisual auteur became constructed: 'Katy is clearly delighted with the wealth of history that Russell has given Jo, which reveals much about her life since she left the Doctor in *The Green Death* to get married and travel up the Amazon'.[23] This sentiment was also stated in other sources, since Manning is quoted in an interview with *SFX* magazine as having said:

> When I read the script I thought he'd done the most wonderful job on what would have happened to her. ... What a wonderful man, and didn't he do this country a huge service by bringing back this remarkable programme with the love and passion that he did? What's lovely is that everything Russell did is in absolute keeping with everything that she was 40 years ago.[24]

Both of these statements drew upon romantic discourses of the author as creative genius by highlighting the rounded characterisation given to Jo Grant. Although this was not the only way in which Davies was constructed in romantic terms – Matt Smith is quoted as having said that it was 'an honour and a privilege' to be working on a Davies-penned script[25] – the underlying assumptions behind this construction are common within academic discussion of televisual auteurs. Television Studies work in this area has previously mobilised a discourse that celebrates specific writers for their understanding of characterisation. Moreover, such character-based appraisals are typical of discourses concerning 'quality' television since depth of character is usually identified as a hallmark of this televisual form.[26]

However, identifiable alongside this romanticised discourse of authorship in the above quotes is another discourse concerning fan authenticity. This second discourse positioned Davies not only as a 'good' television writer but also as an author displaying an excellent understanding of the metatextual world of *Doctor Who* by implying that Davies developed Jo Grant in a manner consistent with the character's previously established traits.[27] The presence of this second discourse within constructions of Davies-as-auteur provides an entry point for addressing why discussions of authorship should consider issues of context concerning how, where and when specific authors become constructed. Song Hwee Lim alludes to this point – albeit from the discipline of Film Studies – by asking 'in what sense, and for whom, is ... an auteur?'[28] Similarly, in an analysis of how David Lynch's position as auteur for *Dune* (1984) has been negotiated, Tony Todd suggests how constructions of authors respond to issues arising from historical and industrial contexts by identifying that

> On its theatrical release *Dune* was not promoted, nor widely read, as 'a Film by David Lynch'. His emergence in the promotion and reception of his films only properly occurs through the release of *Blue Velvet* (David Lynch, 1986), written and directed by Lynch sequentially following *Dune* (and for the same production company, DEG). This fact points to the historically transient and volatile nature of meanings.[29]

Todd's analysis of Lynch and *Dune* thus highlights how 'the identification of a creative source will differ according to its marketing and publicity contexts' and so suggests that analyses of authorship need to address the historical and industrial contexts in which discourses of authorship become constructed (or avoided).[30]

A contextually rooted approach to authorship is suggested in Michel Foucault's work on author-functions through its identification of the author as a status linked to industrialisation.[31] This idea can be used to analyse the presence of a discourse of fan authenticity within publicity material concerning Davies and 'Death of the Doctor'. Cult texts such as *Doctor Who* are partly defined by their seriality and, subsequently, their ability to construct vast ongoing narrative worlds.[32] At the same time, as John Tulloch and Henry Jenkins have argued, 'fans…dr[a]w on the textual history of the series to establish the "common ground" of their interpretive community'.[33] Given the propensity for cult TV fans to occupy a reading formation that proffers interpreting their favoured programme in terms of its series history,[34] it can be assumed that characters returning to the programme's narrative world after a period of absence need to display consistency with their established textual past to win fan approval. Mobilising a discourse of fan authenticity to construct Davies-as-auteur suggests a promotional strategy having being implemented within the context of fan-orientated magazines such as *SFX* and *Doctor Who Magazine* in order to (re)affirm Davies's credentials with fans of 'classic' *Doctor Who*. Foucault's notion of the author-function focuses primarily upon 'practices or assumptions in textual reception or dissemination' and considering this point suggests that discourses of fan authenticity were employed to construct Russell T Davies within the context of niche-orientated fan magazines to mirror fan reading preferences.[35] Thus, by combining analysis of the discursive mixture utilised in the construction of an auteur with consideration of the promotional micro-context in which articulation occurs, greater understanding of how and why specific discourses become employed in the construction of an individual auteur can be provided.

It has been necessary to consider one of the strategies used for securing Davies's position as auteur for 'Death of the Doctor' here since it has allowed for a contextual approach to authorship to be outlined. The next section extends these ideas by considering a range of alternative discourses used for discussing Davies's role as writer of 'Death of the Doctor' within extratextual material. It will be argued here that, when these discourses are aligned with a contextual approach to studying authorship, the discourses used to construct Davies's role writing for the Eleventh Doctor related to the programme's brand management and the need to maintain authorial hierarchies on post-2009 *Doctor Who*.

Distancing the Doctor: Authorship Management Strategies for 'Death of the Doctor'

Working alongside the aforementioned strategies for construct-ing Davies as a televisual auteur within niche-targeted publicity material are another set of statements which ultimately com-plicated Davies's claims to this status. One example of this can be seen in how 'Death of the Doctor' became contextualised in some of its coverage amongst institutional production practices within the BBC. Andrew Pixley's outline of the story's production history alludes to this by stating:

> [w]hen work on the stories for the fifth series of *The Sarah Jane Adventures* took priority for Phil Ford, [producer] Nikki Wilson called Russell in Los Angeles and asked him if he would be will-ing to write the Doctor/Jo story himself.[36]

Moreover, Davies self-construction in articles also intersected with this discourse. In an interview with *Doctor Who Magazine,* Davies used 'ratings discourse'[37] to account for his involvement with the story by suggesting that one of the key motivating fac-tors behind the story's development was the success achieved by David Tennant's appearance in *The Sarah Jane Adventures* during the previous season:

> [W]hen ratings lift like they did for *The Wedding of Sarah Jane Smith*, then the whole of BBC One's shift increases, so you get a very happy Channel Controller, which is good for all of us! So some sort of boost every year would be good. But really,

it was just perfect timing – David appeared during his swan-song, which then automatically suggested that Matt should visit Bannerman Road.[38]

In both of these cases, discourses became mobilised that drew attention to the problems of discussing authorship in relation to television since industrial working practices place limitations upon the agency of creative individuals.[39] When read within the context of this discourse, then, Smith's (as well as Manning's) appearance in 'Death of the Doctor' were readable as 'clever marketing'[40] strategies used by *The Sarah Jane Adventures'* producers since their guest roles were implemented with a view towards 'increas[ing] the possibility that a viewer hooked on one ... series ... may become an avid viewer of the other'.[41] Thus, whilst Davies's role as televisual auteur was offered up in press material for 'Death of the Doctor', romanticised constructions of his authorship within certain publications existed alongside an industrial discourse that constructed him as a professional television worker.

Multiple interpretations of Davies's divided construction can be offered. On the one hand, this discursive representation offers a variation upon Hills' characterisation of Davies as 'a (de)materialising auteur – present and absent' within publicity material for pre-Moffat *Who*.[42] This is because his authorial role was simultaneously secured (Davies-as-subculturally – valued creative force) and displaced – (Davies-as-working professional) within coverage of the story. However, addressing contextual issues regarding how, where and when authorial discourses are constructed provides a more nuanced understanding of Davies's representation here. Industrial discourses stressing the production background for 'Death of the Doctor' appeared in fan-targeted magazines and it has been recognised elsewhere in work on fandom that fans place high value upon gaining 'access to behind-the-scenes information and "insider" knowledge' about their chosen object.[43] Production history information provides fans with an opportunity to accrue subcultural capital by making such readers aware of production details.[44] So, by providing such information in niche-targeted publications, the presence of an industrial discourse could be read as an(other) example of fan reading preferences being appropriated by media industries and sold back to fans within niche-targeted magazines.

This reading appears further valid if a statement accredited to Matt Smith, which appeared in both the *Radio Times'* coverage of 'Death of the Doctor' and the official BBC press release, is considered. In both of these sources, Smith singled out the story's aliens – intergalactic vulture-like undertakers named the Shansheeth – for praise by saying they are 'very impressive. We should get them into an episode of *Doctor Who.*'[45] On the one hand, this statement again drew upon romanticised discourses to position Davies as a valued television writer. However, if this construction is contextualised, it demonstrates how different authorship strategies were mobilised in publications addressing alternative readerships. Recent distribution information for the *Radio Times* shows it has an average weekly circulation of around 900,000 copies with this figure including a slightly higher percentage of female than male readers and high popularity with ABC1 demographics (75 per cent of its readership).[46] The *Radio Times* thus has significantly more readers than the 31,000 average circulation for *Doctor Who Magazine* each month and this indicates of how the former extends beyond niche fan appeal to address a wider section of the TV audience.[47] If a contextual approach to constructions of television authorship is mobilised, then, an account can be provided regarding why different constructions of an established auteur occur in different publications. Fan-targeted magazines appropriate fan reading preferences by combining romanticised discourses of authorship with allusions to industrial factors,[48] whereas listings magazines with wider appeal offer different, arguably more singular, characterisations of figures such as Davies by only drawing attention to romantic issues such as creativity.

However, if some sources suggested the potential for Davies's alien creations to move across the wider franchise, a different discursive strategy was employed across all publicity material concerning the issue of Davies writing for the Eleventh Doctor. Some publicity material avoided engaging with this topic altogether – such as coverage of 'Death of the Doctor' for the *Radio Times*[49] – consequently suggesting that this issue would not be a concern for certain audience groups. However, when the concept of intra-franchise authorship was raised in publicity material for 'Death of the Doctor', specific discursive strategies became identifiable that could be related to the aforementioned issues concerning Moffat's position as hyphenate-brand for post-2009

Who. For example, Pixley's research into 'Death of the Doctor' identifies that, when asked about writing for Smith's Doctor, Davies's self-construction combined an industry professional discourse with one concerning the brand's authorial hierarchy:

> By the time I came to write *Death of the Doctor*, I'd only read the scripts for *The Eleventh Hour* and *The Time of Angels*, then I'd stopped, not wanting to be spoiled! But then I had to research Matt Smith's Doctor, so ... Steven [Moffat] kindly sent me copies of finished edits of *The Time of Angels* and *Flesh and Stone*. ... I also emailed Steven about the Eleventh Doctor's character in general ... And Gareth Roberts filled me in on [the Doctor saying] 'Come along, Pond!' which I adapted to 'Come along, Smith!'[50]

Davies positioned himself here as a combination of 'jobbing writer' (e.g., working with the materials of others in this instance) and 'everyday television viewer' by drawing attention to how wider knowledge of Moffat-era *Who* might disrupt the pleasures of watching the programme within its scheduled position. This approach to self-presentation recurred elsewhere in interviews for the story, however, such as Davies's response of '[o]h I love him. He's limitless, isn't he?' when questioned about Smith in an article with the *Guardian* newspaper.[51]

In both of these instances, Davies's construction as auteur drew upon distancing discourses to remove associations between himself and the Eleventh Doctor – arguably one of the cornerstones of Moffat-era *Who*. A variety of inflections of this distancing discourse could be identified in a range of other publications: an interview with *SFX* saw Davies joke about the situation Moffat would be in as *Doctor Who*'s hyphenate at different times of the year and so connoted his separation from this area of the franchise.[52] Alternatively, a different set of distancing discourses was evident in comments made in an interview with the CBBC website's *Sarah Jane Adventures* page. Within this context, Davies widened out issues concerning authorship and writing for the Eleventh Doctor by refocusing them upon his involvement with the programme which he still operated as hyphenate for:

> That was the greatest attraction of taking this commission – not just introducing the Eleventh Doctor and Jo to SJA-world, but

getting to write for Lis, Daniel and Anjli. (And even Tommy too, briefly, as you'll see!) I've spent so long creating these characters, and working on every draft of the scripts, every edit and dub, without being able to give them words myself.[53]

The presence of this distancing discourse between Davies's authorship and the character of the Eleventh Doctor suggests that there was an attempt to construct rigid discursive boundaries around different eras of the *Doctor Who* franchise within publicity material. What's more, the recurrence of inflections of this discourse across a range of sources addressing divergent audience groups (fans, children and beyond) suggests that securing a correlation between the Eleventh Doctor's character and Moffat's author-function formed a key part of *Doctor Who*'s post-2009 rebranding and reformatting.

This point can be further explored by considering these distancing discourses within the context of media ownership. Martin Flanagan touches upon issues surrounding how ownership of publicity outlets such as magazines impacts upon press coverage of movie releases by highlighting how

many of the reviews and reports of blockbuster movies to be found in mass-market film publications like *Empire* and *Total Film* in the UK or *Premiere* in the USA stay faithfully 'on-message' with the studio sanctioned party line.[54]

From this perspective, popular publications targeted towards an audience of cinema fans predominantly fulfil 'an unabashed cheerleading function ... frequently proffering on-set access that is essentially uncritical and designed to convey studio-vetted information to anxious fans'.[55] A similar, less cynically toned, point can be made in relation to the presence of discourses distancing Davies's auteur status from the Eleventh Doctor in publicity for 'Death of the Doctor'. For example, until recently, the *Radio Times* was owned by BBC Worldwide[56] – the BBC's commercial arm. If this ownership knowledge is aligned with the absence of questions concerning Davies and the Eleventh Doctor within this publication's coverage of 'Death of the Doctor', the avoidance of this line of questioning can potentially be read as having been a promotional strategy implemented by the BBC to maintain the integrity of post-2009 *Doctor Who* as a Moffat-authored product. Similarly, since *Doctor Who*'s 2005 re-launch, *Doctor Who Magazine* has operated under an official licence from BBC Worldwide despite being outsourced to Panini UK[57] whilst BBC Online (which houses the official *Sarah Jane* site) remains an in-house production.[58] Given the distancing strategies observable within the coverage of 'Death of the Doctor' in publicity material from these official sources, these discourses can be read as having been different branches of the same promotional strategy where potential challenges to *Doctor Who*'s post-2009 author branding were avoided by positioning Davies away from Matt Smith's Eleventh Doctor.

Of course, although Davies's authorship was managed in a way that distanced his author-function from specific aspects of post-2009 *Who* in some publicity material, other non-licensed material has nevertheless read the story in terms of his authorial signature(s). A review of the story by Dan Martin in the *Guardian*, for example, stated that

> This could hardly been more of a Russell T Davies script, his familiar tropes turned up to ... Eleven. There were animal-headed aliens. There was a jolly chase around a ventilation shaft. There were lashings of brazen sentimentality. ... Moreover, Death of the Doctor established Matt Smith in the role as much as any of his episodes in the main show.[59]

This comment is significant to the focus of this chapter since it occurred within the context of press material that is external to the control of BBC publicity. The review subsequently contributed towards what Jonathan Hardy names 'the non-corporate controlled axis'[60] of the commercial intertextuality characterising individual television programmes at present where "'independent' news, commentary, previews and reviews in public media ... together influence relations between texts and readers'[61]. The aspects of 'Death of the Doctor' mentioned above (as well as other textual markers such as references to the Tenth Doctor visiting previous companions prior to regenerating, and a nod to the Time Lords and the Time War) may have aided different contextually located audience groups like reviewers or fans to have classified the story in relation to Davies's authorial voice. However, the outspoken tone adopted by Martin could not have occurred within the context of BBC-owned/-licensed press material since such statements represent officially sanctioned challenges to the brand value of post-2009 *Who* as a product authored by Steven Moffat. Thus, whilst Martin's review indicates how audiences could read the Eleventh Doctor's characterisation in the story through Davies's author-function, these statements occurred within a reception context that is separate from the BBC's current branding practices for the series.

Conclusion

This chapter has investigated authorship discourses relating to the *Doctor Who* franchise post-2009 and used these as a case study for thinking about intra-franchise brand management strategies. By examining how Russell T Davies, *Doctor Who*'s former executive producer and ongoing auteur-hyphenate for *The Sarah Jane Adventures*, was constructed in publicity material for 'Death of the Doctor' it has been argued that a variety of overlapping discourses (romantic, fan authenticity, industrial, distancing, etc.) were drawn upon to construct and contest his ongoing status as televisual auteur. However, to account for where and when the range of discourses identifiable in press material for the story became used, a context-based approach to studying Davies's author-function has been employed. This approach involves addressing how and why certain discourses became utilised in different press sources and relating these constructions to the reading formations adopted by specific target audiences. The fact that fan-orientated publications such as *Doctor Who Magazine* constructed Davies in a manner which recognised his status as auteur, but complicated these claims via addressing industrial-production issues, can be read as an approach to authorship that was aligned with fan reading preferences for behind-the-scenes information. Going further, though, this chapter has also argued that, if a contextual approach to studying constructions of authorship is to be taken, attention also needs to be paid to a range of micro-contextual issues arising from the cultural site of articulation including ownership. Placing authorial constructions against a backdrop of who owns or licences the publication where a TV auteur becomes constructed can provide subsequent insights in to the strategies utilised for accruing distinction to a series. In the case of 'Death of the Doctor', the fact that a variety of distancing discourses were identifiable when lines of questioning concerning Davies writing for Matt Smith's Eleventh Doctor were explored becomes suggestive of there having been an attempt on behalf of the BBC Press Office to remove associations between Davies's name and a version of the Doctor assigned to Moffat's authorship. Having aspects of the Eleventh Doctor readable through an alternative author-function may have devalued the post-2009 *Doctor Who* brand by disrupting the authorial hierarchy set-up elsewhere in the series' promotion.

In conclusion, then, addressing the concept of televisual authorship from a discursive perspective, and placing such analysis against a backdrop of micro-contextual factors arising from the site of articulation, can move beyond the auterist paradigm that is still observable in some TV Studies work on authorship.[62] Instead, by combing a focus upon contextual issues with the analysis of discourses of authorship, the latter concept can be aligned with key debates concerning the TVIII era such as its focus on brand management.

Notes

1. Ross P. Garner, '"Don't You Forget About Me": Intertextuality and Generic Anchoring in *The Sarah Jane Adventures*', in Ross P. Garner, Melissa Beattie and Una McCormack (eds) *Impossible Worlds, Impossible Things: Cultural Perspectives on Doctor Who, Torchwood and The Sarah Jane Adventures* (Newcastle upon Tyne, 2010), p. 161.
2. Richard Lewis, *The Encyclopaedia of Cult Children's Television* (London, 2002).
3. John Caughie, 'Introduction: Part Three – Fiction of the Author/Author of the Fiction', in John Caughie (ed.) *Theories of Authorship: A Reader* (London, 1981), p. 200.
4. BBC Press Office, 'Press Packs – *The Sarah Jane Adventures*: Introduction'. 30 September 2010. Available at www.bbc.co.uk/pressoffice/pressreleases/stories/2010/09_september/30/sja.shtml (accessed 27 July 2011).
5. Kim Newman, *BFI TV Classics: Doctor Who: A Critical Reading of the Series* (London, 2005), p. 113.
6. Matt Hills, '*Doctor Who*', in David Lavery (ed.) *The Essential Cult TV Reader* (Lexington, 2010), p. 99.

7. Catherine Johnson, 'Tele-Branding in TVIII: The Network as Brand and the Programme as Brand', *New Review of Film and Television Studies*, v/1 (2007), p. 6.

8. Robin Nelson, 'HBO Premium: Channelling Distinction through TVIII', *New Review of Film and Television Studies*, v/1 (2007), pp. 25–9.

9. Roberta Pearson, 'The Writer/Producer in American Television', in Michael Hammond and Lucy Mazdon (eds) *The Contemporary Television Series* (Edinburgh, 2005), p. 17.

10. Timothy Corrigan, 'The Commerce of Auteurism', in Virginia Wright Wexman (ed.) *Film and Authorship* (New Brunswick, NJ, 2003), p. 100.

11. Michel Foucault, 'What is an Author?', in Paul Rabinow (ed.) *The Foucault Reader* (London, 1991), p. 107.

12. Matt Hills, *Fan Cultures* (London, 2002), p. 133.

13. Matt Hills, *Triumph of a Time Lord: Regenerating Doctor Who in the Twenty-First Century* (London, 2010), p. 26.

14. Foucault, 'What is an Author?', p. 107.

15. Steven Moffat, 'The Ultimate Episode Guide', *Radio Times*, 16–22 April 2011 and Steven Moffat, 'The Ultimate Episode Guide by Executive Producer Steven Moffat', *Radio Times*, 27 August–2 September 2011.

16. Steven Moffat, 'Who's Ready for the Ghost Train?', *Radio Times*, 16–22 April 2011 and Gareth McLean, 'Who is My Hero? Steven Moffat Chooses ...', *Radio Times*, 1–7 October 2011.

17. For complications of this point see Matt Hills, 'Steve Thompson's Steven Moffat's *Doctor Who*: A Pirate Copy?', 9 May 2011. Available at http://blog.commarts.wisc.edu/2011/05/09/steve-thompsons-steven-moffats-doctor-who-a-pirate-copy/ (accessed 10 May 2011).

18. Neil Perryman, 'Doctor Who and the Convergence of Media: A Case Study in Transmedia Storytelling' 14/1, *Convergence, pp.* 21–39.

19. BBC Press Office, 'Final Series of The Sarah Jane Adventures starts on CBBC'. 27 September 2011. Available at www.bbc.co.uk/pressoffice/pressreleases/stories/2011/09_september/27/sj.shtml (accessed 30 September 2011). See also BBC Press Office, 'Russell T Davies Creates New Series for CBBC, starring *Doctor Who*'s Sarah Jane Smith', 14 September 2006. Available at www.bbc.co.uk/pressoffice/pressreleases/stories/2006/09_september/14/sarah.shtml (accessed 2 January 2007) and BBC Press Office, 'The Doctor to Appear in CBBC Drama *The Sarah Jane Adventures*', 26 May 2009. Available at www.bbc.co.uk/pressoffice/pressreleases/stories/2009/05_may/26/sarah_jane.shtml (accessed 25 August 2009).

20. BBC Press Office, 'Interview with Phil Ford', 27 September 2011. Available at www.bbc.co.uk/pressoffice/pressreleases/stories/2011/09_september/27/sj2.shtml (accessed 30 September 2011).

21. Foucault, 'What is an Author?', p. 111. See also Mark Duguid, 'That was Then, This is Now', *Sight and Sound* (June 2010).

22. John Ainsworth, 'Funeral for a Friend', *Doctor Who Magazine* 427 (2010), p. 16.

23. Ibid.

24. Ian Berriman, 'Grant: An Audience', *SFX Collection 47: Doctor Who – A Celebration* (2011), p. 46.

25. Ainsworth, 'Funeral for a Friend', p. 20.

26. Sarah Cardwell, 'Is Quality Television Any Good?: Generic Distinctions, Evaluations and the Troubling Matter of Critical Judgement', in Janet McCabe and Kim Akass (eds) *Quality TV: Contemporary American Television and Beyond* (London, 2007), pp. 26–7.

27. Roberta E. Pearson and Máire Messenger-Davies, 'You're Not Going to See that on TV' *Star Trek: The Next Generation* in Film and Television', in Mark Jancovich and James Lyons (eds) *Quality Popular Television* (London, 2003), p. 114.

28. Song Hwee Lim, 'Positioning Auteur Theory in Chinese Cinema Studies: Intratextuality, Intertextuality and Paratextuality in the Films of Tsai Ming-Liang', *Journal of Chinese Cinemas*, 1/3 (2007), p. 224.

29. Tony Todd, 'Meanings and Authorship in *Dune*', *Film-Philosophy*, 13/1 (2009), p. 69.

30. Ibid., p. 75.

31. Foucault, 'What is an Author?', p. 108.

32. Hills, *Fan Cultures*, pp. 138–9.

33. John Tulloch and Henry Jenkins, *Science Fiction Audiences: Watching Doctor Who and Star Trek* (London, 1995), p. 141.

34. Tulloch and Jenkins, *Science Fiction Audiences*, pp. 134–42.

35. Rachel Blay DuPlessis, 'Agency, Social Authorship, and the Political Aura of Contemporary Poetry', *Textual Practice*, 23/6 (2009), p. 987. See Tom Steward, 'Author Who? Masterplanners, Scribermen, and Script Doctors; The Producers, Writers, and Script Editors of *Doctor Who*', in Christopher J. Hansen (ed.) *Ruminations, Peregrinations, and Regenerations: A Critical Approach to Doctor Who* (Newcastle, 2010).

36. Andrew Pixley, *Doctor Who Magazine Special Edition: The Sarah Jane Companion Volume Two* (2011), p. 77.

37. Ien Ang, *Desperately Seeking the Audience* (London, 1991).

38. Davies in Ainsworth, 'Funeral for a Friend', p. 19.

39. Virginia Wright Wexman, 'Introduction', in Virginia Wright Wexman (ed.) *Film and Authorship* (New Brunswick, NJ, 2003), pp. 11–12.

40. Angela Ndalianis, 'Television and the Neo-Baroque', in Lucy Mazdon and Michael Hammond (eds) *The Contemporary Television Series* (Edinburgh, 2005), p. 90.

41. Ibid.

42. Hills, *Triumph of a Time Lord*, p. 26.

43. Matt Hills, 'From the Box in the Corner to the Box Set on the Shelf', *New Review of Film and Television Studies*, 5/1 (2007), p. 53.

44. Sarah Thornton, *Club Cultures: Music, Media and Subcultural Capital* (Cambridge, 1995).

45. Benjamin Cook, 'Who's My Favourite…?', 2010. Available at http://benjamincook.net/writing/radio-times/interviews-and-articles/the-sarah-jane-adventures/ (accessed 17 July 2011). See also BBC Press Office, 'A Few Words with Matt Smith about Appearing in *The Sarah Jane Adventures* …', 30 September 2010. Available at www.bbc.co.uk/pressoffice/pressreleases/stories/2010/09_september/30/sja3.shtml (accessed 27 July 2011).

46. 'Radio Times advertising', 2011. Available at www.bbcmagazinesadvertising.com/Magazines/Radio_Times.html (accessed 28 October 2011).

47. *Doctor Who Magazine*, 2011. Available at www.abc.org.uk/Certificates/17593399.pdf (accessed 28 October 2011).

DOCTOR WHO, *THE ELEVENTH HOUR*

48. Matt Hills, 'Defining Cult TV: Texts, Inter-Texts and Fan Audiences', in Robert C. Allen and Annette Hill (eds) *The Television Studies Reader* (London, 2004), pp. 514–16.

49. Cook, 'Who's My Favourite ... ?'

50. Pixley, *The Sarah Jane Companion Volume Two*, p. 78.

51. Vicky Frost, 'Interview: Russell T Davies's, *Guardian*, 26 June 2011. Available at www.guardian.co.uk/media/2011/jun/26/interview-russell-t-davies (accessed 25 July 2011).

52. Ian Berriman, 'Interview: Russell T Davies Talks About THAT *Sarah Jane Adventures* Line', October 26 2010. Available at www.sfx.co.uk/2010/10/26/interview-russell-t-davies-talks-about-that-sarah-jane-adventures-line/ (accessed 25 July 2011).

53. CBBC Online, 'We Sit Down with Russell T Davies to Find Out How he Approached Writing his New SJA Story', 2010. Available at www.bbc.co.uk/cbbc/sja/theattic/russell-t-davies-q-and-a (accessed 25 July 2011).

54. Martin Flanagan, '*The Hulk*: An Ang Lee Film', *New Review of Film and Television Studies*, 2/1 (2004), p. 25.

55. Ibid., p. 26.

56. Mark Sweney, 'BBC Worldwide Agrees £121m Magazine Sell-Off', 16 August 2011. Available at www.guardian.co.uk/media/2011/aug/16/bbc-completes-magazines-sell-off?intcmp=239 (accessed 28 October 2011).

57. Andrew Reynolds, 'BBC Worldwide sells BBC Magazines – What about *Doctor Who Magazine*?', 17 August 2011. Available at www.kasterborous.com/2011/08/does-bbc-magazines-sale-mean-uncertainty-for-dwm/ (accessed 28 October 2011).

58. BBC Trust, 'BBC Online Service Licence', 2011, pp. 1–2. Available at www.bbc.co.uk/bbctrust/assets/files/pdf/regulatory_framework/service_licences/online/2011/bbc_online_feb11.pdf (accessed 28 October 2011).

59. Dan Martin, 'Doctor Who: Matt Smith in *The Sarah Jane Adventures*', *Guardian*, 27 October 2010. Available at www.guardian.co.uk/tv-and-radio/tvandradioblog/2010/oct/27/doctor-who-matt-smith-sarah-jane-adventures (accessed 25 July 2011).

60. Jonathan Hardy, 'Mapping Commercial Intertextuality: HBO's *True Blood*', *Convergence: The International Journal of Research into New Media Technologies*, 17/1 (2011), p. 8.

61. Hardy, 'Mapping Commercial Intertextuality', pp. 8–9.

62. See, for example, Jonathan Bignell and Andrew O'Day, *Terry Nation* (Manchester, 2004).

LIST OF EPISODES

CS = Christmas Special; 6a and 6b and 7a and 7b = the seasons were split into two

Specials by Steven Moffat

Comic Relief	'The Curse of the Fatal Death' (1999)
Children in Need	'Time Crash' (2007)
Comic Relief	'Space'/'Time' (2011)

Steven Moffat writing for the Russell T Davies era

1.09/1.10	'The Empty Child'/'The Doctor Dances' (2005)
2.04	'The Girl in the Fireplace' (2006)
3.10	'Blink' (2007)
4.08/4.09	'Silence in the Library'/'Forest of the Dead' (2008)

The Steven Moffat/Matt Smith era

Note: Matt Smith made a brief appearance at the close of 'The End of Time' Part 2 (2010)

Series 5 (2010)

5.01	'The Eleventh Hour'
5.02	'The Beast Below'
5.03	'Victory of the Daleks'
5.04/5.05	'The Time of Angels'/'Flesh and Stone'
5.06	'The Vampires of Venice'
5.07	'Amy's Choice'

5.08/5.09 'The Hungry Earth'/'Cold Blood'
5.10 'Vincent and the Doctor'
5.11 'The Lodger'
5.12/5.13 'The Pandorica Opens'/'The Big Bang'

CS 'A Christmas Carol' (2010)

Series 6a (Spring 2011)
6.01/6.02 'The Impossible Astronaut'/'Day of the Moon'
6.03 'The Curse of the Black Spot'
6.04 'The Doctor's Wife'
6.05/6.06 'The Rebel Flesh'/'The Almost People'
6.07 'A Good Man Goes to War'

Series 6b (Autumn 2011)
6.08 'Let's Kill Hitler'
6.09 'Night Terrors'
6.10 'The Girl Who Waited'
6.11 'The God Complex'
6.12 'Closing Time'
6.13 'The Wedding of River Song'

CS 'The Doctor, the Widow and the Wardrobe' (2011)

Series 7a (Autumn 2012)
7.01 'Asylum of the Daleks'
7.02 'Dinosaurs on a Spaceship'
7.03 'A Town Called Mercy'
7.04 'The Power of Three'
7.05 'The Angels Take Manhattan'

The Sarah Jane Adventures Series 4

'Death of the Doctor'

The Doctor Who Adventure Games
01 'City of the Daleks'
02 'Blood of the Cybermen'
03 'TARDIS'

| 04 | 'Shadows of the Vashta Nerada' |
| 05 | 'The Gunpowder Plot' |

Further Adventures of the Eleventh Doctor

CS 'The Snowmen' (2012)

Series 7b (Spring 2013)

7.6	'The Bells of Saint John'
7.7	'The Rings of Akhaten'
7.8	'Cold War'
7.9	'Hide'
7.10	'Journey to the Centre of the TARDIS'
7.11	'The Crimson Horror'
7.12	'Nightmare in Silver'
7.13	'The Name of the Doctor'

50th Anniversary Special: 'The Day of the Doctor' (2013)
CS Regeneration Episode (2013)

…and introducing Peter Capaldi as the Twelfth Doctor!

INDEX

DOCTOR WHO, *THE ELEVENTH HOUR*

audiences – *continued*
  and technology 124–5, 126
  and trailers 187
  US 110, 116
  see also children; fans
Auntie 41, 42
auteurs 247–54, 256, 257, 260–1
Avery, Henry 62–3, 191
'Aztecs, The' (serial) (1964) 57

Bailey, Bill 100
Baker, Colin 14, 16–17, 19
Baker, Tom 17, 26, 100, 110, 217
  and character 16, 19, 113
Barthes, Roland 142, 143
Batman (film) 34
Battlestar Galactica (TV series) 110, 234
BBC (British Broadcasting Corporation) 76, 115, 131, 136, 185, 190
  and audiences 110–11, 135, 206–7
  and branding 260, 261
  and Christmas 89, 92
  and overseas sales 107
  and policy 58, 59
  and technology 125
  and transmedia 233, 237, 240
BBC America 98, 116, 190
BBC convention (2012) 2–3
BBC Editorial Guidelines 58
BBC iPlayer 211, 230
BBC National Orchestra of Wales 160, 162
BBC Online 228–9, 259
BBC Outreach 182, 185
BBC Proms 182, 241
BBC Wales 130–1, 250
BBC website 135, 183, 195, 211
BBC Worldwide 116, 117, 125, 148–9, 239, 258–9
'Beast Below, The' (episode) 27, 36, 37, 65, 66, 67
  and Amelia 75
  and Britishness 112
  and the future 53
  and music 168
Benjamin, Floella 247

'Big Bang, The' (episode) 34, 39, 65, 66–7, 74–5, 241
  and character 130
  and music 161
  and River Song 78, 79
  and special effects 127
Big Finish audio plays 205, 210
Black Guardian 231
'Blink' (episode) 35, 36, 48, 49, 118, 129
  and sexuality 70
  and Weeping Angels 186
Blitz, the 54, 66–7
Bonneville, Hugh 191
Bracewell 54, 67, 75
branding 142, 181, 197, 200, 248–9, 261
  and design 144, 147, 148–50, 156
  and theme music 160–1
  and trailers 185–6
Brian Williams 183
Bride of Frankenstein (film) 42
Brides of Dracula (film) 60
(Brigadier) Sir Alistair Gordon Lethbridge-Stewart 247
Britishness 108, 111, 112, 113, 114–17, 118, 138
  and history 55
  and the US 106, 107
  see also Englishness
budgets 5, 117, 118, 124, 130, 136, 138
  and music 160, 175
Buffy the Vampire Slayer (TV series) 73, 75, 249
Burton, Tim 134, 185

Cabinet War Rooms 53–4, 55
Cal 35, 36, 38
camerawork 32, 131–2, 164, 165
Canadian Broadcasting Corporation 107–8
Captain Jack Harkness 70, 210
'Carnival of Monsters' (serial) (1973) 241
Casanova (TV series) 61
catchphrases 35, 36, 54
'Caves of Androzani, The' (serial) (1984) 101–2